MASTERS OF
MAKE-UP EFFECTS

Actors can have their highs and lows. Directors do. Producers do. Almost everyone does. But the make-up artist can't. They don't have that luxury. They have to keep that calm hand and head in the middle of what can sometimes be absolute madness.

Richard Taylor

The friendships I made doing this stuff, and the good times we had together, that's really what it's all about, man. We've been in the trenches together, and now we get to tell the stories.

Norman Cabrera

Dedications

Howard

I dedicate this book to the ones who have always told me the truth: my wife Mirjam, and my children Kelsey, Travis and Jacob. Thank you for tolerating my obsession with Monsters, Movies and Make-up.

Marshall

This book is for my daughters, Martyna, Maia and Phoebe. You're excellent sports, wonderful fun, and I love you even more than robots, aliens and monsters.

Published in 2022 by Welbeck
An Imprint of Welbeck Non-Fiction Limited,
part of Welbeck Publishing Group.
Based in London and Sydney.
www.welbeckpublishing.com

Design and layout © Welbeck Non-Fiction Limited 2022
Text © Howard Berger and Marshall Julius 2022

A CIP catalogue record for this book is available from the British Library.

ISBN 978 1 80279 001 6

Editors: Ross Hamilton & Roland Hall
Design: Russell Knowles, Darren Jordan
Production: Rachel Burgess

Printed in China

10 9 8 7 6 5 4 3 2 1

MASTERS OF
MAKE-UP EFFECTS

A CENTURY OF PRACTICAL MAGIC

HOWARD BERGER & MARSHALL JULIUS

FOREWORD BY
GUILLERMO DEL TORO

AFTERWORD BY
SETH MACFARLANE

WELBECK

CONTENTS

INTRODUCTION

BY HOWARD BERGER

At eight years old I found my calling to become a Special Make-up Effects Artist like my idols Stan Winston, Rick Baker, Dick Smith and Rob Bottin. I lived, dreamed and breathed monsters and make-up 24/7. From the time I saw *Planet of the Apes*, when it first opened in 1968, I figured there were people who created these characters and I wanted to be one of them.

After years of destroying my parents' home with clay and plaster in the carpets, and my mother's oven smelling like foam latex – and yes, everything that came out of it tasted like rubber back then – I was able to forge a path towards my one and only dream. Of course, I was very fortunate to grow up in Los Angeles, CA. My father was in the film industry, working as a post-production sound editor, so his love of films rubbed off on to me, and we would watch everything we could.

I think my first exposure to horror was 1972's *The Thing With Two Heads*, with Ray Milland and Rosey Grier. There was this two-headed gorilla in the opening of the film, which to me was amazing. I asked my dad how it was made, and he came home with an issue of *Famous Monsters of Filmland* that featured the gorilla and the name of the person who made it and played it! This was the first time I ever saw Rick Baker's name, and I immediately had to know more about him.

Now it's important to always be proactive and take initiative, so I went to the White Pages phone book and hunted for Rick Baker, but to no avail. Shortly after that, though, 1981's *The Incredible Shrinking Woman* came out, and there was another great gorilla in that film – my favourite by the way, named Sidney – that had also been made by Rick Baker, and played by Richard A. Baker.

I'd found the Holy Grail: Rick's full name! Again, I grabbed the White Pages and low and behold – BOOM! – there was Richard A. Baker's address and phone number. I called that number for six months, annoying Rick's then-wife, Elaine, every night by asking to speak to him. And finally she said, "OK, you really want to talk to Rick, so here's his shop number and he knows you're calling."

My heart beating out of my chest, my throat dry, I ran through what I would say to my idol. I dialled the number, Rick answered, and I went into what felt like cardiac arrest. Rick identified this and just said, "Calm down, take a breath, I'm just a person."

I blurted out, "NO, YOU ARE RICK BAKER AND YOU ARE A GOD!"

Anyway, Rick kindly invited me to his shop in North Hollywood the next day. My mother let me skip school to go spend the day with him. It was beyond magical and there I was, with a box of my crappy masks, drawings and sculptures, showing Rick I was serious about this. That was a hell of a day and there were many more like it as I continued to harass as many make-up artists as possible until they let me come and visit.

The inspiration for the book you are about to read comes from remembering the first time I laid my eyes on the book, *Making a Monster*, by Al Taylor and Sue Roy. In that book were all the secrets of monster making, peppered with amazing photos that I would stare at for hours upon hours. The book became my bible, and I never went anywhere without it. It lived in my backpack when I went to school, as I lived in Hollywood, so I never knew when I might stumble across one of my idols, and be able to get them to sign my book. Which, by the way, did happen. Through the years I was able to fill up that book with messages of encouragement and autographs from most of the artists featured in it.

I still think of it fondly, and always thought it would be great to create a follow-up. So when my good friend and co-author, Marshall Julius, contacted me at the beginning of the pandemic lockdown, I had no excuse not to work on the book with him. Since I was stuck at home, and everyone we wanted to speak to was also stuck at home, it was the perfect time to do it.

I hope you find this book filled with amusing, insightful and funny adventures. It really was a labour of love, plus I learned so much more about my friends after all these years. Enjoy, and I hope you laugh a lot, as that's what keeps us all going and alive: great stories and laughter.

Best,
Howard

INTRODUCTION

BY MARSHALL JULIUS

I was invited to interview Howard Berger for *The Sunday Express*. He'd just won an Oscar for his remarkable work on *The Chronicles of Narnia: The Lion, The Witch and the Wardrobe*, and after a hit cinema release, with the movie bound for DVD, Howard had flown to London to help spread the word about that.

That was in April, 2006, and one of my all-time favourite interviews. Not only because the chat was friendly, interesting and uncommonly candid, but also because, by the end of it, Howard had transformed me into Mr Tumnus, or at least, his older, stockier cousin. So there I was, with hair for the first time in years, and faun ears for the first time, well, ever, and god, it was all just so much fun.

Through it all, Howard could so easily have played the Hollywood Bigshot. I wouldn't have even minded, because, fair dues, the guy's a legend. Having played a part in so many classic, fantastic films, and worked with so many legendary filmmakers and make-up effects artists, he could have exuded BIG I AM vibes, and I'd have just lapped them up, happily fanboying out.

Except, Howard's not like that at all. You see, I'm a big, dorky nerd. That's my tribe. We love films and TV. We collect, we create and we obsess, because it's all just so damn meaningful to us. So we're defined, I'd say, by our enthusiasm, and immediately, I could tell that Howard was one of us.

"I'm still such a fan," he told me then, "and I get so excited about everything. I love it all. I love the movies. I love the effects stuff. I love every aspect of it.

"And you know what? Everything I do now, I did as a kid. I played with puppets, I made monsters and practised make-ups on my sisters. The only difference is that now I get paid to do it!

"It's still a great big hobby for me, and I'm as excited about it today as I was when I was 10 years old."

We've stayed in touch ever since.

Around 2010, I think after Howard first told me about his all-time favourite movie book, Al Taylor and Sue Roy's *Making a Monster*, we had our first conversation about how great it would be to write something together. Howard wanted to interview his friends about their adventures in movie making, so not a dry, instructional thing, but rather something focusing on the fun of it all. Fun being Howard's operative word.

But he was always so damn busy! Always working on something new with Sam Raimi, or Quentin Tarantino, or

Mark Wahlberg… But I never gave up on the idea. So every six months or so, for ten years, I'd check in with Howard, see how things were with him, and drop in a mention of the book. So maybe, yes, there was the faintest whiff of stalker about me, but Howard never sent me packing, or nixed the idea, so I always thought of it as something we'd hopefully get to one day.

And then HOORAY! Yes! Finally… The Pandemic.

Suddenly everyone was home with too much time on their hands, and so, without shame or delay, I reached out for a Skype, and within minutes we'd agreed that the time was finally right to get on with our book. And that was that. We were instantly all in, and worked diligently to make it happen for the best part of the next two years.

And what a grand collaboration it's been. Conducted entirely by email, WhatsApp, Facetime and, of course, Zoom, with Howard in LA, and me in London. In fact, at the time of writing – October, 2021 – we've still only met in the real world once, all those years ago for the Narnia interview. So it's a very modern friendship we've built, and honestly, collaborating with Howard on this book kept me going through the lockdown.

So Howard reached out to legend after legend after legend… Most of whom responded almost immediately, and cheerfully made time to chat. Certainly that aspect of the process proceeded with greater speed and success than I'd ever experienced before. Without Howard at the helm, I doubt this book could have ever happened.

There's just no way an outsider, a journalist like myself, could have gathered such a dizzying array of talent, or gotten them to share so much of themselves, or dig through their archives for personal pictures that no one's seen before. No. Creating this book demanded the sort of access only enjoyed by a handful of industry folk. And beyond that, someone with a lot of friends, who's always put himself out for others, and generated a tremendous amount of good will.

Essentially, then, creating this book required Howard – specifically, Howard – and what a privilege it was to join him on that journey. To be privy to all those relaxed, revelatory catch-up sessions with people I've admired for years. Most of whom turned out to be geeks like us! Just friendly, fun, approachable people, excited to talk monsters and make-up, and happy to share their stories, thoughts and photos.

I hope we've captured the fun and warm familiarity of those lively, unguarded interviews in the chapters ahead.

After discussing the format at great length, we settled on quotes alone, as we wanted to pack as many stories as we could into the book, cutting straight to the good stuff every time. So this isn't a definitive history of the make-up effects industry. And it's not a detailed how-to either. Neither of those options was ever the plan.

What we wanted to produce, and hopefully what we've achieved, is something much more inclusive, intimate, and fun. And though Howard was initially reticent about being included as a make-up master in his own book, I insisted on interviewing him as there's no way I'd deny you his amazing stories.

Enjoy!

FOREWORD

BY GUILLERMO DEL TORO

A FAMILY ALBUM

I have said it before – many times – but, perhaps it's worth repeating here: I love monsters. They are my religion, my light, my life.

Therapists would call it, I believe, a counterphobic reaction, because – truth be told – as a small infant (in my crib) I was terrified of them. But the mechanism of loving them, of delivering myself to them, like St Paul would deliver himself to the Savior on the road to Damascus, well, that mechanism was implanted deep inside me at an almost pre-verbal age.

Every testimony in this book has been collected from Monster Kids everywhere. We are an odd breed: no matter where you were born, no matter what your background, if you love monsters with a passion, if you want to dedicate your life and labor to creating them, you belong to this hidebound society of misfits.

Obsessive-compulsive loners, dramatic, fixated one-track minds and many more unflattering adjectives that result in creature perfection. These traits, and a common family tree – one that includes ancestors dating back to Lon Chaney or Jack Pierce or William Tuttle or John Chambers or any of the big make-up families that dominated the North American film industry through the Golden Era: the Westmores, the Burmans, etc.

These names are the Houdinis, the Thurstons, the Malinis of our magic: the ones who figured out misdirection and sleight of hand. The ones who tested the trapdoors, the bullet-catching gang.

But the one father figure most of us have in common is Dick Smith. The gentlest giant who this industry ever had. Demanding, truthful and loyal to a fault, Dick Smith advanced the art of make-up and popularized its allure more than any other artist before him. He birthed us all – even a deity like the brilliant Rick Baker.

He answered probably every letter ever written to him, and he attended to every need ever presented to him. Almost every person in this book has handwritten cards or neatly-typed letters that he always signed: "All The Best, Dick Smith".

He was Cronos, our Titan, and he gave birth to the universe of modern make-up effects.

In his wake we found a brotherhood that, albeit dysfunctional on occasion, is full of passion and fire. The testimonies here collected attest to that. They chronicle what I have come to believe were the golden years of our craft.

Some of the Titans have passed away, while others have retired or, in Rob Bottin's case, they have become J.D. Salinger-level mysteries to puzzle about for generations to come. But most everybody else is here, talking shop, sharing, praising, gossiping or revealing secrets and stories. And most of them are true, or at least truthfully remembered, by the teller. And that, my friends, makes for great reading.

To memorialize the voices of the post-classicists, the make-up prog-rockers, the punks, the metal gods and everyone who came after those early masters. To repeat the names and spread the anecdotes, is an act of love and a prayer for immortality.

What has been done with an art that started with an "out-of-kit" method and a light-and-shadow painterly approach to the human face, has become a tale of fantastic proportions: here are the scientists, the muralists, the punctilious ones and the fabulous crazies who elevated, enshrined and executed the impossible into a glorious, epic tale.

It's good to remember our stories and to repeat our names so that we can recognize each other, as we have done for the love of our monsters past, present and future. So we can survive and continue a lineage that existed before cinema, before theatre, when man first donned a mask to invoke a God in an ancient temple.

Allow this book to provide you with the solace of coming home, the voices of your siblings and the embrace of family.

Guillermo del Toro
Santa Monica, CA, 2022

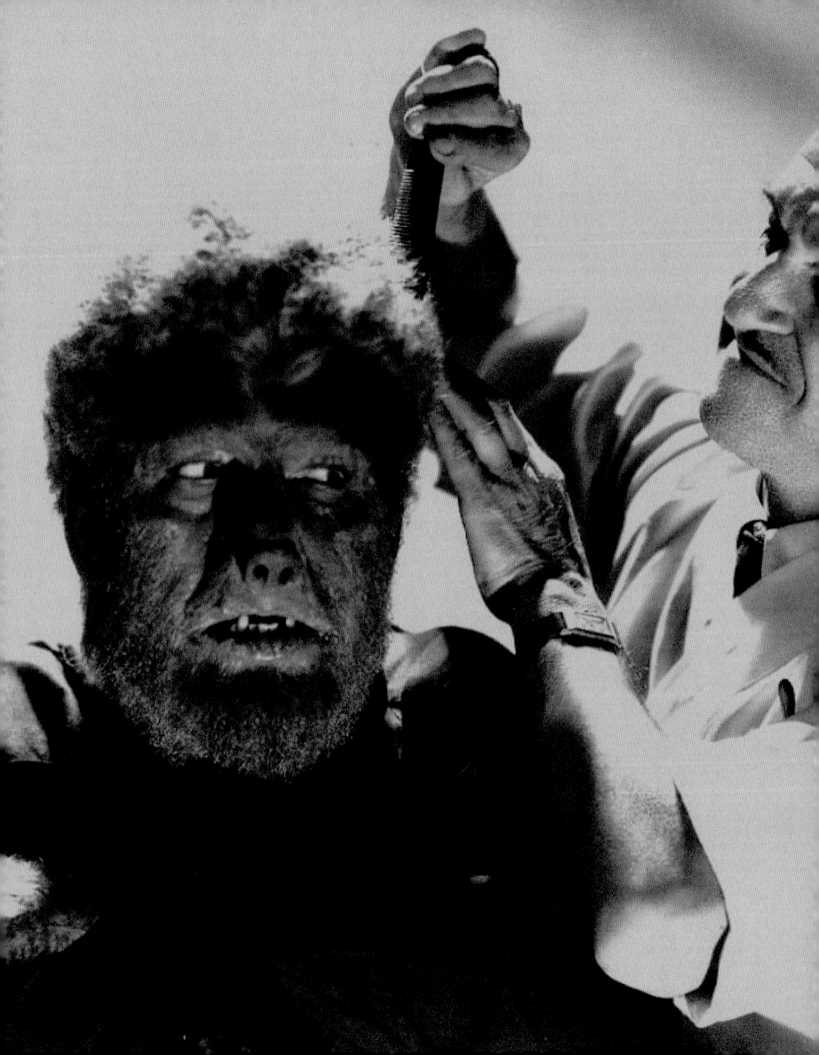

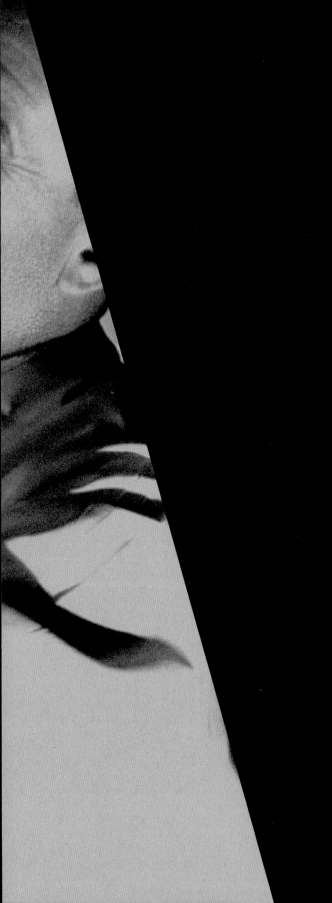

1

HALL OF FAME

With a century of cinema to choose from, our masters faced a fiendish challenge when we asked them to single out their favourite make-up movies, their favourite movie make-ups, and the make-up movie masters who have come to mean the most to them over the years.

It's a lot to digest in an opening chapter, a wealth of artists and timeless artistry to absorb, but a perfect primer for the glued and grease-painted, prosthetic-packed pages that follow.

My grandpa used to say, you leave something at the beach and the sand will come cover it. The sands of time. It's like important people. Legends like Jack Pierce, John Chambers . . .

Over the years their memory gets covered with sand, so you have to bring their names back up. Celebrate what they did, and remember what they meant to us. Dust the sand off.

Rob Freitas

My godfather was the top distributor for a major publisher and an entire room in his big old ranch house was full of coffee-table books. My favourite was a thick red book called *The Movies*. I remember an image in it from *Dracula's Daughter* (1936), and one from *Frankenstein* (1931), but what I remember most is spending a lot of time reading about Lon Chaney, the Man of a Thousand Faces.

There were a series of postage stamp-sized pictures in the

book of all the different make-ups he'd not only worn, but also had done on himself. There was one, I particularly remember, where he was playing a blind man and had put egg membranes over his eyes to make them look milky and dead.

This was for a silent movie and it looked great! For all intents and purposes, it was probably the first contact lens, too. The man was a genius.

Robert Englund

Previous pages: Universal's monster maker Jack Pierce gives Lon Chaney Jr's Wolf Man a trim.

Above, left: John Chambers (left) and Vern Langdon (right) flank David McCallum's Six-Fingered Alien from *The Outer Limits* (1963-64).

Above, right: Lon Chaney cheerfully models his Phantom of the Opera make-up, created for the 1925 chiller of the same name.

Left: Simon & Schuster's *The Movies* (1957), written by Richard Griffith and Arthur Mayer, was an inspiration to many growing up, including Robert Englund. See here a montage of Lon Chaney's brilliant transformations from the book.

"IT'S A CENTURY OLD, BUT STILL, IT PREYS ON THE MIND."

I've always found Count Orlok, from Murnau's *Nosferatu* (1922), particularly disturbing. Though it's a simple, minimal make-up, combined with the costume, the use of shadow, the style of filming and, of course, Max Schreck's eerie performance, it's very powerful.

It's a century old, but still, it preys on the mind.

Montse Ribé

Right and below: Max Schreck, simply nightmarish as Count Orlok, from F.W. Murnau's *Nosferatu* (1922).

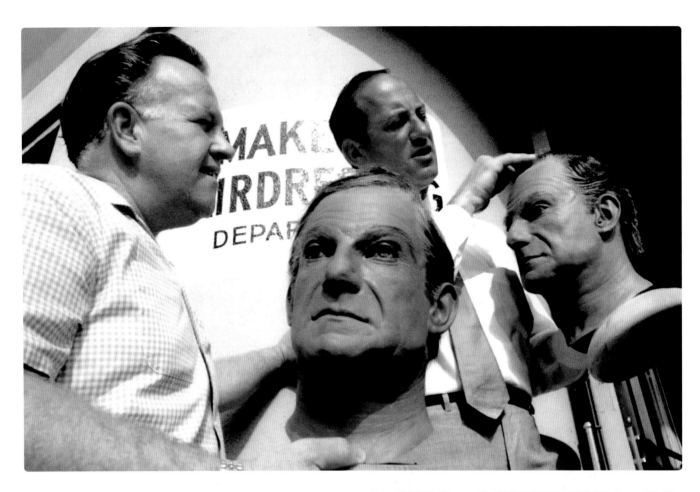

Jack Pierce, William Tuttle and John Chambers were the Famous Monsters triumvirate, and thank God Forry [Ackerman] brought them to our attention. Otherwise, how would we have known about them?

They were the trailblazers. They hadn't grown up dreaming of making monsters. They just did whatever it was they were called upon to do, and they developed make-up effects without even realising they were creating an entirely new art form.

Mick Garris

It doesn't get any better than *Frankenstein* (1931).

To me, Frankenstein's monster is the greatest make-up achievement in the history of film. Even though he's built up of shit on his forehead, it's brilliant. It doesn't even make sense when you think about it – that weird flat top.

Yet that motherfucker works, right? Why? Because of the genius of Jack Pierce, Boris Karloff's acting, Arthur Edeson's cinematography and James Whale's directing. They brought the whole thing to life.

That film demonstrates more than any other what the magic of collaborative film-making is all about.

Mike McCracken Jr

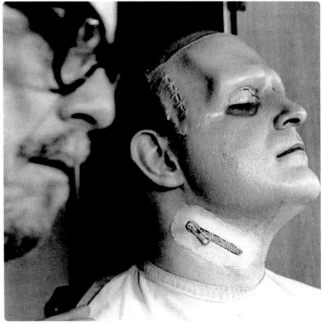

Top: John Chambers (left) and Daniel Striepeke, outside the make-up department at 20th Century Fox Studios, displaying the life-like masks they created of Jonathan Harris as Dr Smith for *Lost in Space* (1965-68).

Above: William Tuttle transforms Peter Boyle into The Monster for Mel Brooks' classic spoof, *Young Frankenstein* (1974).

Opposite: Charles Laughton, impeccably made up as the tortured and twisted Quasimodo, from *The Hunchback of Notre Dame* (1939).

The first monster movie I have a clear memory of watching was *The Hunchback of Notre Dame* (1939). I was six and absolutely terrified by Quasimodo. I asked my mum if he was a real person.

She told me he wasn't. That it was an actor, Charles Laughton, wearing make-up, which is something people did for movies. I sort of understood, but he still frightened me!

What a flawless make-up that was. You can't see a single edge, and it moves so naturally. Also on his body, the bumps of his spine are so real.

Even after all these years, it's still a beautiful make-up. One of the best of all time.

Norman Cabrera

"EVEN THOUGH HE'S BUILT UP OF SHIT ON HIS FOREHEAD, IT'S BRILLIANT."

"YOU JUST CAN'T BEAT THE UNIVERSAL MONSTERS!"

As a kid, I was obsessed with the Creature from the Black Lagoon. You just can't beat the Universal Monsters! They have so much character.

I was excited when Stan Winston asked Matt Rose and I to build the Gill-man for *The Monster Squad* (1987). Stan designed it and Matt and I refined it. The biggest challenge, for us, was figuring out how to create a seamless suit. We were twenty years old and didn't really know what we were doing, but somehow got by on gut instinct.

The funny thing about the Gill-man is, I never thought of him as the Creature from the Black Lagoon. To me, it was an entirely different fish monster. So when people tell me how much they love my Creature, I always have to bite my lip.

It's awesome they appreciate it so much, and yeah, it's cool, but it's not the Creature. There's only one Creature and he's still my favourite monster.

He's the dude.

Steve Wang

Top: Ben Chapman, who played the Gill-Man on land in *The Creature From the Black Lagoon* (1954), chats with Bud Westmore in the Universal Make-up Department. Ricou Browning played the Creature underwater.

Above: Steve Wang airbrushed the Creature suit from *The Monster Squad* (1987) while working at Stan Winston Studios.

Below: The completed Creature from *The Monster Squad* (1987), played by Tom Woodruff Jr.

The three best monster make-ups of all time are Boris Karloff's Frankenstein's Monster, Charles Laughton's Hunchback of Notre Dame and Oliver Reed's Werewolf.

I like them best because I still see the actors in there: they're not completely covered with prosthetics and hair.

Karloff's face is fully on view, and it's beautiful. The sadness on Laughton's face is plain to see and breaks your heart. And when I watch *The Curse of the Werewolf* (1961), it's Reed's face I see, trapped within that demon.

I love those make-ups because they don't hide the actors wearing them. They just enhance them.

Mike Hill

Right: Mike Hill with his brilliant replica of Oliver Reed from *The Curse of the Werewolf* (1961).

Below: Oliver Reed in all his werewolfy glory, transformed by Roy Ashton for *The Curse of the Werewolf* (1961).

Roy Ashton did a lot of Hammer's movie make-ups in the Sixties. I met him when he was a very old man and he was lovely. I wish I could have worked with him.

Everything he did was done with materials you could find in the kitchen cupboard.

I'm inspired by people who finesse something technically to a very high level. But I also admire people like Roy who produced wonderful things using next to nothing.

Totally different disciplines, but equally powerful.

Nick Dudman

There is a long list of stuff that we could talk about when it comes to picking the greatest make-up effects, but I'll limit myself to three.

One: Frankenstein's Monster by Jack Pierce could so easily have gone awry. But there's just something about the gauntness, the heavy lids and the look in Karloff's eyes. Plus that collodion and cotton forehead . . . It's perfect.

Two: Rick Baker's Wolfman. That has totally replaced Lon Chaney Jr's Wolf Man in my lexicon of films.

And three: Everything Rob Bottin did in *The Thing* (1982). That's the epitome of splatter. People call me the King of Splatter, but I'm not. Rob is!

Tom Savini

To me, Jack Pierce's Bride of Frankenstein is a perfect aesthetic. The two- and three-dimensional make-up elements are beautifully designed and executed. Everything melds so perfectly, including the hair. The wig work is gorgeous and iconic.

Sarah Rubano

Above: Elsa Lanchester as the Monster's Mate, with hair and make-up by Jack Pierce, for Universal's classic *Bride of Frankenstein* (1935).

Right: Boris Karloff, back in Jack Pierce's iconic Monster make-up, for *Bride of Frankenstein* (1935).

Frankenstein's Monster is the perfect combination of actor and make-up. It's wonderful when things works out that way.

Like on *Nutty Professor* (1996) with Eddie Murphy. The make-ups were good, I thought, but when I saw what Eddie did with them, he just took them to a whole other level.

It's great to see your pieces of rubber become a person.

Rick Baker

Even today, there are people who don't realise that Eddie Murphy was the old Jewish guy in *Coming to America* (1988). I didn't know myself until the end of the movie, when they revealed it during the credits. Everyone in the cinema was like, "OH, MY GOD!"

That make-up by Rick Baker is the ultimate magic trick. It's everything I love about make-up.

Carey Jones

"IT'S GREAT TO SEE YOUR PIECES OF RUBBER BECOME A PERSON."

One of my earliest inspirations was Rick Baker. Not as a make-up artist, per se, but as a performer. It was the late Seventies, I was about fourteen or fifteen years old. My dad was working for Rick, sculpting on the gorilla for *The Incredible Shrinking Woman* (1981).

Bear in mind this was long before Rick had a huge studio. This was at Rick's home studio in his garage at his home on Hortense in North Hollywood. Rick asked my dad if I'd be interested in building a shed for him in his back garden to store his moulds in. I went to Rick's and started building one of those big metal sheds, the kind you'd buy at Sears.

While I was in the back garden, building this shed, every hour or two Rick would come out and perform. He was practising playing Sydney the Gorilla. Sometimes he would practise with arm extensions on, sometimes with a gorilla head on. I was the only one in the back garden watching him. It was as if he was performing just for me. It was literally the most mind-blowing thing I'd seen in my life. Watching Rick perform was truly magical. He was completely convincing as a gorilla. It made me want to be a suit performer.

Years later I had the opportunity to play a monkey in one of my dad's creations. It was for a TV show he was working on called *Tales of the Gold Monkey* (1982–83), and it was a dream come true.

Mike McCracken Jr

Above: Eddie Murphy as Sherman Klump shares a laugh with Rick Baker on the set of *The Nutty Professor* (1996).

In addition to being given a load of great make-ups to apply, I was asked to make up Rick [Baker] for his cameo as a big-brained alien for *Men In Black 3* (2012). He was so patient in the chair, considering he was really under the weather AND it was his birthday.

Rick's wife comes over and she's like, "So, are you nervous doing make-up on the boss?"

To her surprise, I was calm and focused. Rick, through it all, paid me a wonderful compliment. He said, "You have a really great touch," and I'm practically blushing!

Mike Smithson

I got the *Cinefex* issue on Rick Baker. The one with the Greystoke ape on the cover. It was my bible. I read it so many times, I actually memorised parts of it.

There was a quote in there from Rick that sort of became my mantra. Something like, "The only reason I ever became any good was that I kept doing it and doing it and doing it."

I wrote it on the ceiling above my bed, and I'd stare at it every night before going to sleep.

Mike Marino

Top: Rick Baker's cameo as the Brain Alien in *Men in Black 3* (2012).

Above: The ultimate monster kid issue of *Cinefex*, with Rick Baker's Kala from *Greystoke: The Legend of Tarzan, Lord of the Apes* (1984).

Whenever I'm asked, "What's the quintessential make-up effects movie?," my go-to effects guy answer is *An American Werewolf in London* (1981). I put that on whenever I want to feel like I'm eight years old and get really excited about what I do for a living.

Vincent Van Dyke

Jack's flap of skin was a happy accident. I'm not saying it wasn't planned. It was always there. But it wasn't nearly as prominent until I meddled with it. I kept saying, "It's not wet enough!"

So they put K-Y Jelly on it. But it still wasn't wet enough. Eventually I said, "Just get me the spray."

And Rick goes, "You're always spraying everything. I do all this detailed work and you're always covering it with water and blood!"

So I spritzed the flap with water, and it's foam, you know. It swelled up and started flapping. We all loved it! Except Rick claims he didn't notice it until he saw the movie, and he was like, "Oh, Shit!"

But the audience around him loved it. They were going, "EWWW!"

It was a big hit!

John Landis

"JACK'S FLAP OF SKIN WAS A HAPPY ACCIDENT."

Above, left: One of Rick Baker's startling Nazi Demons from David's massacre nightmare in *An American Werewolf in London* (1981).

Below: Rick Baker adds the final touches to Griffin Dunne's Jack Stage 1 make-up for *An American Werewolf in London* (1981). "That little dangly piece of chicken skin affected everybody," observed Garrett Immel.

The Thing (1982) is the quintessential, balls-to-the-wall, blowout make-up effects movie. Rob Bottin, that fucking guy was my first protégé. He took everything we ever talked about and put it in that film. Only he did it ten times bigger than I ever imagined.

Rick Baker

Even now, when I watch The Thing (1982), I'm not certain how everything was done. The way the creature keeps transforming in the spider-head scene, the way the effects just keep constantly upping themselves . . .

Between the artistry, the creativity and the sheer gross-out factor, it's gotta be the ultimate make-up effects set piece.

Fred Raskin

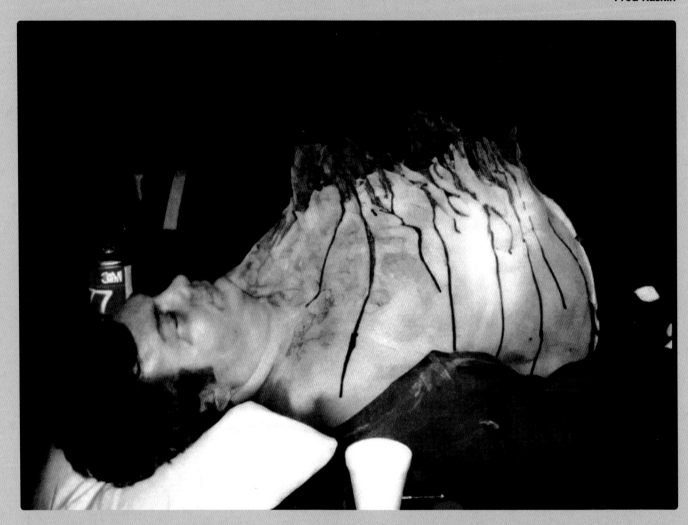

I was on the set of The Thing (1982), shooting a 'making of' documentary. Right from the start I could tell that movie was going to be special. John Carpenter had given Rob Bottin carte blanche to go nuts, and I knew Rob was planning lots of really experimental stuff.

I saw them filming the scene where the guy's head comes off and becomes the spider monster. Watching it was revelatory. No one had ever done anything like that before and I felt so privileged to be there. Like I was looking behind the curtain of the Wizard of Oz.

In terms of practical make-up effects, that scene has never been outdone.

Mick Garris

"NO ONE HAD EVER DONE ANYTHING LIKE THAT BEFORE."

Above: Charles Hallahan as Norris at the start of one of the greatest make-up effects sequences ever filmed, from John Carpenter's The Thing (1982).

I've always been drawn to the fantastic and other-worldly. Anything dreamy and different from reality. Ridley Scott's *Legend* (1985) was a huge inspiration. I was obsessed with Darkness, by Rob Bottin. I'd sculpt him over and over in Plasticine as that's all I had when I was small.

I'd use all the colours, too – green, blue, yellow, red – as I was only really interested in the sculpt and didn't care if my Darkness was rainbow-coloured!

Pamela Goldammer

I remember one day we went over to Universal Studios' Alfred Hitchcock Theater to see a rough cut of the 'chest-chomp, head-stretching' sequence. Vince Prentice, Art Pimentel and I were walking back to the car afterwards, when I told them, "Man, I don't know how anybody's gonna ever top this."

Here I had been thinking that we were just a bunch of kids having fun, but it was at that point that I first realised *The Thing* (1982) was going to be something special.

Ken Diaz

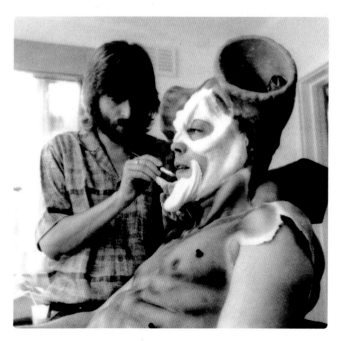

Above: A close-up Polaroid photo of Tim Curry as Darkness from Ridley Scott's *Legend* (1985).

Above, right: Tim Curry as Darkness, in make-up designed and created by Rob Bottin, and applied by Nick Dudman and Lois Burwell, for *Legend* (1985).

Right: Nick Dudman applies Tim Curry's legendary Darkness make-up.

Bib Fortuna, from *Return of the Jedi* (1983), is an incredibly cool make-up. The colouration is so unique and vivid and intense. He's so pale, and with that blue veining, it really looks like flesh. And with those orange eyes, he's just so weird!

Jamie Kelman

Something that really got under my skin and fascinated, confused and inspired me was the Dawn of Man sequence from *2001: A Space Odyssey* (1968). I saw it at the cinema ten years after its original release and those chimps, they were so real. What Stuart Freeborn achieved, with nothing to draw on, was years ahead of its time and you still believe it now.

Neill Gorton

Top: Under the supervision of Stuart Freeborn, Nick Dudman handled the task in creating Bib Fortuna, played by Michael Carter in *Return of the Jedi* (1983).

Above: Stuart Freeborn grooms his Primal Man apes from Stanley Kubrick's *2001: A Space Odyssey* (1968).

Right: Stuart Freeborn's wife Kay helps an actor into his Primal Man suit and head for *2001: A Space Odyssey* (1968).

Stuart Freeborn was a true Renaissance man. He could paint your face; he did beautiful hair; he could work a lathe; he understood electronics. Plus he was ambidextrous! Really anything he turned his hand to, he seemed able to do.

It was almost annoying!

Nick Dudman

Right: Nick Maley works on the Yoda puppets, under the supervision of Stuart Freeborn, for *The Empire Strikes Back* (1980).

Below: Stuart Freeborn frosts Christopher Reeve for a scene ultimately cut from the theatrical version of *Superman: The Movie* (1978).

"STUART FREEBORN WAS A TRUE RENAISSANCE MAN."

Star Wars (1977) is the first movie I remember seeing as a kid. I was three when it came out and I was like, 'I want this, or something like this, to be in front of me all the time.'

I can't fathom how they achieved what they did. Still. Even though I've been in the business for years. It's just so far above and beyond, and that's probably because so many great artists worked on it together.

Of all the characters in the original trilogy, I think Yoda is the most significant.

Muppets were the most popular thing in the world when I was growing up. More popular than humans for a while, and they had a real grip on me. Yoda was this incredible mix of puppetry and animatronics who was every bit as believable to me as the human characters.

Yoda was so central to the movies, if he hadn't worked, the entire trilogy might have collapsed under the weight of his failure. He was a huge risk, but he worked because everyone worked so hard – together – to make him work.

It wasn't like, "Just bring him to set and turn him on."

It took Stuart Freeborn and George Lucas. It took Irvin Kershner and Peter Suschitzky, who's just a master of light and colour and texture and photographed everything so beautifully. And of course, it took Frank Oz, who's probably the greatest puppeteer of all time. I mean, yes, Jim Henson was a legend, but if he was the Rick Baker of puppeteers, Frank Oz is the Rob Bottin.

Yoda's success proved that, with enough care, anything was possible. And he had a profound effect on my childhood. Both as a fabricated creature that sparked my imagination, and as a living, breathing character. Honestly he was as much a parent to me, a voice of wisdom and authority, as my actual parents!

Jamie Kelman

For me, a great make-up is something that perfectly complements the movie it's in: John Mills in *Ryan's Daughter* (1970); Dustin Hoffman in *Little Big Man* (1970); Jeff Goldblum in *The Fly* (1986).

They should be gorgeous, but grounded, and absolutely real.

David White

Left: Dick Smith and Carl Fullerton test one of the crushable mummy busts for *The Hunger* (1983).

Below: Linda Blair as poor, possessed Regan, demonically made up by Dick Smith for *The Exorcist* (1973).

The make-up movie that made the earliest impression on me was *The Exorcist* (1973). I saw it way too young. It messed me up and I'm still messed up.

I remember once in Dublin, I was making a movie and staying in this fancy converted barn. The bedroom was this long, narrow, stone-walled room. Like a Viking banquet chamber. There was a four-poster bed at one end, and at the other, this tiny wood fire and stove.

I woke up once, in the middle of the night, and the embers were still glowing from a fire I'd built earlier. I immediately thought, "Wouldn't it be terrible if I start thinking about scary things right now?"

Of course, my mind went straight to *The Exorcist* and that was it. I was awake for the rest of the night. But not just awake. I was standing on the bed, screaming at Satan, "Come on then you bastard! Try and take me! Fucking try it!"

I was so certain he was coming. Because I saw *The Exorcist*, way too young.

James McAvoy

"IT MESSED ME UP AND I'M STILL MESSED UP."

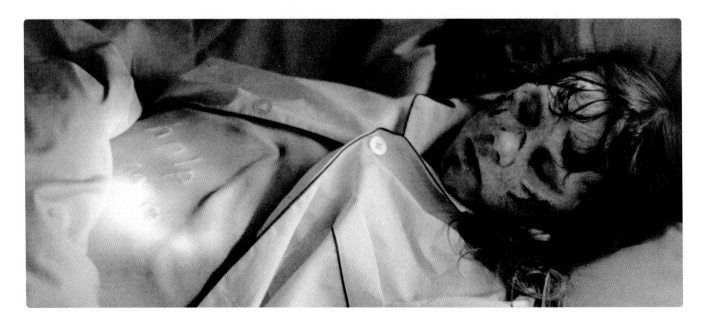

I don't consider my skills as being anywhere near Dick Smith's. His sensitivity to sculpture and what I call skin-flow is unrivalled. He understood how skin moves, the effect of gravity and how posture plays a key role in affecting a make-up.

He was able to capture realism because he'd devoted so much hard work and practise to his art. I remember watching him back then; it was a great time to learn how he saw and did things. He was truly an innovator and I'm appreciative for everything he gave to me and others.

Carl Fullerton

Left: Catherine Deneuve cradles David Bowie in his final-stage age make-up for *The Hunger* (1983).

Below: David Bowie in a mid-stage age make-up created by Dick Smith for *The Hunger* (1983).

Dick Smith's extreme, old age make-up of David Bowie in *The Hunger* (1983) is my all-time favourite make-up effect. Being both a huge Bowie fan and Dick Smith enthusiast, seeing Bowie in Dick's foam latex make-up was therefore startlingly powerful to me.

My all-time favourite creature from any movie has got to be Rick Baker's Sasquatch suit from *Harry and the Hendersons* (1987). A perfect creation, in my opinion!

Richard Taylor

Dick Smith's transformations on [David] Bowie in *The Hunger* (1983) are just jaw-droppingly astonishing.

I know how Smith did it. I know what the pieces look like. I've seen the moulds. But no matter how carefully I examine shots like that close-up of David Bowie's eyes in the elevator, there's not a seam, there's not a line, there's not a mark. It wasn't cleaned up digitally. The illusion is so complete, you can even see sweat on his skin through his glasses.

It's just astounding, the subtle things Dick Smith achieved in that movie. It should have won an Oscar.

Todd McIntosh

"YOU CAN EVEN SEE SWEAT ON HIS SKIN THROUGH HIS GLASSES."

After graduating from high school in 1969, my parents took me on a trip to New York, and that's when I met Dick Smith for the first time.

They drove me to his house in Larchmont, and I thought it was going to be a very short visit, but he sent my parents away, telling them, "I'll get Rick back to you when we're done."

We ended up spending the whole day together. He gave me a legal notepad and pencil, saying, "I'm going to tell you all this stuff. You'd better write it down so you don't forget it."

Anything I wanted to know, he told me. Like, "How do you make a wrinkle that looks like a wrinkle? When I do it, it just looks like I cut the clay with a knife."

He told me to use a brush and alcohol, which wasn't something that had occurred to me before. And that was just one of a ton of things he taught me that day.

First thing I made when I got home was an old man mask. Thanks to Dick, it was better than anything I'd done before.

Rick Baker

"HOW DO YOU MAKE A WRINKLE THAT LOOKS LIKE A WRINKLE?"

The Exorcist (1973) marked a turning point from the past to the present of make-up effects. Rick Baker was Dick Smith's assistant on that.

So I'm with Toni G in Rick's trailer on *Planet of the Apes* (2001) and *The Exorcist* is playing on the monitor. Suddenly Rick says, "Everybody stop and watch the movie."

Father Merrin's talking and when his hand enters the frame, Rick goes, "That's my work! That's what I did! I did that hand!"

I loved that Rick got so excited about such a little thing. But of course, it's an iconic movie, and we all want to leave our footprints in the sand.

Jamie Kelman

Right: Max Von Sydow was only in his early forties when cast as Father Merrin in *The Exorcist* (1973), flawlessly transformed into the elderly priest with a best-in-class age make-up by Dick Smith.

Opposite, top: The Weta team greet Dick Smith upon his arrival at their workshop in Wellington, New Zealand.

Opposite, bottom: Richard Taylor was overjoyed to host legendary make-up master Dick Smith at Weta.

In our early years at the Weta Workshop, we were a group of technicians fairly isolated from the world's industry here in Wellington, so when we were fortunate enough to win our first Oscars, [my wife] Tania and I wanted to give our crew the most special present we could think of. We decided to invite Ray Harryhausen and his wife Diana to come to New Zealand, and they ended up spending two wonderful weeks with us. Later, when we were incredibly fortunate to win again, we wanted to do something equally special, so we invited Dick Smith.

He was somewhat frail and elderly at that point, so it took a while to convince him to come, but eventually he agreed and, having travelled across the world by himself, I picked him up from Wellington Airport and took him the short trip back to our workshop. What happened next was really one of the most beautiful moments in my career.

As I drove him through the front gates of our workshop, there were about a hundred-plus people standing outside, waiting to greet him. As we pulled into our gate, everyone started clapping and cheering, one or two even springing a tear because, well, it was Dick Smith. And he just broke down in front me and started sobbing. He said to me, "I never thought anyone would care enough to do this again. I didn't think anyone cared any more."

I couldn't quite believe he felt that he'd fallen into obscurity to that degree – because, of course, he hadn't.

Everyone loved him, and, just like Ray, he was so gracious with his time. On the last night of his visit, he did an incredible talk. He was so animated and excited. Over a two-week period we got to watch this frail, elderly man turn back into this energised, enthusiastic artist and superhero. He told us later that he went home and started sculpting again, and it was just so lovely to hear.

Richard Taylor

Dawn of the Dead (1978) gets a lot of shit but there are some great technical make-ups in that movie. A lot of it's just colour, which is really neat. I love what Tom Savini did with highlight and shadow.

Flyboy is one of the best zombies, still, and he's basically all colour, with just a few little extra things and some stipple. It's incredible.

Mikey Rotella

"I LOVE WHAT TOM SAVINI DID WITH HIGHLIGHT AND SHADOW."

I'm proud of the big part The Walking Dead (2010–22) played in introducing practical make-up effects to a new generation. To show there's more to film-making than digital effects. And it meant a lot to me that the network celebrated that aspect of the show. Like, the first promotional photo they ever released wasn't of Rick or Daryl, but the Bicycle Girl zombie.

People often come up to me at conventions to tell me they want to do what I do because of The Walking Dead. That makes me feel good because it's kind of the exact same thing I said to Tom Savini about following in his footsteps, because of Dawn of the Dead (1978).

Greg Nicotero

Above: Bicycle Girl paved the way for countless creative zombies on The Walking Dead (2010-2022).

Right: David Emge lurched his way into the hearts of horror fans as the ill-fated Flyboy in Tom Savini's make-up for George A. Romero's Dawn of the Dead (1978).

Opposite, top: David Kindlon helps John Vulich apply Sherman Howard's Bub make-up for Day of the Dead (1985).

Opposite, bottom: Sherman Howard's Bub enjoys a tune in Day of the Dead (1985).

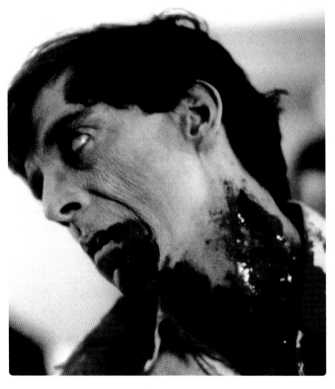

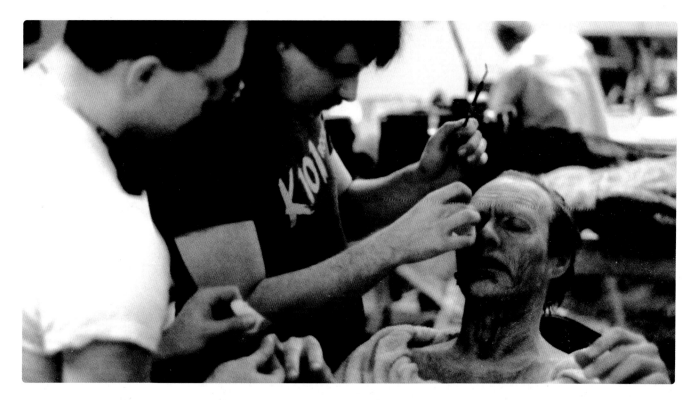

In terms of zombie make-ups, John Vulich's Bub from *Day of the Dead* (1985) will never be topped. He's just so instantly recognisable! Credit also to Howard Sherman, of course, the actor who was able to bring him to life from under all that make-up.

That zombie was a real character. More human than most of the actual humans in the movie.

Fred Raskin

When I first saw *Planet of the Apes* (1968), those talking chimps and gorillas totally blew my mind.

Then I saw this documentary that showed, step by step, how John Chambers transformed Roddy McDowall into Cornelius. First the life casting, then the mould making, casting the foam rubber, gluing the pieces on . . .

I realised make-up was as interesting as monkeys!

Gino Acevedo

The first time I saw the original *Planet of the Apes* (1968), I was six I think, and that's definitely what triggered my love of make-up. I mean honestly, at first, I thought they were real. I wondered how they got gorillas to ride on the backs of horses?

But eventually finding out they were people in make-ups was actually no less amazing to me. The make-ups were unbelievable, of course, but my favourite was Dr Zaius. I loved his orange hair, and with his wrinkled skin, he really looked the best.

Kevin Yagher

"THOSE TALKING CHIMPS AND GORILLAS TOTALLY BLEW MY MIND."

I take my hat off to Kazu's make-up for *Darkest Hour* on Gary Oldman. It was a bloody good sculpt that was beautifully applied.

That sculpt was informed. It was not just Kazu sculpting Winston Churchill. It was Kazu sculpting a machine that allowed Gary Oldman's muscle structure to be Churchill.

It was a sculpt that allowed Gary Oldman to do his job.

Nick Dudman

Kazu's Churchill make-up might be the finest make-up that's ever been achieved. I mean, is it even a make-up? You look at Churchill and that's a real guy, right? You're just looking at a person.

Garrett Immel

Opposite: Kim Hunter as Zira in a test make-up for *Planet of the Apes* (1968). "The true definition of a good movie," says John Landis, "is one with someone in a gorilla suit."

Above: Gary Oldman as Sir Winston Churchill in Kazu Hiro's Oscar-winning make-up for *Darkest Hour* (2017).

"IT WAS A CONCERTED EFFORT BY A WHOLE COUNTRY OF PEOPLE."

After Peter [Jackson] told us we were going to be making *Lord of the Rings*, [my wife] Tania and I, and our small crew of initially thirty-eight people, were given charge of designing and fabricating the armour, weapons, creatures, miniatures, special make-up effects and prosthetics. Ultimately our team – which would grow to 158 people – delivered 48,000 separate things for the trilogy, including more than 10,000 make-up components. It was a massive undertaking.

When we started, many of our crew were very young and had never worked on a movie or TV show before. We were pretty inexperienced ourselves and had certainly never done a film close to this size. It possibly wasn't like making a movie in the United States at the time where you could turn to a relatively seasoned group of highly skilled professionals. One of our staff had been a pine tree planter. One had painted cars. One was an undertaker! And, you know, Tania and I were pretty young and inexperienced ourselves. We'd never done anything on this scale before. But the crew and ourselves had this incredible conviction that this was our opportunity. That it was New Zealand's opportunity to make a mark in the industry.

I've often thought the *Lord of the Rings* wasn't made by a single director. It wasn't made by a film company, or a studio. It was a concerted effort by a whole country of people. *Lord of the Rings* was made by New Zealand.

We did a lot of fun make-ups for *Lord of the Rings*. Seven of the nine leads were in some form of prosthetic every single day for two-and-a-half years. Really most of the cast were in prosthetics every single time they walked on to the set. But if I was to pick a single favourite character, without question, it would be Lurtz, the Uruk-hai who shoots Boromir in the forest, the character played by Lawrence Makoare.

Why do I like Lurtz? When we first meet this character in the first film, it's in the caverns below Isengard. For this, Lawrence endured ten-hour make-up application sessions exquisitely carried out by Gino Acevedo and Jason Docherty, a full body prosthetic with a combination of complex make-up and foam latex suit components for the torso, arms, hands, face, eyes and teeth.

Although it wasn't the cleverest make-up we ever did, Lawrence's performance through the make-up captured something truly remarkable, that intrinsic evil you feel exists in some people. And though he's only in the movie for a short length of time, for me he's absolutely unforgettable.

Also the contortionist who played the birthing Uruk-hai is the only actor in special effects make-up that I've ever known to get an ovation at rushes. At the dailies, everyone applauded him because of what he put himself through for this scene.

Born of alchemy, the birthing Uruk-hai was like an ill-formed potato being dug out of the ground. It was the most extreme make-up process we ever did on the trilogy of films. Every inch of his body was covered in prosthetics and his mouth was held open into a scream-like expression. Then we put him inside the Hot Melt birthing sack and filled it with glycerine. To achieve the visual we wanted, this amazing and crazy actor was contorted, as if underwater with his mouth held open, totally blind, on and off for eleven hours. It was remarkable.

That was a fun day of make-up!

Richard Taylor

Opposite: Richard Taylor prepares to seal the birthing Uruk-hai in a sack filled with glycerine for a standout scene in *The Lord of the Rings: The Two Towers* (2002).

2

WHAT
DREAMS ARE
MADE OF

What witches' brew created the Monster Kids now
running amok through the pages of this book? It was the
rise of the late-night fright flick, televised treasures from
Hammer, Universal and the like. Then from the stores
they came: magazines and models, costumes, masks and
make-up kits.

It was a world of gods and monsters, where our
masters discovered they could be anything they wanted,
simply by slapping crazy stuff on their faces. Here, then,
are their origin stories.

Things would come and go like parties and school and cheerleading… But it always came back to monsters and make-up.

Eryn Krueger Mekash

Previous pages: Eryn Krueger Mekash applies make-up during the early days of *Sabrina the Teenage Witch* (1996–2003).

Above: James Cagney made up as the Hunchback of Notre Dame for his portrayal of make-up artist and actor Lon Chaney in *Man of a Thousand Faces* (1957).

Opposite: Bud Westmore (centre) makes up James Cagney as Lon Chaney for *Man of a Thousand Faces* (1957).

I was ten when I first saw *Man of a Thousand Faces* (1957). That movie changed my life forever. After seeing it I wanted to follow in Lon Chaney's footsteps, to learn about make-up effects and figure out how everything was done. Even now, if I could go back in time, I'd go to MGM in 1925 to watch Chaney do his Phantom make-up.

As a kid I'd shine shoes to make enough money to buy things, such as bald caps from a local novelty store, but it frustrated me that you could always see the edges. There was another place, a better place, a proper make-up store, but it was farther away. It took a bus and a streetcar to get there, and cost me some of my shoeshine money, but it was worth it. I still remember the smell of nose putty and spirit gum when you walked into the place. It fed my senses.

I bought crepe hair and mortician's wax. At first I'd experiment on myself, but then I realised I could make up my friends. They'd go home with cut throats and burn scars, just make-up, of course, but their parents didn't like it and eventually my friends were all banned from playing with me.

Tom Savini

"EVENTUALLY MY FRIENDS WERE ALL BANNED FROM PLAYING WITH ME."

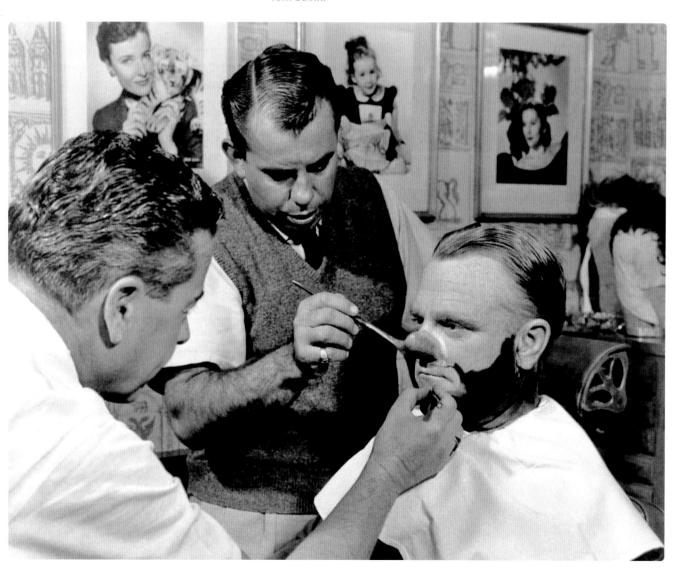

My father was a make-up artist.

I remember him doing a bloody scab on my arm, saying, "When your mother comes home from church, tell her one of the kids dragged you along the sidewalk."

He was a lot of fun!

Every Christmas, he'd put beards on the three wise men. Every Halloween, he'd turn the local kids into monsters. He was a big hit.

Unfortunately, he died when I was eleven, but I inherited his make-up cases and starting experimenting with everything. Then suddenly it's me turning the kids into wise men at Christmas.

By the time I was thirteen, I knew I wanted to be a make-up artist.

Leonard Engelman

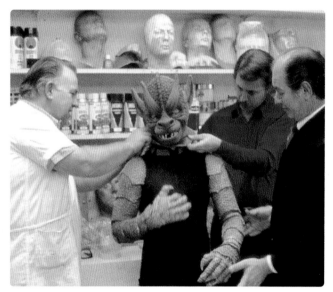

I was small. Still a toddler. My mother had put me in my crib upstairs to sleep. I was being unnaturally quiet, so she came to check on me, only to find I'd reached through the bars, grabbed her Max Factor lipstick, and turned myself into a Lipstick Person.

I'd rubbed it into my face, into my hair, absolutely everywhere, including the wall. And I'd rubbed it in so significantly, it took three weeks for me not to be red!

I'm not certain if that's what inspired me to become a make-up artist, but it was definitely my first make-up!

Lois Burwell

Left: Leonard Engelman stands for a snap with his creation for the *Night Gallery* (1969-73) episode *Pickman's Model* (S02E11).

Above: John Chambers and Leonard Engelman test fit the *Pickman's Model* creature suit at the Universal make-up staff shop.

Creature features on TV. *Famous Monsters* at the newsstands. Aurora model kits in toy stores. For kids like me in the Seventies, it was a perfect storm of stuff that sparked a lifetime obsession with monsters.

Norman Cabrera

When my parents bought their house, the front yard and backyard were all dirt. In just a few years, however, it had beautiful brick-laid paths and gardens, a wishing well, a koi pond lined with abalone shells, and that was all my grandfather's work. He was a concrete mason. A brick mason.

I'd watch him work and absorb it all.

I remember reading an article in a *Famous Monsters* magazine on *Revenge of the Creature* (1955). It showed gentlemen in their ties and lab coats – isn't that cool? – and they had the moulds open for the Creature suit. There were the plaster moulds in the little wooden cradles and they were stippling in coloured latex. I looked at what they were doing and something just clicked.

I went to my grampa and showed him the magazine. I said, "So, what you do… This is how they make monsters."

And he's like, "Theirs is a little sloppy, but… yes."

I always loved monsters, but, when you're a kid, you don't think much about how they're made. At least I didn't. But after I made that connection, I just felt compelled to learn how to do it.

Rob Freitas

This page: *Famous Monsters of Filmland* fueled the imagination of many a Monster Kid. Editor Forrest J. Ackerman ensured that, each month, the magazine had a great cover and was loaded with behind-the-scenes photos and stories from everyone's favourite horror, fantasy, and science fiction movies of the day.

Opposite: Bob Dawn and Jack Kevan ensure their monster is fighting fit on the set of *Creature from the Black Lagoon* (1954). Chris Mueller Jr. was instrumental in the design and sculpture of the Creature, under the supervision of make-up department head Bud Westmore.

My older brother Jeff was the driving force behind my interests. He bought Aurora model kits and *Famous Monsters* magazines. We made movies together, practiced make-up… He's a great big brother.

I remember once we had a dinosaur kit each. Accidentally, Jeff squeezed the Testors glue too hard and it squirted all over his Brontosaurus's head. You can't get that stuff off, you know. It just melts the plastic. So he took it and whipped it at the wall, smashing it into pieces. I always learned a lot from his mistakes! About being patient, and knowing when to walk away.

Another time, I was maybe ten, I saw Jeff lying on our workout bench. He was by himself, putting plaster of paris on his face, and I asked him what he was doing. He couldn't talk, or see, so he motioned for me to get a pencil and paper. He scribbled that he was making a cast but needed me to finish it. He started to panic, because the plaster was really heating up. So I did my best, laid on the gauze strips, but, when it dried, it locked behind his jaw and didn't separate from his skin easily. He didn't use any kind of release, such as Vaseline, so it pulled out all his eyebrows and all but two of his eyelashes!

Besides Universal Monster and Hammer horror movies, Jeff and I loved Ray Harryhausen stuff and made our own 8mm stop-motion movies. We'd turn G.I. Joe into a cyclops and stuff like that. Once,

"IT PULLED OUT ALL HIS EYEBROWS AND ALL BUT TWO OF HIS EYELASHES!"

we were maybe eleven and twelve, we spent three weeks making a movie, frame by frame, Jeff doing the main work and me assisting him. We took the film to a drug store to get developed.

The woman we gave it to asked Jeff, "What's in this honey?"

Then she untaped it, opened the canister to look inside, and totally exposed the film. Ruined it. Jeff's face went white. And that was it for our movie. After that, I focused more on make-up as you got results much quicker and they weren't so easily ruined.

Kevin Yagher

Opposite: Kevin Yagher at seventeen, sculpting Yoda.

This page: Aurora Monster model kits were a favourite of every Monster Kid. James Bama's box art hypnotised them into buying everything from The Creature and Godzilla to The Forgotten Prisoner.

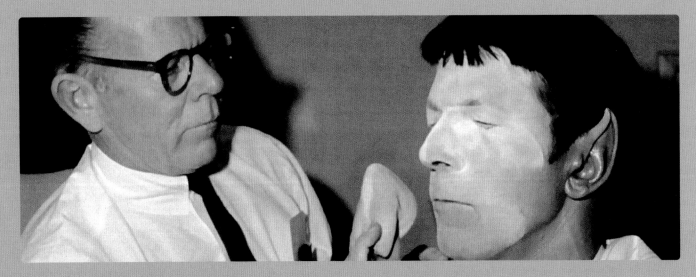

When I was six years old, my mom made me up as Mr. Spock. She gave me wax ear tips and even cut and dyed my hair.

That's when I realised, "I'm REALLY into this stuff!"

Garrett Immel

Above: Fred Phillips makes up Leonard Nimoy as Mr. Spock for the original *Star Trek* (1966–69) TV series. The ears were created by make-up legend John Chambers.

Below: A young David Grasso shows off the fearsome creature head he made growing up in Massachusetts.

After I saw *Planet of the Apes* (1968), I cut up a gorilla mask into an appliance and stuck it on my face with Elmer's glue.

After I saw *Star Wars* (1977), I was obsessed with Darth Vader and made a cardboard helmet and costume for myself.

I was a huge fan of Godzilla, too, and using brown paper bags that my mother brought home from the supermarket, I cut and taped them up into Godzilla, Rodan, and Ghidorah costumes.

That was me as a kid, and, honestly, not much has changed!

David Grasso

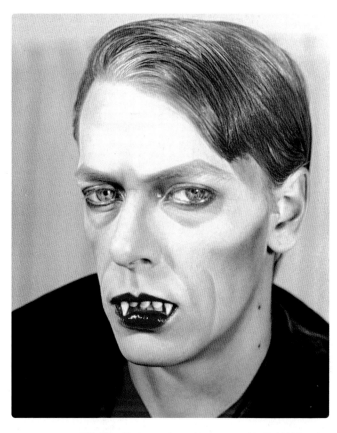

This Page: Early vampire make-up created by Todd McIntosh. That's Todd, thirsty for blood, below.

I used to hide behind my stepfather's chair while *Star Trek* (1966-69) was on, because it terrified me. My parents explained to me that these things weren't real – that those pointed ears on Spock were something that had been put on the actor, and that no, that actor on *Dark Shadows* (1966–71) doesn't really have fangs.

That started me experimenting.

So, at six years old, I began cutting out shirt collar stays to make fangs and used my mother's eyebrow pencil to paint lines on my face. After that, a kind neighbour, who worked in local amateur theatre, saw what I was doing and decided to encourage me by buying me the Leichner make-up book. That led to Corson's book, which, of course, became the make-up artist's bible in those days. Later, I discovered Lee Baygan's books and began my deeper journey into the craft of make-up.

All the while I was practicing on myself, and, by the time I was twelve, I was already doing make-up for local stage productions.

The first show I was involved with was *The Threepenny Opera*. I remember taking these pieces of joke shop plastic dog vomit, cutting them up, and sticking them on faces for syphilis sores – not that I knew what syphilis was. I asked an actor once and he told me to go home and ask my mother.

I was on my way!

Todd McIntosh

"INSTEAD OF JUST BUYING ME AN EXPENSIVE MASK, HE SAID, 'WHY DON'T WE MAKE OUR OWN?'"

My dad encouraged my interest in make-up effects. He thought it was all really cool. Once I asked him for a Don Post Timber Wolf mask. I wanted it so bad! But instead of just buying me an expensive mask, he said, "Why don't we make our own?"

He'd get me everything I needed to practice and learn new things: clay and latex, nose putty and rubber mask greasepaint... He was all in. And he'd tell me, "This is a real job. You could do this!"

Bill Corso

Stan Winston's store was just 2 miles [3km] from my house. I was twelve when I found out it was within walking distance, and after finding the number in the Yellow Pages, I immediately called to ask if I could come visit.

I packed up a box of shitty stuff I'd done and carried it over there. I got to spend the day and it was fantastic. I still remember the way everything looked. The way it smelled. The way Stan presented the studio – so clean and organised.

Stan started to nurture me, and would let me visit from time to time and bring new things to show him. But I always had to bring my report card, because he wanted me to maintain my grades.

I'd say, "But Stan, this is all I want to do."

And he'd reply, "That's great. You can do this when you're grown up. But right now, school's your job and you have to focus on getting good grades. If you get As and Bs, you're good to go. But anything below a B, you're not coming in the shop."

So I maintained As and Bs the whole time I was at school, because, god forbid, I couldn't visit Stan. And eventually I got to work there, on *Aliens* (1986), *Invaders from Mars* (1986), *Predator* (1987), and *Pumpkinhead* (1988).

Howard Berger

Opposite: Concept art for Frankenstein's Monster, and the frightening finished make-up, designed by Bill Corso when he was just starting out.

Top right: Howard Berger with his high school friend Allan Eto, pictured here wearing the first multipiece prosthetic make-up ever created by Howard, in 1980.

Right: Howard Berger surrounded by a selection of the latex masks he created while in high school.

"RED WAS THE ONLY COLOUR I CARED ABOUT, BECAUSE IT LOOKED LIKE BLOOD."

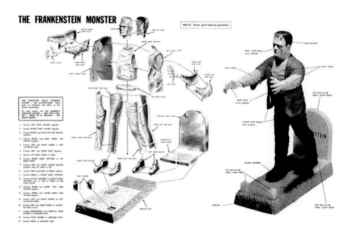

My parents would go out to dinner every Saturday night and, on the way home, they'd go to Burland's Hobby Shop to pick me up an Aurora model kit. Every week there would be a different monster.

I'd build them in the basement, laying out all the pieces on a bar top. Because there was no superglue at the time, you couldn't accelerate anything. So using Testors glue, I'd slowly stick the model together, one piece at a time, taping each piece in place while it set.

Once the model was built, I'd get out all my little enamel paint pots, although red was the only colour I cared about, because it looked like blood. I'd slather it all over everything, and then I had another model to display in my bedroom.

Greg Nicotero

This page: 1972's Aurora model kits had glow-in-the-dark parts, reinvigorating a slew of vintage terrors, and introducing them to a new generation of Monster Kids.

Opposite: Christopher Lee as The Mummy, courtesy of British make-up master Roy Ashton.

As a kid, the movie that resonated the most deeply with me was Hammer's *The Mummy* (1959). I saw it at the perfect age, where anything cheesy just went over my head. I thought it was magical!

I was eleven years old and I loved it so much, I wrote a short play about it, based on the burial scene. I cast myself as The Mummy and tried several make-up transformations that always left me looking like an accident victim. It never occurred to me to age my bandages, which I made by ripping up clean, white bedsheets.

I was a shy kid, so I can't actually fathom what possessed me to perform it at my school's talent show. Maybe I was just so excited, it squelched the kind of stage fright that plagued me for the rest of my life. Or maybe it was the suit. The perfect thing to hide behind. All of a sudden, you're no longer you.

Blair Clark

I was born in the Sixties, so I grew up around women with great cat eyes and eyelashes. I spent hours in the hair salon with my mother and grandmother getting these high, Marge Simpson hairdos. And I was always in my mother's make-up. It all just fascinated me.

I did my first successful make-up – without realising it – when I was about four. I'd found a bottle of Flintstones vitamins in the bath-room and had eaten them all. Then I mixed face powder with water and painted my face with it. I rubbed it in really good!

When my mother found me, she saw the empty vitamin bottle, and me looking an unnatural colour, and immediately thought I'd overdosed. It was only after getting my stomach pumped at the hospital that she realised what actually happened. I'll never forget her asking me, "Is that make-up on you?"

Toni G

As a teenager, I got a lot of inspiration from Tom Savini's book *Grande Illusions*. I made Tom's Boris dummy, sat him on a BMX bike, and pushed him off the edge of a quarry. I'd go to school with a fake axe in my face and freak everyone out.

I was into painting and illustration, sculpting and mould making, and I would spend hours in my bedroom making bodies and then cutting their heads off. Fortunately, my parents were very understanding.

Paul Katte

"FORTUNATELY, MY PARENTS WERE VERY UNDERSTANDING."

Opposite: Paul Katte in his bedroom in Australia, surrounded by make-up items and creatures he'd created. Monster Kids were truly international!

Left: HUGO was sold as Man of a Thousand Faces. You could start with a clean slate and turn him into anything. It was a toy that most aspiring make-up effects kids dreamed of owning.

Above: Paul Katte and Nick Nicolaou pose with the maestro of gore, Tom Savini, and a friend.

I did a magic act for my school talent show, but I bombed. It was pitiful. I realised the stage was not for me, but maybe I could do behind-the-scenes stuff. I'd do these little cuts and wounds on myself. And then I got my favourite ever toy: Hugo – Man of a Thousand Faces!

It was a bald puppet with a ton of prosthetic parts and hair pieces. I'd put the cuts on the puppet, then the cuts on me. The moustaches, the chin pieces… It was awesome. I caught the bug!

Louie Zakarian

was eight years old. There was a magic store in South Side, Pittsburgh, not too far from where I lived. They had a Bob Kelly make-up kit. It had brushes, greasepaint, and a tiny bottle of latex. But it was, like, ninety bucks, and I couldn't afford it. Once a week I'd go back to the store, however, just to look at it.

I went around the city collecting bottle and cans, looking in bushes and going through trash, until I'd made two dollars from the deposits left on them. I then convinced the guy behind the counter to sell me just the latex. He said they'd had the set

forever and didn't expect to ever sell it, so at least this way they'd make a few dollars.

Although I didn't actually know what to do with the latex, I figured out that if you put it on stretched skin, when you let go it would wrinkle. And I remember seeing a picture of the Mummy and realising that's how they must have done that. So I did this wrinkled Mummy make-up on my face – the first make-up I ever did – and it was terrible! But I thought it was amazing and ran around the house showing everybody.

Carey Jones

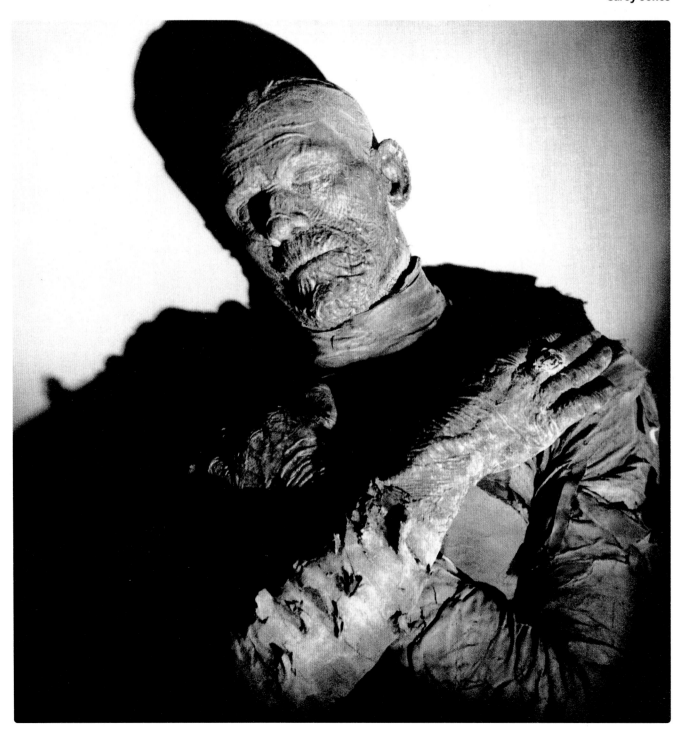

"IT SAID 'NON-TOXIC' ON THE BOX, SO I RECKONED WE'D BE FINE."

As a kid, I didn't do a lot of make-up on myself. I always preferred doing it on my friends, because I hated that shit on me. One Halloween, however, I did us all up as the band Kiss. We couldn't afford real make-up, but I found some poster paint at Kmart. It said "non-toxic" on the box, so I reckoned we'd be fine.

So I was painting my friend Andy, and it was going on cool, but then he said, "It's starting to sting a bit."

I'm like, "It's just drying. It'll be alright."

I finished everyone else, then did myself. I had this round, bowling ball face and looked like a chubby, Mexican Gene Simmons. But now my face was stinging, too, and getting hot, and shit, we hadn't even gone out trick-or-treating yet.

I don't think we made it even a block before my friends started wailing, "We can't take this any more! Take it off! TAKE IT OFF!"

We ran back to my house, and we're all in the bathroom, scrubbing it off. Obviously the paint had reacted with our skin and our faces were all now beet red.

Later on, we took a second look at the package, and noticed the warning, "Not intended for use on skin."

Lesson learned.

Gino Acevedo

Opposite: Boris Karloff in Jack Pierce's wonderful make-up for *The Mummy* (1932). Karloff described the one-time application of the seven-hour make-up, and the fourteen hours he subsequently spent in it, as "the most trying ordeal I ever endured."

Above left: Glam rockers Kiss in all their finery.

Above: Gino Acevedo strikes a pose in his Gene Simmons-inspired Kiss make-up. The group delivered everything that Monster Kids of the Eighties loved: make-up, horror, rock 'n' roll, and blood.

Above: The godfather of make-up, Dick Smith, poses with
a larger-than-life bust of himself, by Kazu Hiro.

Opposite: Kazu's wonderful Dick Smith bust reflects the
artist's remarkable attention to detail.

When I was in high school, I wasn't into special effects make-up, because I thought it was just about monsters. I don't like horror, so it didn't interest me.

Then I came across a copy of a *Fangoria* magazine in a bookstore in Kyoto, Japan, where I grew up. There was an article in it about Dick Smith and the Lincoln make-up he applied on Hal Holbrook for *North and South* (1985–86). I understood then that special effects make-up was also about creating characters, and that was much more interesting to me.

There are so many different aspects to special effects make-up, I realised it touched on almost everything I was interested in – nature, technology, art…

The next day, I gathered the materials I'd need to create the Lincoln make-up on myself. I made five attempts. Dick's address was in the back of the magazine, so I sent him photos of, I think, my third attempt, and that's how we began our correspondence.

Years later, in 2002, I wanted to make something special to celebrate Dick's eightieth birthday, a gift that reflected a skill I'd learned from him. So I decided to make a portrait, a bust of Dick, but doing it life size didn't interest me. Because he was my father figure, and I have looked up to him as a child sees a parent, I made it giant size.

Once I'd finished, I wanted Dick to be the first person to see it, and he was really touched. He cried. It was a special moment.

Later, when the portrait was displayed in public, I got to see how other people reacted to it, too. Make-up paraphernalia that you create for a movie is seen by audiences staring up at a screen. You can't really stand there and watch them. But with Dick's portrait I could, and seeing how people connected with it, and how emotional some of them got, really touched something in me. So now, besides make-up for movies, I also create portraits.

Ultimately, everything I do reflects my fascination with human faces.

Kazu Hiro

"ULTIMATELY, EVERYTHING I DO REFLECTS MY FASCINATION WITH HUMAN FACES."

ick Smith's *Do-It-Yourself Monster Make-up Handbook* was one of the few things I ordered from the back of a *Famous Monsters* magazine that actually arrived. It was amazing. My Bible!

I'd skip past the little kid's make-up articles and go straight to the tough ones at the back, such as Frankenstein's Monster. I made the flat top of his head out of lead. It was at least one-quarter inch thick and so heavy, I thought my neck was going to give way.

Blair Clark

started painting my face at the age of five. It wasn't so much that I wanted to wear make-up. It was more that the only face available to experiment on was my own!

I used my mother's make-up bag, sat in front of the mirror, and started by doing something clean and traditional, but then kept going until it became strange and interesting.

I was ten when I cut off my eyelashes, just to see the effect – what it did to my face. It was weird and uncomfortable growing back, but worth the trouble, because it fueled my fascination with transformation.

Pamela Goldammer

"I CUT OFF MY EYELASHES JUST TO SEE THE EFFECT."

hen I was nine years old, E.T. was my best friend. My grandmother was a sculptor and she made me this awesome E.T. costume. My dad was also an artist, so growing up I was encouraged to draw and express myself.

My friends like to remind me that I spoke like E.T. all summer long. So embarrassing! So I guess maybe I expressed myself a little too much sometimes.

Jamie Kelman

This page: *E.T.* superfan Jamie Kelman preparing to phone home in a costume created by his grandmother, and possibly searching for Reese's Pieces in a T-shirt featuring his out-of-this-world best friend.

Opposite, above: Jamie Kelman, menaced by an early werewolf creation of his own.

Opposite, below: Jamie Kelman applying his version of fan-favourite Freddy Krueger. Most aspiring make-up effects artists tried their hand at a version of either David B. Miller or Kevin Yagher's inspiring designs.

When I was small, I didn't have this whole, like, Guillermo del Toro, "I'm in love with monsters" thing. I was afraid of them.

I didn't relate to them. I didn't feel sorry for King Kong. He scared me shitless.

I didn't consider myself an outsider. I didn't commiserate with Frankenstein. He was horrifying to me.

I was, however, obsessed with them. I wanted to make them. And the more I learned, I was more intrigued than frightened.

There's nothing wrong with being scared! I mean, that's an appropriate response, yeah?

Mikey Rotella

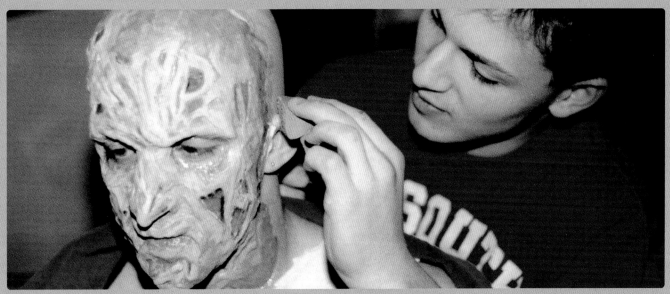

Unlike so many of the guys in our industry, I was terrified of monsters until my early teens. Honestly, I was deathly afraid and went to a therapist, because I couldn't sleep at night.

I had friends who'd tell me the stories of entire horror movies, because I couldn't go to see them. That's how I experienced *A Nightmare on Elm Street* (1984). It sounded really interesting, but I couldn't bear to actually watch it, because anything scary I saw would just play over and over in my head at night. It was torture.

Eventually, I was forced to confront my fears when I was invited to a get-together where they were watching *Silent Night, Deadly Night* (1984) and *A Nightmare on Elm Street Part 2: Freddy's Revenge* (1985). I had the cutes for one of the girls there, so I couldn't be a wimp.

I was twelve years old. In between the two movies, one of the girl's dads ran into the room dressed like Santa from *Silent Night, Deadly Night*. He was screaming and swinging this giant axe, but it wasn't scary. We were laughing! It was like this button switched on in my brain and suddenly horror was fun.

After that, I remember sitting through *Freddy's Revenge*, realising that instead of it being a string of nightmarish scenes I had to endure, it was full of all these incredible things that people had made with their hands. Like when Freddy pulls his skull open and his brain's pulsing – someone made that! It was the coolest thing ever and I became completely obsessed. A total horror hound. And I wanted to make everything myself.

One of the first things I attempted was the eyeball from *Evil Dead II* (1987) that flies across the screen. I made it in my bedroom with a ping-pong ball, five-minute epoxy, and red latex rolled around a pipe cleaner.

I made a few weird things to understand how moulds and foam latex work, and, about five make-up tries into my experiments, I made a pretty decent Freddy Krueger. It was crude, of course, but it looked like Freddy and I thought, "Hey, I could do this."

Eventually, my therapist told me that by making these monsters, I was taking control of them, and because they didn't frighten me any more, I no longer had to go see him.

Jamie Kelman   061

"I DISCOVERED A CREEK AT THE BACK OF OUR FARM WHERE I COULD DIG UP CLAY AND SCULPT WITH IT!"

I grew up in rural New Zealand, so I don't have the usual make-up artist backstory: Sadly, I didn't grow up watching amazing movies or knowing of the elite of the make-up and effects industry. We had one black-and-white television channel playing mainly British content. Even if we'd owned a VHS player, I wouldn't have even begun to know where to find the specialty tapes to watch on it. Getting to the movies required a one-hour bus trip to Auckland. There were no industry or fan magazines available in New Zealand at the time and, of course, the Internet didn't exist.

It wasn't until my later teens that I discovered all the things I'd been missing. The history of make-up and model effects, of miniatures and matte painting. And I had the good fortune of meeting Peter Jackson in my early twenties. More than anything else, due to his willingness to share his comprehensive knowledge, that gave me the greatest insight into the U.S. effects industry.

But from when I was small, I was driven by this desire to make things with my hands. I had a science teacher mother and an aircraft engineering dad. When we emigrated from Northern England, we moved into a small country cottage with a dirt-floored, single car garage out the front. That garage, however, was a place of wonder and invention.

My dad built our car when we first arrived. Then a sailing yacht, and most of the furniture in our home. He built me a little tin boat from a 2-litre [2-quart] sliced peach can – which I still have as a treasure today – and at five or six I realised that using my hands, and odds and ends lying around the house, I could start making things from my imagination for myself and others.

My first great and early love was papier-mâché. Simple old wallpaper paste and newspaper. Then I discovered a creek at the back of our farm where I could dig up clay and sculpt with it! The first sculpture was a rendition of the Loch Ness Monster. Then I started doing make-up effects on myself using adhesive tape, glue and acrylic paint to create wounds.

I remember once – I was eleven or twelve – I slipped on some wet grass and tore my calf muscle badly on a barbed wire fence. When I showed my mother, she berated me, "You're so bloody stupid. Get up to your room."

She thought it was another one of my ropey make-up efforts – that I was crying wolf – because most days back then, I enjoyed giving myself cut wrists, bleeding necks, damaged limbs… And I was beginning to do them well enough, I guess, that she was convinced that this very real wound was just another one of my dodgy creations.

After about an hour, however, feeling very woozy, I went back downstairs and showed her my wound again. I pulled it open so she could see it was real and give me the patching up I needed!

Richard Taylor

Opposite: Richard Taylor, Peter Jackson, and Tania Rogers puppeteer the Baby Selwyn heads in *Braindead* (1992), an early collaboration from the team that revolutionised the movie industry with their *Lord of the Rings* trilogy (2001–03).

Following pages: Tania Rogers and Richard Taylor prepare one of their many gore effects for Peter Jackson's *Braindead* (1992).

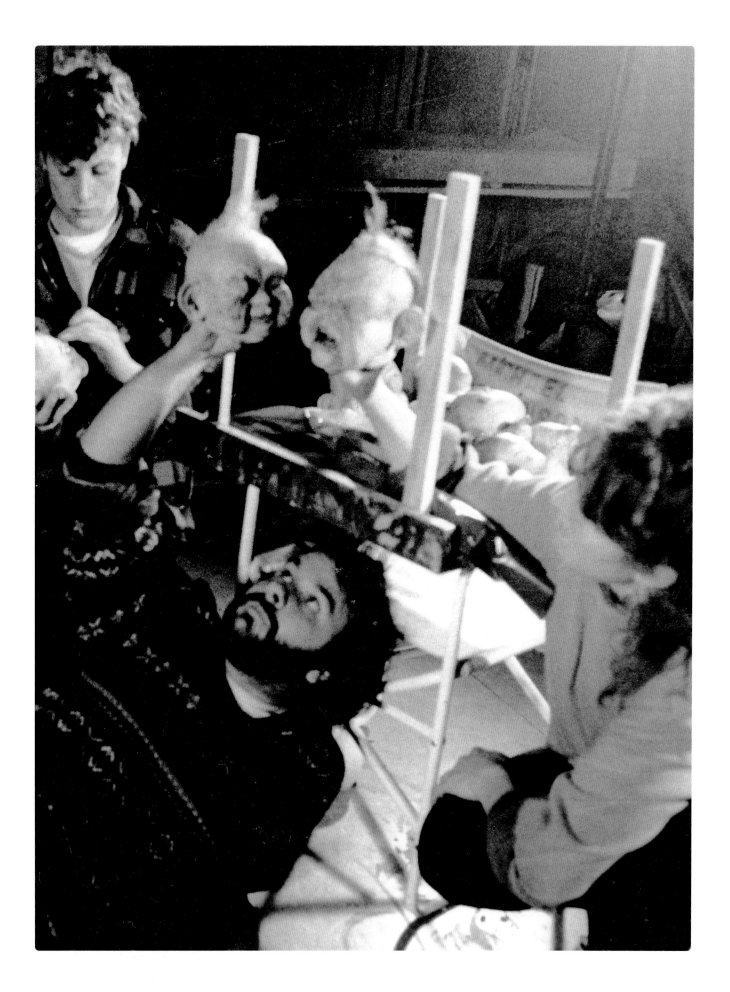

As a youngster in Iowa, I built my own make-up kit. There was a make-up store, and a magic store, where I'd spend my allowance. I'd make noses on myself, do things to try to scare my mother, and eventually that led, not to me becoming a make-up artist, but to storytelling and acting.

Ben Foster

This page: *Fangoria* magazine, originally edited by Bob Martin and then Tony Timpone, was the ultimate Eighties' horror and make-up effects publication.

Opposite: Everyone who aspired to become a make-up effects artist dreamed of being featured in *Fangoria*. Leading with a story on Rick Baker's work on *An American Werewolf in London* (1981), this fan-favourite issue also featured industry icons Tom Savini, Stan Winston, and Chris Walas.

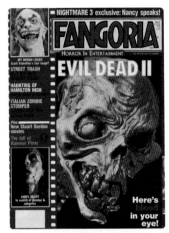
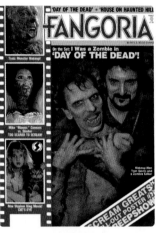

"IT WAS ALL GORE, GORE, MONSTERS AND GORE."

Way before I was in school, back in the late Seventies, every Tuesday I'd go with my mother to the grocery store. She'd put me in front of the magazine stand and I'd just look at all the pictures. I used to like *Mad*, but there was this other magazine, just a little bit off to the right… I got on my tippy toes and reached for it and grabbed it.

This horrible face was on the cover, a bloody, burned thing. I couldn't read, of course – I was probably only four years old. But it had a cool font in red and yellow. It was *Fangoria*! And I just sat there, like, flipping through the pages. It was all gore, gore, monsters and gore, but I was infatuated by it until this hand came from behind me and snatched the magazine out of my hands.

My mother forbade me to look at it. But every time she left me at that stand, I'd grab a *Mad* magazine and a *Fangoria*. And what I'd do is I'd take the *Fangoria* and put it inside the *Mad* magazine. So it looked like I was reading *Mad*!

Tami Lane

SHOCK FX SPECIAL

CARPENTER on Halloween 2 & The Thing!

FANGORIA

$2.25
K49129
#14
DGS
UK
95P

MONSTERS • ALIENS • BIZARRE CREATURES

TOM SAVINI 'The Prowler'

STAN WINSTON 'Dead & Buried'

CHRIS WALAS 'Caveman' & MORE!

Rick Baker & **AN AMERICAN WEREWOLF in London**

BREAKING IN

Like Indiana Jones taking his first step on that invisible bridge, here we detail the various leaps of faith taken by our make-up masters as they rose from the ranks of the hobbyist to, "I could do this for a living?"

Encouraged to venture beyond the safety of their bedroom labs, our young magicians learned their craft from a pioneering earlier generation of industry wizards, who graciously shared their secrets, and generously shepherded our heroes through their earliest professional adventures.

I was twenty-one. My dad said to me, "You're forever sticking bits of rubber on yourself and scaring the hell out of us. Have you ever thought about doing that for a living?"

I went, "Can you do that?"

I'd been to see *Star Wars* (1977) and was absolutely astounded by it. My father found a newspaper article about the cantina sequence and this guy, Stuart Freeborn, who'd done many of the aliens for it.

In the paper, it said he lived in a little town called Esher, which happened to be just 10 minutes down the road. My dad looked him up in the phone book, dialled his number, and handed me the phone.

He said, "Speak to him."

I was terrified, being put on the spot like that, but, luckily, Stuart was wonderful. He asked me if I had any photos of the make-up effects I'd done, and I told him I had a shopping bag full of photos that I'd taken during a film and TV production course.

He said, "Come and see me!"

My father drove me up to Elstree, parked the car in the pub opposite, and got himself a beer while I wandered into the studio to meet Stuart. We talked for a while and then he asked me, "Would you like to see what I'm doing?"

He led me into another room and there, sitting on a table, was this little green guy with pointy ears and a lot of cables falling out of his buttocks. At this point, I had no idea what he was working on. He said, "I'll take you on the set."

I quietly followed him up a flight of stairs, being careful not to trip over any cables. Blue and orange bars of light were everywhere. There was a pit in front of me, and when I looked inside, although I didn't know what it was at the time, there was Han Solo in carbonite. Then, on the other side of the pit, in walked Darth Vader! Him, I definitely knew.

So I'm in the carbon-freezing chamber, grinning, thinking, "This is *Star Wars*! Oh my God! THIS IS *STAR WARS*!"

Then Stuart lead me out and said, "Can you start Monday?"

I raced back to the pub and told my dad, "I've got a job!"

They paid me forty-five pounds [roughly sixty-five dollars] a week, which was more money than I'd ever seen in my life. It was fantastic! Most of the show had already been shot, but the Yoda stuff they'd saved for the end, because it had taken so long to make the damn thing.

Stuart had built this incredible mechanism inside Yoda's skull, but we were looking at a bunch of loose cables at the other end, because he hadn't given a lot of thought, yet, to the control system. He asked me to help him with that, but honestly I knew as much about controls as I did about flying a spaceship.

As it turned out, however, Stuart mainly wanted me to hold things and pass things and run out and find things. And to make him colossal amounts of tea. Honestly, I've never met anyone who drank as much tea as Stuart.

For me, it was a mad training session with one of the most genuinely clever people I've ever met.

Nick Dudman

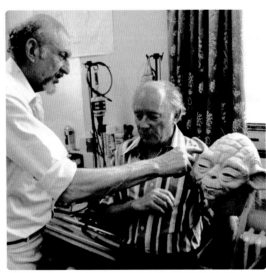

Previous pages: Carl Fullerton completes his Jason make-up for *Friday the 13th Part 2* (1981).

Left: Irvin Kershner, the director of *The Empire Strikes Back* (1980), applies a finishing touch to Yoda creator Stuart Freeborn.

Above: Irvin Kershner (left) discusses Yoda's puppet head with Stuart Freeborn.

The first feature movie I ever worked on was *Gregory's Girl* (1980). A week before we began the shoot, one of the leads — Claire Grogan — had been attacked. Someone had broken a glass and cut her face from cheek to ear and Bill Forsyth and the D.P. Mick Coulter asked how I could cover the wound.

As inexperienced as I was, I told them I wouldn't go anywhere near it. That covering it up could leave her scarred for life and be dangerous for her health. I suggested instead they only shoot her wide, or from the other side, and that's what they did. So my first real professional make-up challenge resulted in me refusing to use make-up on a principal character.

Lois Burwell

"I ALWAYS WANTED MY MAKE-UP EFFECTS TO LOOK ABSOLUTELY REAL, EVEN WHEN CLOSE-UP."

After I got back from Vietnam, I was stationed in Fort Bragg, North Carolina. One night I happened to be walking past a local theatre. I went in on a whim to watch the rehearsal and that was that: I was there for eight years!

That theatre became my second home. I was in a play every night, and besides acting, I did the hair work and make-up, too.

Chaney's make-ups were stage make-ups. The Phantom make-up was a stage make-up. He was able to lift up his nose with silk organza. People later said he used fish hooks, but it was actually a fabric called fish skin. And he painted his mouth and nostrils black to make them look bigger. It was a beautiful stage make-up and it inspired me.

On stage, since the audience is far away, and because the lighting is so forgiving, you can get away with anything. But I always wanted my make-up effects to look absolutely real, even when close-up. I needed to look in the mirror and be totally convinced by what I'd done.

It was great practice for movie make-up effects, where your face is 40 feet [12m] high and 60 feet [18m] wide.

Tom Savini

Left above: Tom Savini with an early alien creation.

Left below: Lon Chaney in full Phantom guise, displaying his famous make-up kit.

Dawn of the Dead (1978) changed everything for me. Although I'd been fascinated with make-up for a long time, besides Planet of the Apes (1968) and The Exorcist (1973), there weren't a lot of make-up movies that really grabbed me. But Dawn was just so in-your-face.

Plus it was a local production. I grew up in Pittsburgh, Pennsylvania, a long way from Hollywood, but the two guys who were mainly responsible for Dawn of the Dead lived within 40 minutes of my house: George Romero was in Shady Side, and Tom Savini lived in Bloomfield. They were within arm's reach!

Now, my parents had spent years telling me, "You've got the brains so you're gonna be the doctor of the family," and I never questioned that. I respected them and believed that was what I was going to do.

I was just a kid, really, when I first met George, but my uncle Sam had been in The Crazies (1973) and that was enough of an in for me to strike up a conversation. As I got to know him, and he could see how interested I was in what he did, he'd say things like, "You still want to be a doctor, right? You're not going to quit school and do something stupid like start making movies? I don't want a call from your parents telling me I ruined everything by seducing you into the dark side of horror filmmaking."

Still, I only ever thought of movies, make-up and model making as a hobby.

I first met Tom Savini when I visited George on the set of Creepshow (1982). George was busy filming, so I ended up spending a lot more time with Tom. I felt lucky to be hanging out in the studio of a guy who created incredible make-up effects at a time when special effects make-up was being introduced to the world via The Fog (1980), Friday the 13th (1980), The Howling (1981), and An American Werewolf in London (1981).

Pretty much every week, back then, another big genre movie came out. The studios were spending big money on major productions that everyone was going to see and, finally, horror, sci-fi and fantasy were getting the respect they deserved.

Still, as much as I loved spending time with Tom and being on movie sets, I was still very much focused on becoming a doctor, so I went to college to study biology and pre-med.

Three years later, it's summer vacation and I'm having lunch with George. He said, "We just got the green light for Day of the Dead (1985) – would you like a job?"

How could I possibly refuse working on the sequel to Dawn of the Dead? So I said yes, but just for this one, and came aboard as Tom Savini's assistant. One of the advantages to having me manage the department was that it gave Tom the opportunity to collaborate with George and other members of our crew and brainstorm the variety of ways in which zombies could be dispatched. With me in place, Tom didn't have to concern himself with management stuff like collecting résumés, hiring the crew, doing script breakdowns and ordering supplies.

So I got hired on July 23, 1984, and my plan was to take some time off school, work on Day of the Dead, and then in January, go back to college.

But nothing was ever the same after that. I just loved everything about it. I loved the collaboration. I loved the ingenuity. And I learned so much! Like how to make moulds and run pieces. I'd make chopped-off arms and body parts and it was all so much fun!

When the movie wrapped and everyone left, I was like, "But I'm not done. I want to keep going." So I never went back to college.

I was hooked.

Greg Nicotero

"FINALLY HORROR, SCI-FI AND FANTASY WERE GETTING THE RESPECT THEY DESERVED."

Opposite, top: Greg Nicotero (centre) and Howard Berger (right) complete a few final touches on Michael Trcic as Day of the Dead's (1985) Gut Lab Zombie.

Opposite, left: Galen Ross and Ted Danson as the waterlogged lovers from Creepshow (1982).

Opposite, centre: Connie Nicotero poses with her son Greg, made up as one of the many zombies he played in Day of the Dead.

Opposite, right: Tom Savini (left) and Greg Nicotero ready an explosive blood bag on the head of a zombie extra for Day of the Dead.

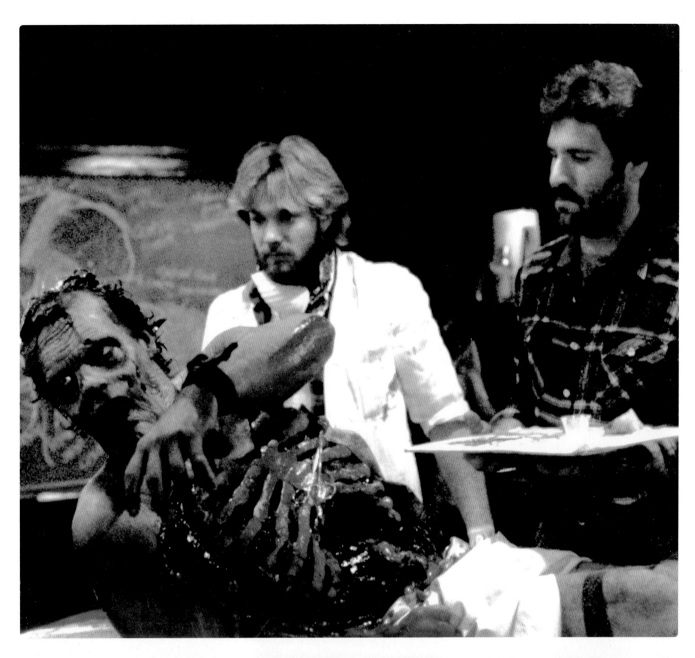

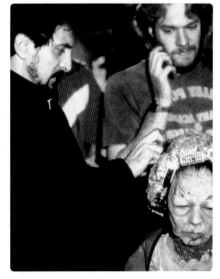

The first movie I ever went on location for was *Day of the Dead* (1985), with four months in a 175-mile [280-km] limestone mine in Beaver Falls, Pennsylvania. What a crazy place that was. We'd go in early and come out late. The only time we saw sunlight was on our day off.

I was young, however, and up for anything, so it didn't matter. And it was so much fun, working for Tom Savini. And dangerous, because Tom is a big practical joker. So sometimes you'd get hurt. Everyone gets hurt, working for Tom!

One day I was sitting at my desk, concentrating on something, unaware that Tom was shuffling along on the floor like a soldier, planting gunpowder and an igniter beneath my chair.

Suddenly he said, "Hey, Howard."

I went, "Yeah, Tom?"

Then he pushes the button on a box that said "DETONATOR" on it, and there's a massive BOOM, BOOM, BOOM, BOOM – and smoke everywhere. No destruction, because there weren't projectiles in it, but still, this incredibly loud, echoing bang.

And Tom's like, "I blew you up!"

That made him super happy... One day, Tom triggered an explosion that was so loud, everyone thought the cave was collapsing and ran out.

Also there were golf carts. Every department had one, and during shooting, they'd all be lined up. That's when Tom would have us stop work. We'd jump in the carts and speed through the mine. It was cold as shit, pitch black, and you could hear bats flying overhead.

"THE ONLY TIME WE SAW SUNLIGHT WAS ON OUR DAY OFF."

Tom would bring a little boom box that he'd play the *Raiders of the Lost Ark* music on, and we'd smash into each other, jump from one cart to another, and play fight.

People used to store their cars and boats in the mine to keep them from getting damaged by winter weather. Little did they know that we were down there, screwing around. One time we turned all the carts' lights off, and suddenly there was a "CRASH!"

We turned the lights on and, oh shit, we'd smashed a golf cart-size hole in the side of this big boat. Nobody ever found out, though, because it was winter, and we were long gone before anyone came to pick the boat up.

We just backed up, got out of there, and never said a thing... Until now.

I've just always loved to play, and have fun – and a lot of that, I'm sure, I got from Savini.

Howard Berger

If you'd told me when I was fifteen, that one day I'd be at KNB doing zombies and stuff, I'd have said, "Get the hell out of here."

When I first came out to L.A., one of my first stops was KNB, the old shop on Woodman Place. I just walked in there, cold, with my book. And I asked, "Can I go look at the shop?"

And they replied, "What are you doing here? You can't just walk in here."

But I'm like, "Is there anyone I can talk to?"

And they said, "Hold on. We'll see if someone's here."

So one of the girls went back and, a few minutes later, Howard Berger comes out! He said, "Hey, what's up?"

And he gave me a whole tour. Like, an hour-long tour of the shop. And then he sat down and looked at my book. It was nuts.

When I left, I thought, "I got to get in that place. Someday I'm going to work there."

And then it happened, about thirteen years later! It was the coolest thing ever. A little nerve-racking at first, but it has a real homey vibe and I started having fun almost immediately, making crazy over-the-top zombies for *The Walking Dead* (2010-22).

Mikey Rotella

Opposite: Howard Berger makes up John Vulich for his cameo as the Shovel Zombie in *Day of the Dead* (1985).

Above: A scary selection of masks, and their maker, Mikey Rotella.

I grew up in Illinois and didn't know the first thing about make-up effects. Hollywood might as well have been Mars. I loved the idea, however, and swung a trip to Los Angeles via a communication class. The best part was visiting KNB. As soon as I walked in there, I fell in love.

That's where I first met Howard [Berger]. He gave a talk about make-up, and while he was doing it, gave me a rubber chin and teeth. I asked him, "How can I do this?"

Tami Lane

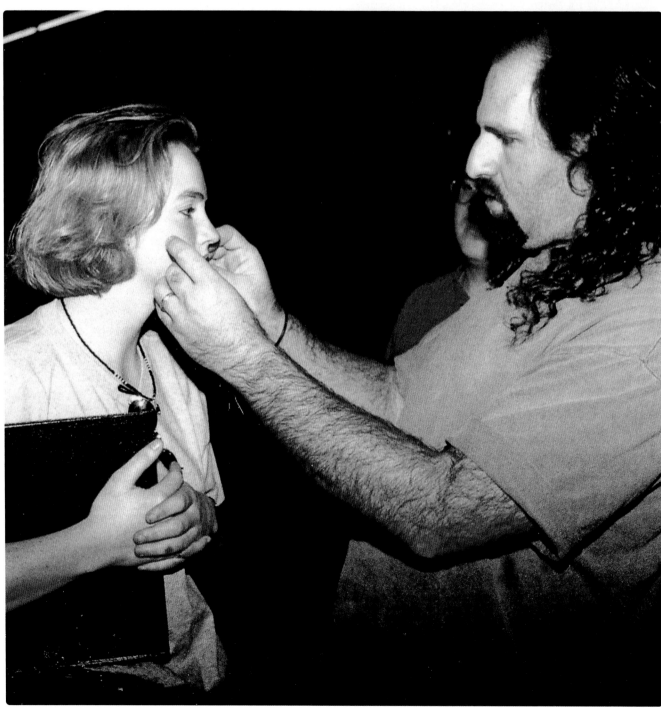

M att Rose and I had a mask company called Bizarre Creations. We ran it out of his backyard. We created about a dozen masks and they all had crazy names, such as Ungeryaw, Booboid, and Budda Budda Budda.

It's one thing to sculpt something, but the first time I ever pulled a mask out of a mould I'd made – THAT was the best thing ever. It felt like opening a door to an amazing new world.

Nothing will ever beat the smell of R&D latex and baby powder. It's magical!

Steve Wang

"HOLLYWOOD MIGHT AS WELL HAVE BEEN MARS."

Opposite, top: Tami Lane at twenty-one, back when she first started working at KNB EFX.

Opposite: Tami Lane and Howard Berger's first meeting at KNB EFX Group in 1995.

Above: Matt Rose (left) and Steve Wang (right) as The Ghoul Brothers, their entry in *Fangoria*'s Monster Makers contest, held by the magazine in the early Eighties.

Dick Smith was the most wonderful man in the world. He brought everyone in our industry closer together and encouraged us to share information. It's amazing that kids starting out could just get him on the phone.

It must have driven his wife crazy, with kids calling from all over the world, all hours of the night, asking him questions – and he'd answer them!

Kevin Yagher

Right: Kevin Yagher (left) and Dick Smith (right) pose for a photo. Dick was dedicated to encouraging and inspiring all young and up-and-coming artists.

Below: Dick Smith applies his old-age Barnabas Collins make-up to Jonathan Frid for *House of Dark Shadows* (1970).

Opposite: Gino Acevedo with a batch of the Frankenstein's Monster masks that he painted for Imagineering.

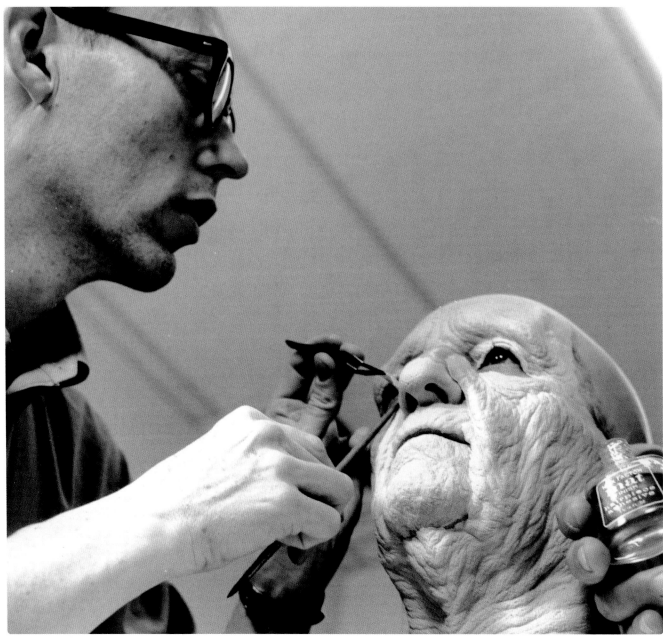

My first job, straight out of high school, was designing masks at Imagineering, a Halloween company in Phoenix, Arizona. I was eighteen years old.

A friend of mine, Dave Ayres, who was one of the first people I knew in the business, told me he was friends with Dick Smith. I said, "You know Dick Smith?!"

And he went, "Yeah. You should really start sending him photos of your sculptures. Here's his number. Give him a call and introduce yourself. Tell him you know me and he'll probably let you send him some pictures. He looks at everyone's stuff. He's always helping people out."

Finally, one day, I got brave enough to call Dick. He answered, "Hello?"

I went, "Hi, Dick. My name is Gino Acevedo. I'm calling you from Phoenix, Arizona. I'm a friend of David Ayres."

Dick said, "Oh, I know David. He's a great guy."

I said, "I work at a Halloween company, sculpting masks, and David suggested that, if I send you some of my work, maybe you'd critique it and hopefully give me some tips."

And he said, "Oh, well, Dino… You realise I'm a very busy man. I'm really sorry, but I'm going to have to deny."

I'm like, "OK. All right. No problem."

He said, "But you keep going and keep practicing. OK. Bye-bye!"

And that was that. I was devastated.

I called David Ayres back. He said, "Did you ever call Dick?"

I said, "Yeah. I just got off the phone with him."

He replied, "Great! What did he say?"

I told him, "He said he had to deny, because he's too busy."

So David said, "You're kidding?! He looks at everybody's stuff."

Years later, I was working on *Death Becomes Her* (1992) with Alec [Gillis] and Tom [Woodruff Jr.], when Dick came over to the shop, because he was consulting on some of the make-up stuff. While he was there, we took him to lunch.

It was first time I'd actually met Dick and now I'm sitting right across from him. So I said, "Dick. I called you years and years ago."

He said, "Really?"

I said, "Yeah. I'm originally from Phoenix, Arizona, and my friend David Ayres…"

He said, "I know David. He's a great guy."

I said, "Well, David suggested I send you some pictures of my work."

And he said, "Well, did you send them?"

I said, "No, because when I called you, you said you were busy and had to deny."

He went, "You're kidding?! I look at everybody's stuff."

I said, "Yeah. That's what I heard."

So he went, "Well, Gino, you can send me your stuff now!"

would love to say that from the age of ten I was reading *Fangoria*, watching classic movies, and desperate to be a make-up artist. But the truth is I fell into it completely by accident.

I did a degree in graphic design and spent many years as an art director on *Cosmopolitan* and other magazines, but I got bored. I was at a dinner party one night when one of the other guests mentioned she needed to find cheap labor to punch hairs into Robert De Niro's chest. It turns out she was talking about appliances for *Frankenstein* (1994).

I thought it sounded like fun. I took the job, but it turned out I was useless at punching hair. So they asked me, "What else could you do? Can you paint?"

I told them I had experience in illustration, so they had me painting pieces. Then they needed someone to work on the stunt double's prosthetics. It didn't need to be as precise as De Niro's make-up, because it was never going to be seen up close.

Dan Parker partnered me with Michelle Taylor and took us through the make-up process. Then on day one, they threw us on the set. We didn't really know what we were doing, but somehow we got away with it. It was a baptism of fire!

After that, Dan Parker took me on as a trainee for the next few years, and that's how I learned. After working newspaper hours, 10 a.m. to 6 p.m. with a two-hour lunch, it was a shock to the system getting up at 4 a.m. and not finishing until late, but I was young, so it was fine.

Jeremy Woodhead

"THE TRUTH IS I FELL INTO IT COMPLETELY BY ACCIDENT."

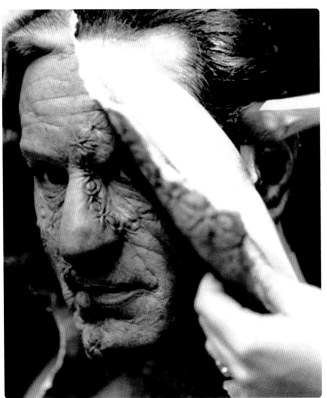

Top: Daniel Parker poses with his creations for *Mary Shelley's Frankenstein* (1994).

Left: David White touches up Robert De Niro as the Monster.

Above: The removal process is every actor's favourite part of the day.

W hen you arrive in Hollywoodland and are 6 feet 3½ inches [191.75cm] tall with a long neck, you weigh 140 pounds [63kg], have a background in mime, and "Contortionist" is on your résumé because you can put your legs behind your head, what do you think your agent sends you out for?

LOTS of otherworldly things.

Doug Jones

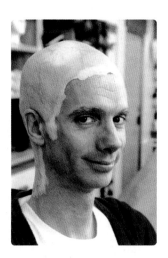

Top, right: New to the entertainment industry, Doug Jones played McDonald's "spokes-moon" character, Mac Tonight, for three years, in twenty-seven commercials. Mac was a cool Steve Neill creation.

Above and right: Doug Jones prepares to play one of The Gentlemen for the fan-favourite *Buffy the Vampire Slayer* (1997–2003) episode, *Hush* (S04E10). The character was designed and created by Optic Nerve Studios and applied by Todd McIntosh.

I spent a year-and-a-half trying to get on *Saturday Night Live* (1975-Present), and finally started on the last two shows of the '94/'95 season. The first thing I did was make a bunch of exploding heads for a pre-tape. The following week, David Duchovny was hosting and they got me in to do an alien make-up on some dude.

So I'm sitting on the set and the director comes up to me, he's like, "The actor who was going to do this page of dialogue didn't show up. Can you memorise it and we'll shoot you for the pre-tape instead?"

Of course, I did it, but they shot, like, seven other people at the same time, so I figured maybe I'd be in there for a little second or something.

Saturday night comes around and I'm working on the show. I think I was taking care of Chris Elliott that day. So I'm sitting in the make-up room. I'm the new guy. I don't know anybody. I don't know what the hell I'm doing. So I'm just sitting quietly, cleaning my brushes, when all of a sudden the pre-taped segment starts and who pops up on the freakin' thing? Yours truly, and they used my whole bit. Like, everything I shot.

I couldn't believe it. Suddenly every make-up artist and hairstylist in that room are shooting me daggers, like, "Fucker's only been here two days, he's on-camera and has dialogue."

I've been at *SNL* ever since and it's been awesome.

Louie Zakarian

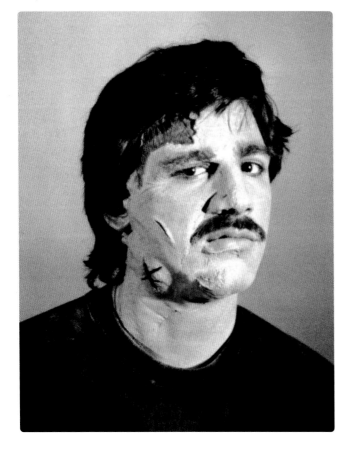

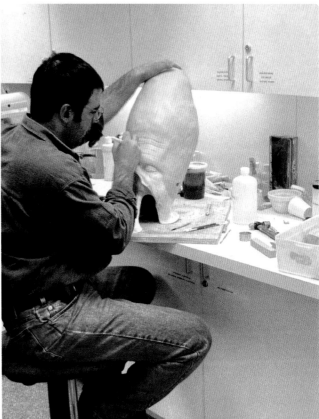

Top: Louie Zakarian (left) stands for a snap beside the first creature suit he ever made for a movie, 1993's *Wonderguy*, assisted by Vincent Schicchi (right).

Above: Louie Zakarian working at 30 Rock, preparing an iconic Coneheads prosthetic for an SNL (1975-present) sketch.

Left: Louie Zakarian models an early test make-up.

Opposite: Louie Zakarian transformed Stephen Colbert into Dr. Zaius for an SNL skit. Virtually every make-up effects artist has created their own take on a *Planet of the Apes* (1968) character, because the film influenced an entire generation of Monster Kids.

"SUDDENLY EVERY MAKE-UP ARTIST AND HAIRSTYLIST IN THAT ROOM ARE SHOOTING ME DAGGERS."

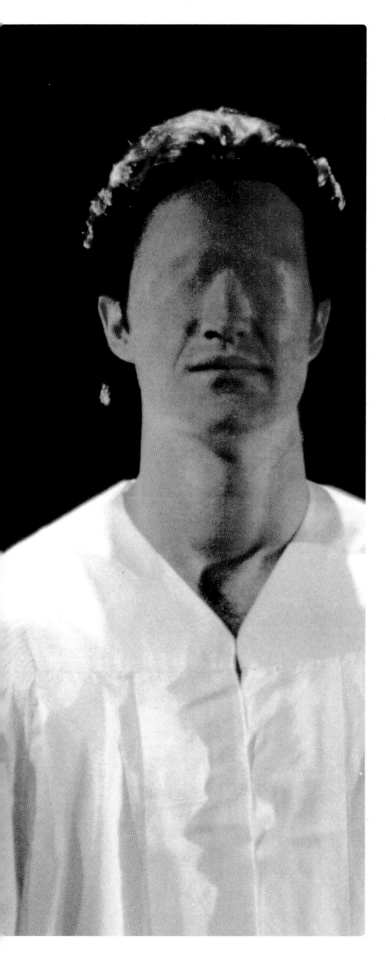

"I DON'T WANT TO SCREW IT UP BY COVERING EVERYTHING WITH BLOOD."

When we were in film school together, Jamie [Kelman] would do these beautiful sculptures. He created a make-up effect for one of my movies where this guy was walking around with such a massive head wound that part of his brain was exposed. And Jamie had done all this detailed painting to give the brains depth and shading.

As we were getting ready to shoot it, Jamie said, "OK, I'm going to apply the blood now."

And I had to stop him. I told him, "It looks so good. I don't want to screw it up by covering everything with blood. Let's just put a little around the edges."

So Jamie replied, "But it's not gonna look real!"

And I just told him, "I don't care!"

Fred Raskin

Left: Fred Raskin stands between a pair of Jamie Kelman creations for his NYU senior thesis film, *Lost Souls* (1995).

Above: Jamie Kelman was the brains behind this gory effect from Fred Raskin's *Lost Souls* (1995).

Ever since I was a little kid, my mother was unbelievably supportive. I was starting to make a connection with all these make-up shops, with Burman Industries, Cinema Secrets and places like that. So she'd drive me to school – I was fourteen or fifteen, not long before I dropped out – and I'd say, "Hey, you know, I got a call. They're going to blow up a head…"

And she'd just turn the car around, saying, "All right, I'll drive you there."

It was incredible. I'd walk into these shops and be able to work. They were like, "As long as your mom says it's OK."

I'd sweep floors, do a little sculpting – whatever they needed me to do. I was ditching school to start my freelance career and everyone was cool with it. I really don't think that would slide today!

Vincent Van Dyke

"I WAS DITCHING SCHOOL TO START MY FREELANCE CAREER AND EVERYONE WAS COOL WITH IT."

Above: Young Vincent Van Dyke's first make-up kit.

Right: A wide shot of one of KNB EFX Group's studio spaces, revealing the scope of what's required to make monsters every day.

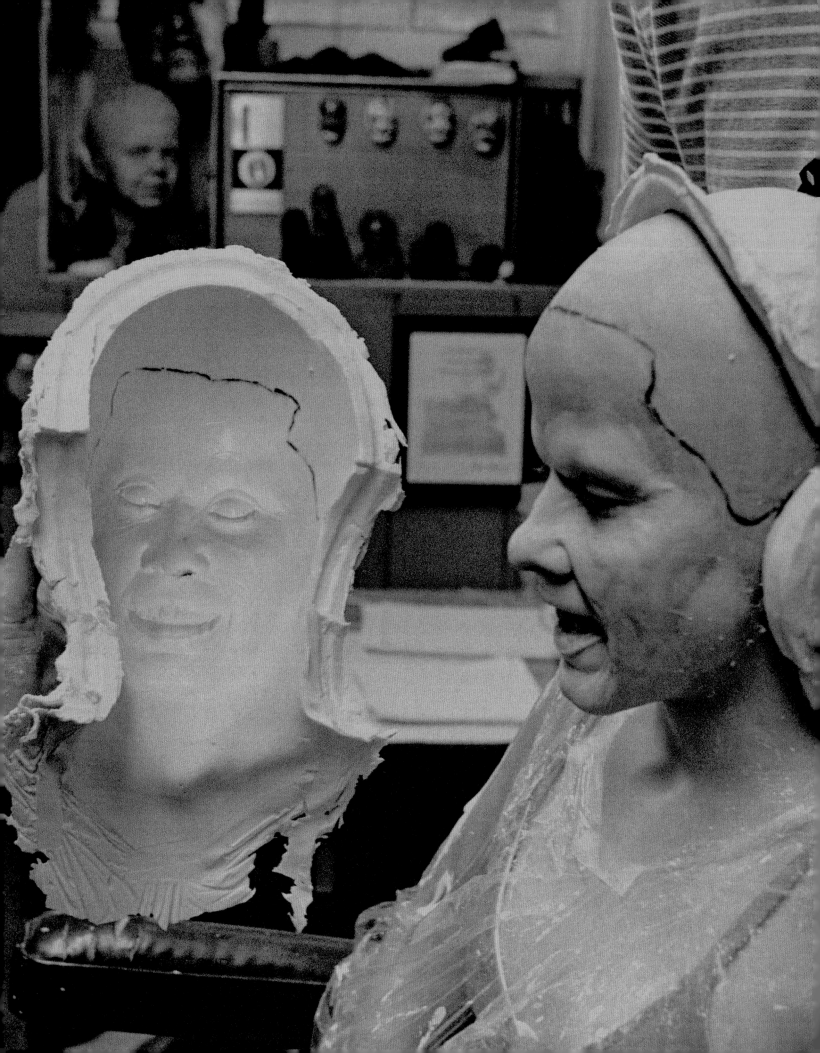

4

THE SEED OF INVENTION

Beyond the eureka moment of a creature's creation, that big bang of inspiration where a character is first conceived, there's an additional series of little bangs, of painstaking creative steps where dreams are dragged from the printed page into the labs of our make-up masters and finally, on to the frames and faces of our favourite suit performers.

From sketches and maquettes to prosthetics and test, discuss, revise, repeat, here's how they slog their way towards the remarkable.

What we do is so unique. But we're not sculpting something to go sit in a gallery somewhere – we're making functional, moving, engineered sculptures.

We're less credible than fine artists as generally we're thought of as technicians. Yet we've created an entirely new art form combining sculpture, painting and movement. And beyond that, it's functional.

Then at the end of the day, we rip it off and throw it out. Just like sidewalk art: shit rains and it's over.

Mike Marino

"WE'RE MAKING FUNCTIONAL, MOVING, ENGINEERED SCULPTURES."

My dad worked closely with John Chambers. They were good friends. They trusted each other. *The Island of Dr. Moreau* (1977) was a big movie for both of them.

From the very beginning of Dr. Moreau it was just my dad, John Chambers and Danny Striepeke. The project began with my dad doing a lot of drawings.

My dad spent a lot of time at the LA and San Diego zoos drawing animals. He did hundreds of sketches and drawings, then John would pick out certain drawings and my dad would transpose them into colour illustrations.

John and Danny would select various illustrations my dad made and then have him sculpt those illustrations into maquettes. After he sculpted the maquette, he sculpted the prosthetics. Three characters – Lionman, Hyena Man and Boarman – were transformed into test make-ups.

These three test make-ups were all done in the make-up department at 20th Century Fox. When the make-up application was finished, the actors were paraded in front of the producers: Skip Steloff, Samuel Z. Arkoff and Sandy Howard, and the director, Don Taylor, at the offices of American International Pictures on Wilshire Boulevard. They loved them.

Originally, there were only going to be three make-ups in the movie, but once they saw how incredibly beautiful those make-ups were, the film was put on hiatus to rewrite the script to include more characters, and more make-ups.

So they go and do the film. They go off to St. Croix in the Virgin Islands. They film it. It's cool. It's bitchin. It's getting ready to be released. And I'm excited. So excited for my dad. These make-ups are so cool . . .

It was the summer of 1977, and guess what came out at the same time? *Star Wars*. All anybody talked about was *Star Wars*.

Nobody gave a fuck about Dr. Moreau. So what did that do to a fifteen-year-old me? I was like, "Fuck *Star Wars*."

Mike McCracken Jr

Previous pages: Linda Blair completes her lifecasting session with Dick Smith for her iconic role as poor, possessed Reagan in *The Exorcist* (1973).

Above: Daniel Striepeke (left) and John Chambers' (right) Lionman (Gary Baxley, centre) make-up for *The Island of Dr. Moreau* (1977) was a roaring success.

Opposite: Eddie Murphy in a beautiful make-up ultimately omitted from *Coming 2 America* (2021), designed and created by Mike Marino and his team at ProRenFX. **Insert Photo:** The study sculpture for Murphy's make-up.

A very tall, imposing actor best known for his roles in the *Carry On* films, Bernard Bresslaw played a cyclops in *Krull* (1983), the first film I ever worked on as a trainee. He refused to take off his glasses, though, which really complicated the make-up.

Heavy, thick-rimmed things they were, big and square and, while today an actor would wear contacts, back then the prosthetic make-up had to be built over and around his specs. They tried to disguise the bumps as cheekbones, but it wasn't ideal!

David White

Below: Bernard Bresslaw in his glasses and Cyclops make-up for *Krull* (1983).

Opposite, top: Kevin Yagher (right) was the brains behind Freddy's fearsome make-up for *A Nightmare on Elm Street 2: Freddy's Revenge* (1985).

Opposite, bottom: Robert Englund strikes a scary pose in his full Freddy Krueger make-up for *A Nightmare on Elm Street 2: Freddy's Revenge* (1985).

Although a lot of talented artists left a thumbprint on the Freddy make-up over the years, it was David Miller who set the template. Soon after Wes [Craven] cast me in *A Nightmare on Elm Street* (1984), I remember driving to David's house, excited to play in the world of cool make-up effects.

I was ready to surrender to the process.

I have a thin face and broad shoulders, so when you put prosthetics on me, my head doesn't look too big for my body. The camera can hide that, but if you're not careful with an effects make-up, an actor's head can easily look out of proportion. But with me, you can pile that shit on and I'm still in ratio.

David realised he could exploit that and designed quite thick and heavy prosthetic pieces for me. Later, on *A Nightmare on Elm Street 2: Freddy's Revenge* (1985), Kevin Yagher refined the make-up and made it much lighter and easier to wear. It was porous. The foam latex breathed. Once everything was dry, you didn't feel anything at all.

"YOU CAN PILE THAT SHIT ON AND I'M STILL IN RATIO."

To get David's make-up moving, I had to make quite exaggerated gestures. With Kevin's, it was like my own face: I'd wrinkle my brow, and Freddy would wrinkle his. David's make-up was more dramatic, so great for wide shots. Kevin's make-up was subtler, which meant it looked great in close-up, but for the wider shots I'd have to physicalise more. Freddy's signature posture really grew out of that.

Both make-ups were wonderful in their own ways, and both presented unique challenges. Of all the Freddy looks, though, my favourite is the Freddy Demon who bursts out of the water in *Freddy vs. Jason* (2003). Bill Terezakis did a great job with that.

He made a lot of subtle changes that I really liked. The ears weren't quite Spock, not exactly elfin, but just a little bit satanic. There was a teeny bit more cheekbone, and the chin was a little more pointed.

It was like Freddy had been through a wind tunnel in Hell!

Robert Englund

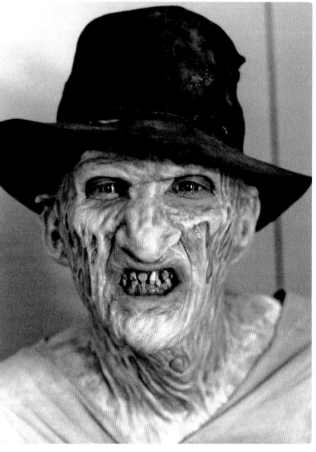

"RICK'S ATTENTION TO DETAIL WAS INSPIRING."

When I first got into the business, I had the privilege of being part of Rick Baker's crew on *Harry and the Hendersons* (1987). Harry is easily one of the best movie creatures of all time.

Rick's attention to detail was inspiring. I had the privilege of putting the armature together for him to sculpt the maquette, and then I got to watch as Rick created this walking, living, breathing, beautiful thing.

Watching Harry's birth is just a perfect, untouchable memory for me.

Norman Cabrera

Make-up is an analogue craft requiring so many different sensibilities, and such incredible attention to detail, that it's about more than transformation.

It's about creating belief.

Ben Foster

Opposite: Kevin Peter Hall shines through Rick Baker's masterpiece creation for *Harry and the Hendersons* (1987).

Top: Working with make-up artist Jamie Kelman, Ben Foster inhabited the role of troubled boxer Harry Haft in Barry Levinson's harrowing biopic, *The Survivor* (2021).

Above: Tim Roth as the evil Thade, a make-up designed by Rick Baker and Kazu Hiro for Tim Burton's *Planet of the Apes* (2001).

I was approached by production designer Anton Furst to do The Joker make-up for *Batman* (1989). Tim Burton told me, "This has to work for Jack."

I went to Tom Burman's shop in LA to do the lifecasts on Nicholson. We did a perfectly neutral one, then a quick one where I asked Jack to give me the biggest smile he possibly could, and hold it.

Back at Pinewood, a producer told me, "This has to be what Jack wants."

Also, "It has to be applied in under two hours, and it's gotta take less than an hour to take off."

Tim Burton gave me some sketches he'd done. He said we needed something familiar enough to please the fans, but also new, and above all else, Jack had to be happy.

I decided the best way to proceed was to duplicate Jack's lifecast and sculpt five different versions of the make-up, from ever so subtle to completely off the wall. I painted them all white with red lips, then invited Tim, the producers and, of course, Jack, to come see them and take his pick.

There they were, one to five, from the sublime to the ridiculous. I knew which one I liked, and then Jack went to the exact same one. The middle one.

He went, "This one."

And everyone else went, "Oh, yeah! That one."

So I did that one.

I sculpted it as a series of prosthetics, but then on set, the first day he went full Joker, I remember saying nervously to Bob Ringwood, the costume designer, "He's painted white. He's got green hair. You've put him in purple clothes. I have no idea whether the sculpt is way over the top or just half what we need."

But when Jack arrived on the set and did his first scene, I just went, "God, Yes! It works!"

Jack was so clever at what he did. So professional, and he made it look effortless. He was kind as well, and very present. Not at all what I expected. And he was hysterical.

I remember one morning he came in, sat in the chair, and said with a smile, "Another day, another $250 thousand!"

Nick Dudman

Below: Nick Dudman tries out various Joker looks on Jack Nicholson's lifecast for *Batman* (1989).

Opposite: Jack Nicholson as Gotham's Clown Prince of Crime, the Joker, from Tim Burton's *Batman* (1989).

"TIM BURTON TOLD ME, 'THIS HAS TO WORK FOR JACK.'"

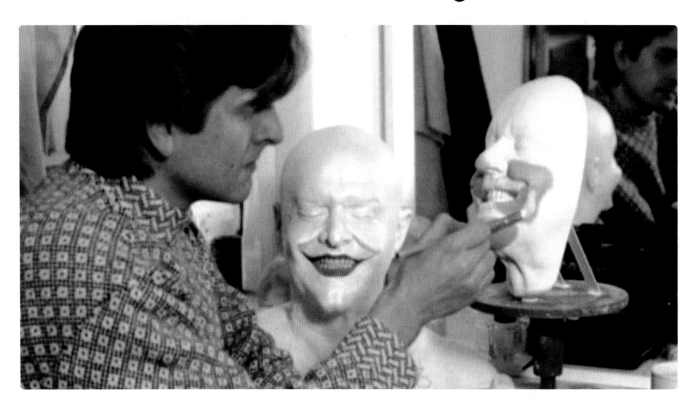

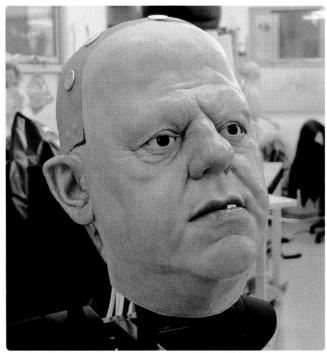

"WE HAD MILLIONS OF FANS TO SATISFY."

From the moment I signed on to the first *Harry Potter* movie, the pressure was laid on thick to get it right. We had millions of fans to satisfy . . .

The producers said, "We've got a problem. We've cast Robbie Coltrane as Hagrid and to digitally make him 8 feet tall [244cm] in every shot is financially insane. How can we cheat it?"

I said, "Well, we could just build a double. You can shoot all your close-ups on Robbie. Just stick him on a box and go in close. And we could make a scaled up Robbie that you can shoot wide, and from behind."

They were suspicious. But the director, Chris Columbus, said to me, "All right. You build this suit. I don't want to see it. I don't want to know how it's done. When it's ready, we'll have a show-and-tell, and only in that moment will I know whether it works or not."

Well, OK then.

We found this guy, Martin Bayfield, who was a rugby player. He was 6 feet 10 inches [208cm], big, and he turned out to be an absolutely brilliant mimic. He took off Robbie like nobody's business. It was quite uncanny.

We did the maths and scaled him up. Made sure his knees and hips and elbows all lined up with Robbie's. Put him on stilts with an animatronic head, and then we had our show-and-tell.

Robbie wore his Hagrid costume and Martin wore his Robbie as Hagrid costume: huge, silicone hands, great, big body suit, whopping boots . . . He had a backpack with servos running up the spine controlling the facial movements.

And out they walked together, from the sound stage into the sunshine, in front of Chris Columbus, the producer David Heyman and various suits.

And, immediately, we just knew. You could see from their expressions that we'd done it. And they used that suit all the time. Certainly on the first four or five shows.

It was a wonderful, theatrical trick that worked a treat!

Nick Dudman

Above, left: Martin Bayfield in the scaled-up Hagrid costume that helped sell the character's giant size in *Harry Potter and the Philosopher's Stone* (2001).

Above: A closer look at the radio-controlled animatronic head of actor Robbie Coltrane, worn by Martin Bayfield in *Harry Potter and the Philosopher's Stone* (2001).

Opposite: Ralph Fiennes frightened a generation of young muggles in his striking Lord Voldemort make-up, designed and created by Nick Dudman and Mark Coulier for *Harry Potter and the Goblet of Fire* (2005).

Ralph Fiennes had just been cast as Lord Voldemort for *Harry Potter and the Goblet of Fire* (2005). Nick Dudman asked if I'd like to head the team in charge of the character, and I was honoured to be given the opportunity.

Paul Catling had drawn several concept sketches of what Fiennes might look like in the role, and I was tasked with turning his ideas into a feasible make-up that could be applied in two hours.

It had to be something that pleased everyone. Obviously, it had to be terrifying, but at the same time, accessible to kids. So not TOO scary. Also, though Voldemort is an evil, corrupt character, we felt he should have an elegance about him. Beyond that, the director and producers wanted to make sure Ralph remained recognisable, plus Ralph himself had to approve the make-up.

We started by casting Ralph's head, chipping off his nose, then sculpting different versions of the make-up. There were five or six of us working on it initially. I think we ended up with about fifteen different heads, all with different snake-like noses.

We worked on these noseless variations for a few weeks but didn't get much response from the producers until one day they came round to view our progress. They responded well to a variation of mine, and I then knew we'd hit upon something and were finally on the right track.

Nick Dudman then asked me to meet with Ralph so we could discuss the make-up. It's always good to study the facial anatomy up close, to get a sense of the performer and start to think about how the make-up might work.

We'd seen him in *Schindler's List* (1993), so we knew he could be terrifying without any make-up at all. So we really just had to enhance what was already there, knowing that Ralph would bring it to life in all its malevolent glory.

For our part, we wanted to explore as many different options as possible, organising several test days to try all sorts of different things. We did so much on that movie that no one ever saw, and fortunately Nick had the budget and the manpower to do that. For example, I made a clear silicone piece for when Voldemort first arrives. The brain tissue wasn't formed properly, but that proved a bit too much. It was a great time to explore the character, though, and hone it down into something interesting.

The biggest decision was whether or not to remove Voldemort's nose. My feeling had always been that he was corrupted in such a way that he was unable to walk around in public as a 'normal' person. The producers were worried that losing his nose might take too much away from him, so the best way to prove the concept was to do a test. We blocked out Ralph's eyebrows, put a bald cap on him as he hadn't shaved his head yet, and did a lot of intricate vein paintwork, which I later achieved more simply with tattoo transfers. Then the VFX department removed his nose.

The test was very promising and everyone was very positive, including producer David Heyman and Ralph himself, so thankfully we were able to keep that important element of the design. We thought that it was something new and interesting and underneath it all, we kept enough of Ralph to keep the producers and Ralph himself happy. We'd managed to tick all the boxes.

It was quite an involved make-up, but working flat out with Stephen Murphy and Shaune Harrison, we were able to apply it in two hours. An hour-and-a-half by the end. It was important to have three people working on it as there were a lot of elements to the make-up and we needed to keep it under two hours.

Every day when we applied the make-up, Ralph paid close attention to what we were doing. We'd do a bit, he'd lean forward and inspect it in the mirror. We'd do it a little more, and again, he'd take a moment to check it over. Usually an actor will only do that for the first few days, and then sit back and read the paper while we get on with it. But Ralph did it every time. So even the seventieth time we applied it, even on our fourth movie doing the character, Ralph was still looking at the edges, still making sure we're painting everything in the same way, and in the same order, too. It really kept us on our toes!

I'm very proud of the make-up, more so now than I was at the time. Back then, I was lost in the technicalities of making it work, weighed down by the intense pressure of doing justice to a character as iconic as Voldemort, and terrified about how it would be received.

People responded really well to the character, though, so I think we did it! That was, and still is, a huge relief!

Mark Coulier

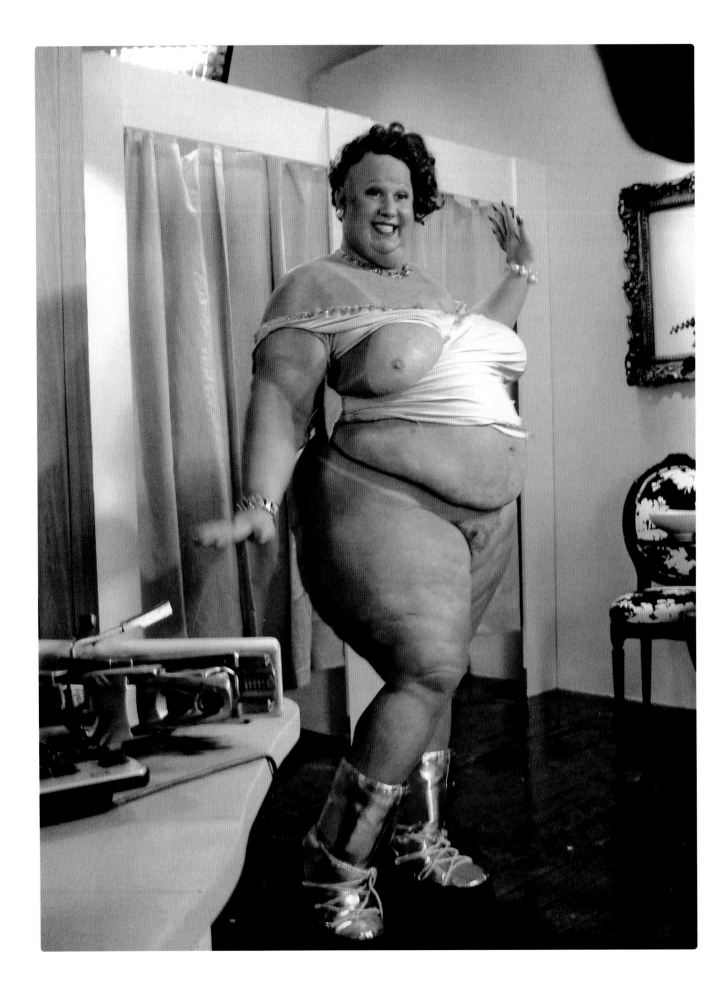

"HOW THE HELL ARE WE GOING TO GET AWAY WITH THIS?"

Matt Lucas and David Walliams really pushed the boundaries with *Little Britain* (2003–06). They didn't want comedy make-ups. They wanted everything to look as real as possible, as that only made everything funnier.

Bubbles was particularly horrifying, I thought. A grotesquely fat, crazy, naked woman, and I'm looking at Matt in the suit and make-up, wondering, "How the Hell are we going to get away with this? This is the BBC, for God's sake!"

But everyone there was like, "Yeah, great, this is fine."

Then I laid some pubes, a Brazilian, to finish things off. Just this little stripe of hair. But I'd gone too far

"Oh, no. You can't do that," they said.

Lesson learned.

Neill Gorton

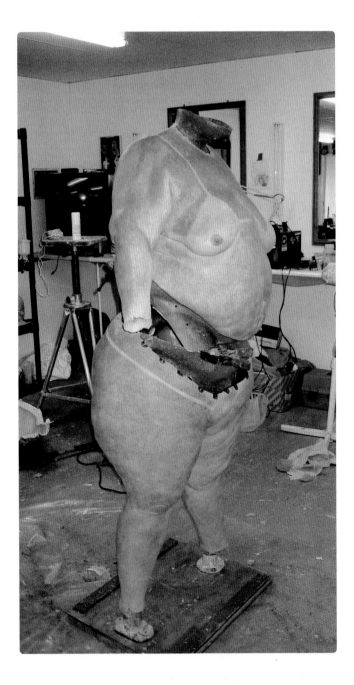

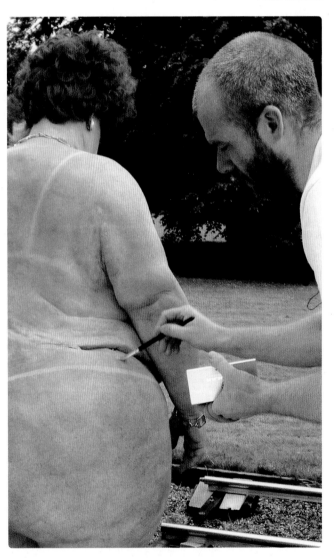

Opposite: Matt Lucas lets it all hang out as Bubbles, in a suit and make-up created by Neill Gorton for the sketch show, *Little Britain* (2003–06).

Left: The Bubbles suit in mid-prep at Neill Gorton's workshop.

Above: Neill Gorton applies the Bubble suit and make-up to Matt Lucas on location for *Little Britain* (2003–06).

We designed a bunch of different versions of Mr Tumnus. Though we were responsible for 175 other creatures on *The Chronicles of Narnia: The Lion, the Witch and the Wardrobe* (2005), to me, it was the most important make-up. Because if we couldn't sell Mr Tumnus, the film just wasn't going to work.

Every Friday, director Andrew Adamson and producer Mark Johnson would come into KNB to see what we'd come up with over the past week. And what I'd always do, the day before, is have my three children, who were all very young at the time, come in and take a look at everything first.

They'd all read the books. They all loved the books. And they didn't have any preconceived points of reference like, "It should look like Alien and Jaws, only different."

My kids had a purer perspective, especially my daughter Kelsey, who had great insight into Tumnus. One time we'd done a bunch of different Tumnus presentation heads, and she pinpointed everything that was wrong with them: "His ears aren't that big. His hair's not that dark . . . "

Once I asked Andrew why the books were so special to him. He said, "I was a sickly child. All I did was sit in my room and read, and I must have read *Narnia* a hundred times."

Then he told me, "This movie is my recollection of the books when I was a child."

That's how I knew it was key to develop Mr Tumnus through my children's eyes, and also, obviously, with the help of all the artists and geniuses I work with at KNB, with James McAvoy, who brought the character to life, and with Tami Lane and Sarah Rubano, who spent three hours every day, by my side, applying the make-up.

It was a great team effort.

Howard Berger

It's easy to connect with Guillermo [del Toro] because he loves all the same things as us. He has a real passion for make-up and knows just as much as we do. He's practically an effects guy himself.

David Grasso

What I enjoy most about make-up is finding that one thing that helps bring a character to life. On one person it could be a beard; on another, a change of eye shape, wrinkles or a shade of lipstick.

Lois Burwell

"MY KIDS HAD A PURER PERSPECTIVE."

Above: David Grasso sculpts the head of the unsettling Fragglewump at Mike Elizalde's Spectral Motion, for Guillermo del Toro's *Hellboy II: The Golden Army* (2008).

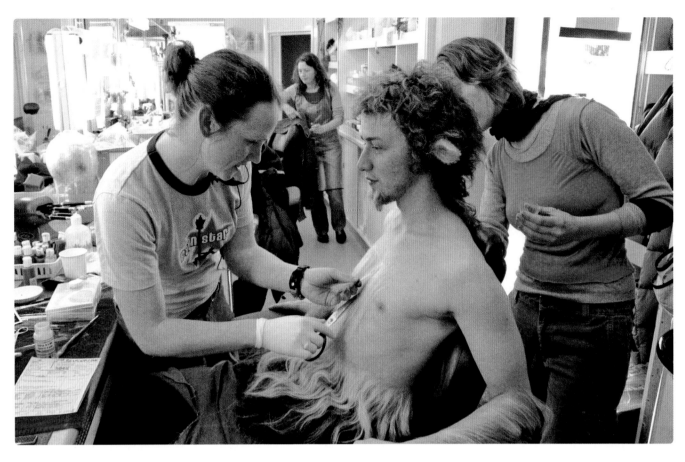

Above: Tami Lane (left) and Sarah Rubano apply prosthetics and heaps of yak hair to James McAvoy for his role as Mr Tumnus in *The Chronicles of Narnia: The Lion, The Witch and the Wardrobe* (2005).

Below: James McAvoy as Mr Tumnus in *The Chronicles of Narnia: The Lion, The Witch and the Wardrobe* (2005).

With every character I've created with Guillermo del Toro, he's never said, "Right, so, this is exactly what I want."

He'll come with an idea and usually some drawings, and from there, it's up to you to develop the concept. It's a process.

The earliest take on the Pale Man, from *Pan's Labyrinth* (2006), was of a wooden man with drawers in his chest. Inside one of them is a dagger that Ofelia has to find, but if she opens the wrong drawer, there's a thin, long, slimy tongue that licks her face.

Guillermo was like, "No, no, no. We need something else."

Next, we came up with a fat, old man, sitting at the banquet table, who suddenly becomes very thin.

Again, Guillermo was like, "No, no, no. Let's change it."

He wanted the Pale Man to be stick-thin with hanging skin, and for reference he gave us that Salvador Dali painting of melting clocks.

But he's like, "I still don't like it . . . Remove his eyes."

I was like, "Remove his eyes? What the Hell? But OK."

We removed his eyes. Then Guillermo tells us to remove his nose as well. I'm like, "How is he going to breathe?"

So Guillermo says, "Do a manta ray sort of thing."

So we did those little, round holes. And we were getting pretty close to what we ended up with in the movie. But then Guillermo's like, "It's not right. Let's do this: When Ofelia eats the grape, he'll transform. He'll open his mouth, his lips will recede, the screaming skull of a horse will come out and he'll turn into a four-legged creature that chases her."

We were in the middle of pre-production, we had no money left, and suddenly Guillermo came up with something that not only required a make-up, but also a mechanical thing, and then a puppet. I told him he'd have to find someone else to do it and he got mad at me.

The thing is, whenever I talk about Guillermo, I always say the same. As a friend, he's the best you could ever have. As a director, he's the most creative person I've ever worked with. But as a producer, his first and only priority is the film itself.

We took some time to cool down and met a while later in Madrid. Guillermo backed down from the screaming horse concept, but the make-up was still not quite there. As he has no eyes, I asked, "How is he going to find Ofelia?"

Guillermo said to me, "Close your eyes and try to find me."

I thought maybe he'd slap my face, but OK, I closed my eyes. First, I felt around on the table on front of me, then I reached out as far as I could, with my hands wide open. Guillermo yells, "Stop there!"

And he comes up to me and draws eyes on my palms. I was like, "That makes no sense! He grabs the fairy with his eyes?"

But he says, "Stop thinking about practical stuff and think about magic."

I was like, "You're right! OK. Let's do this."

The first make-up test we did was with just the face and the hands. Guillermo said maybe we should add some tattoos or something, but I convinced him we didn't need more detail. That the simpler the design, the better.

So Doug Jones is sitting in the chair, playing with the make-up, trying things out. He holds his hands up to his face, like he's staring at us, then he closes his hands, and opens them again, like he's blinking. It was just the most amazing moment.

We painted his pointy fingers black, so they'd look like eyelashes,. And finally, we agreed: we had our Pale Man!

He didn't come from Guillermo's mind, though, or mine. More, a mix of accidents, financial limitations and great ideas from many different artists. Plus Doug, of course, flapping his fingers!

And that's how we somehow created what very quickly became an iconic movie monster.

David Martí

"FINALLY, WE AGREED: WE HAD OUR PALE MAN!"

"IT'S GOOD TO BE PUSHED TO YOUR LIMITS."

Opposite: Doug Jones is ready to head to set as the Pale Man from *Pan's Labyrinth* (2006).

Left: David Martí and Montse Ribé celebrate their Oscar win for Best Make-up and Hairstyling for Guillermo del Toro's *Pan's Labyrinth* (2006).

Below: Doug Jones in all his gory glory as the Pale Man from *Pan's Labyrinth* (2006).

Making *Pan's Labyrinth* (2006) was the most exhausting job that David [Martí] and I ever had.

On one hand, it's good to be pushed to your limits, the way Guillermo [del Toro] pushed us, because you end up using every bit of your imagination and energy to make incredible things like the Faun and the Pale Man.

On the other hand, though, it was just too much suffering.

Even though we won the Academy Award for our work, if we could go back in time, there's no way I'd make that movie.

Montse Ribé 105

At first, when I got the Joker job on *The Dark Knight* (2008), I was thinking like a make-up guy. I was thinking, I do a clown. Not like Nicholson's Joker, of course. That worked great in Burton's *Batman* (1989), but our movie was going to be a whole different style.

My first few attempts were clean and neat. Later, working with Heath [Ledger] and Chris [Nolan] in London, we started looking for a more unkempt look. Only one we could control, which was the tricky part. We were playing with different ideas, shooting tests, and then Chris brought in these Francis Bacon books full of blurred, distorted images of ghostly white and black streaks. They permeated the make-up. So, really, Heath and Chris inspired it, but it was up to me to figure out how to do it technically.

We came up with this crinkling paint design. It had certain strategic lines that were always there, so no matter what went on with the black or the red, if it got blurred or sweated off, some key elements remained that still locked you into a basic design.

Applying it was no big deal. It never took more than half an hour. Depending on where Heath wanted it to go, we went either cleaner or dirtier every day. Still, it's not a film to watch for close continuity. Like, we'd start a scene in Chicago and finish it two months later in London. We took all the pictures we could, and did our best to match everything, but the saving grace of that make-up was its blurriness. As long as you could hit those strategic points, you were always in the right ballpark.

And can you imagine how many kids I made up, like, for three Halloweens after the film came out? Every year I'd go round to my friends' houses and do Joker make-ups on everyone. It was a blast! So much fun.

John Caglione Jr

"THE SAVING GRACE OF THAT MAKE-UP WAS ITS BLURRINESS."

Game of Thrones (2011–19) had a huge art department, but they trusted us to design our own characters. That's a privileged position for a make-up effects department. Of course, back in 2013 when we joined the show, we were still very much within the world of the books so we had a lot of guidance there.

The first major character we designed was The Night King. The White Walkers were already a thing, so that gave us a direction to work in. And David [Benioff] and Dan [Weiss], the showrunners, were eager for him to appear regal. But since he's other-worldly, instead of giving him a costume crown, they suggested we incorporate it in his anatomy. So we had plenty to work with, but it was up to us to deliver.

"YOU CAN ADD TO SOMEBODY MORE EASILY THAN YOU CAN TAKE AWAY."

There's a concept designer called Howard Swindell, who, because he also works in practical effects, understands real world limitations. Like, you can add to somebody more easily than you can take away. So while he's incredibly imaginative, he doesn't get so carried away that he delivers impossible designs.

We told him what we needed. Gave him a colour palette, a sense of texture, and he delivered three or four designs. David and Dan signed off on one and that was it. We just flew into it. Sculpted it. Tested it. And he just worked. Like, when everyone first saw him, they felt that, yes, that was the Night King. No question. No complaints.

Barrie Gower

Opposite: Heath Ledger in John Caglione and Conor O'Sullivan's Joker make-up for *The Dark Knight* (2008).

Left: Richard Brake as the Night King from *Game of Thrones* (2011–19).

Above: Sarah and Barrie Gower enjoy an audience with their creation, the Night King (Richard Brake), on the set of *Game of Thrones* (2011–19).

I didn't know Marvel, I didn't know the comics and I certainly didn't know Red Skull, but when I met with Marvel to discuss designing the character for *Captain America: The First Avenger* (2011), they shared their concept art and I was hooked.

I had a lot of ideas and came up with some designs I liked, but you know, once an actor's cast, everything changes. Hugo [Weaving] came aboard and suddenly I had a specific face to work with. A personality to blend with a character. It took a while to nail, but eventually we did a test with Hugo that everyone liked.

The one thing I was asked to change from my original design was to make it smoother. It was a little too visceral for a family audience. I'd have preferred not to do that, but appreciated why they felt it was necessary to tone it down. Later, I realised that had the design remained so busy, it might have distracted from Hugo's performance. The first thing you want audiences to look at are his eyes, not his cheekbones.

David White

Right: David White applies his Red Skull prosthetics to Hugo Weaving for *Captain America: The First Avenger* (2011).

Below: David White sculpts Red Skull on Hugo Weaving's lifecast for *Captain America: The First Avenger* (2011).

Opposite: Hail Hydra! David White's vivid make-up on Hugo Weaving as Red Skull, for *Captain America: The First Avenger* (2011), was a faithful recreation of the comicbook supervillain.

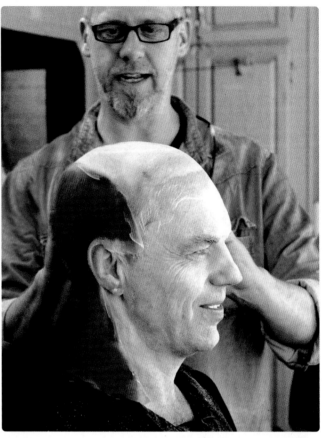

When I seek inspiration, I turn to nature. You're almost guaranteed a good design when you do. I look for colours in *National Geographic*. It's about having an element of realism, even in the most unrealistic thing. Audiences will be much more into something if they recognise something in it. Something that just rings true.

Tami Lane

"IT WAS ABSOLUTELY GRUELLING."

Above: Steve Wang's The Keeper, a salty, snappy creation for a Monster Maker's Halloween Costume Contest.

Above, right: Barrie Gower's Children of the Forest make-up from *Game of Thrones* (2001–19).

In *Game of Thrones* (2011–19), we first saw The Children of the Forest, but only fleetingly, at the end of season 4. It was an impish young girl in a twiggy kind of outfit and no prosthetics at all, so we took the opportunity to redesign them for season 6.

We worked with an incredible concept designer, Simon Webber, on creating these full body make-ups with vines and roots, allowing these scantily clad characters a bit of dignity. Our first test took something like nine hours. I remember thinking at the time, "Oh God, I hope they don't go for this, because it would be hell."

But, of course, they approved it and we're like, "Aargh!"

We realised, however, we only needed the fully made-up characters for hero shots. Those were purely appliances, glued to the skin. For mid-ground shots, we got away with the appliances glued to skin-tight Lycra tops and bottoms. And for our background shots, we did prosthetics for the face, but then digitally printed the patterns onto fabric. To be fair, if you stood a hero and a background character beside one another, and then looked at them from 20 feet [6m] away, you really couldn't tell the difference, so that really saved us a lot of time.

But to have the full-body hero make-ups ready for 8 a.m., we had to get started at ten to midnight, the night before. It was absolutely gruelling.

Barrie Gower

Problem-solving is my favourite part of the job. Elegant and simple solutions are always the goal. We're all gut-level engineers, I think, only with art backgrounds.

Here's an example that's certainly simple, but I'll let you decide whether it's elegant or not: There's a scene in the remake of *Fright Night* (2011) where Evil Ed's arm is severed and flops around on the ground. A remote control arm had been built, but it didn't function as intended.

We needed something motorised and self-contained that we could stick within the arm, and then it hit me: Why don't we just go to a sex shop and buy a motorised dildo?

So that's what we did!

We stripped off the rubber skin, stuck it in the arm and it worked great. OK, well, at first the arm started glowing because we hadn't realised the dildo had lights in it. But once we disconnected those, it was exactly what we needed.

Garrett Immel

"WE'RE ALL GUT-LEVEL ENGINEERS, I THINK, ONLY WITH ART BACKGROUNDS."

Below: Under the supervision of make-up department head Donald Mowat, Eva Von Bahr and Love Larson apply their Baron Harkonnen make-up to Stellan Skarsgård for *Dune* (2021).

Love: When we start a job, we do the breakdown and design the make-ups together.

Eva: Then, when the actual movie starts, we apply the make-ups together.

Since we're married, and always together, we never quit discussing things. So you're doing the spaghetti Bolognese, and saying, "I don't think that nose will work."

Then we'll have some dinner, go do some Photoshop sketches, have a glass of wine, discuss our designs, and really we never let go of a project. That focus, and the time we spend working together, inspiring one another and improving one another, is how we've managed to achieve what we have.

Eva Von Bahr and Love Larson

Before I got involved with helping design The Asset for Guillermo del Toro's *The Shape of Water* (2017), Dave Grasso and David Meng had already sculpted some incredible maquettes. Then Legacy took the best parts of those and sculpted a new maquette of their own.

I was at Guillermo's house and he showed it to me. I thought it was great.

Several weeks later Guillermo asked me to be lead sculptor for the actual suit, which was being created by Legacy. He said, "I want a leading man – not a monster."

So we take another look at Legacy's maquette, and Guillermo asks me straight, "What do you think?"

I tell him, "First, I'd get rid of this Creature from the Black Lagoon plating, because if a lady's going to hold him, and touch him, and want sexual relations with him, she's not gonna want to feel plates. We've got to give her a little something to turn her on. Give him some masculinity."

The other thing I said was, "We gotta lose the fish mouth. He needs kissable lips."

So we gave him voluptuous, male model lips.

Originally, the plan was to create a mechanical head full of servos. I was like, "Isn't it going to be in water all day? It'll short out in a second."

Though the plan was to use waterproof servos, the thing is, nothing's waterproof. Also lots of servos would mean a big head, but Guillermo likes small heads. You put a big head on a creature and don't you think it screams, 'MAN IN A SUIT?' It's a

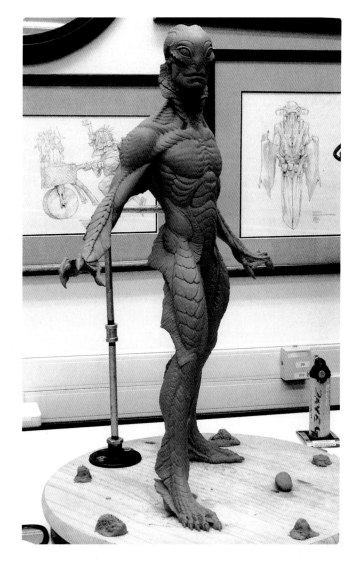

bobblehead, so Shane Mahan and myself decided to do it as a make-up, with CG embellishments.

I made a real quick pencil sketch, which Guillermo loved, followed by a crude maquette. And he said, "That's the one!"

It didn't look quite right on Doug [Jones] though, so I went back to Guillermo's house and spent a few days sculpting. Though I get credit for designing The Asset's face, to be honest, Guillermo gave a lot of input. The whole time, he throws ideas at you. Like, "He's a fish but he has to be handsome" and "Throw a little Jack Kirby in there."

You're like, "What?"

But he's amazing. He has so many wild ideas. You end up trying things you never imagined. And when we were done, though I swear, if you put them side-by-side, you can see how different they are, a lot of people thought it looked like Abe Sapien, from *Hellboy* (2004).

Of course, they're both played by Doug, they both have Guillermo's design sense, they're both blue. In Guillermo's world, they were always going to have similarities and there was nothing I could do about that.

Still, I offered to keep working at it. To make him less Abe-like, but Guillermo said, "Mike, don't work from a negative. If they cross each other, so what? I'm the director, and this is what I want."

And he was right. Avoiding certain attributes would have been forced. Better just let it happen.

Mike Hill

Opposite, top: David Grasso's study sculpture of The Asset for Guillermo del Toro's *The Shape of Water* (2017).

Opposite, bottom: Mike Hill sculpted a variety of facial expressions for The Asset in *The Shape of Water* (2017).

Below: Mike Hill and Shane Mahan from Legacy Studios put the final touches on the make-up suit worn by Doug Jones in *The Shape of Water* (2017).

"I WANT A LEADING MAN – NOT A MONSTER."

What makes an iconic creature?

First, it has to be treated like a living, breathing character. It can't just be a monster. It has to have needs, wants, intention . . . If it's just flailing around without purpose, it's not going to be as effective. All the greatest monsters – the ones that have stood the test of time – have that inner life. That need. From Frankenstein's Monster to Alien.

The original Alien, though it doesn't speak, though it has no eyes, it has clear intention: to reproduce, to survive, to grow. Like the other characters in the film, it's intelligent and has purpose. It's more than just a great make-up or creature suit, and that's one of the reasons it works so well.

The second key element to making a memorable creature is to slow play its reveal. Too often filmmakers let you see too much, too soon, and it kills the magic. The best creatures are teased out slowly, so you have a real payoff at the end.

The third key element is grounding the creature in nature. Grounding it in reality and anatomy. Human beings see real life all the time and have a deep internal sense of what is real and what isn't. So the creatures that work best, to my mind, are the ones that stick to physics and anatomical reality.

Stan [Winston] was a huge believer that the reference images tacked up at work stations around his shop shouldn't be images of other monsters and fantasy characters, but of insects, marine life and other living things. If you want something to be believable, you have to match nature.

Matt Winston

Above: Stan Winston at his Northridge studio with the full-size T-800 puppet from *The Terminator* (1984) keeping watch.

Below: Arnold Schwarzenegger in his Terminator make-up, designed and created by Stan Winston for the James Cameron classic, *The Terminator* (1984).

Opposite: Joel Harlow's take on artist Bernie Wrightson's Jenifer, from a story written by Bruce Jones that originally appeared in *CREEPY #63* (July 1974).

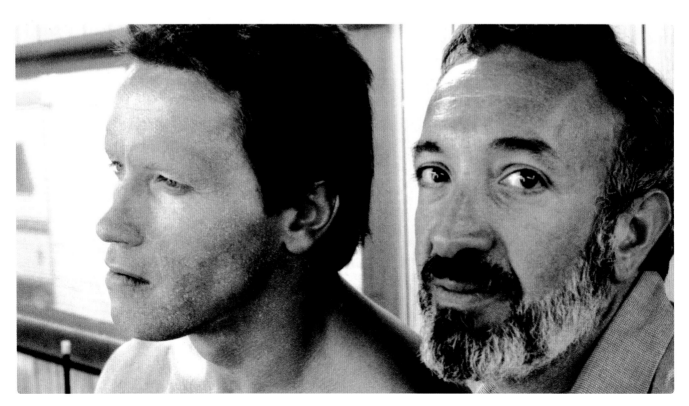

"IF YOU WANT SOMETHING TO BE BELIEVABLE, YOU HAVE TO MATCH NATURE."

THE MONSTER CLUB

Everyone knows that if you're bitten by a vampire, you become a vampire. Yeah? That if you're non-terminally nibbled by a werewolf, come the next full moon, you'll be hirsute, howling and hungrily roaming the moors. Right?

Wrong. Rick Baker makes werewolves. Greg Cannom makes vampires. And Tom Savini makes Crate Beasts named Fluffy. They are the monster makers. So let's give credit where credit's due, and recall the creation of some of Hollywood's hairiest, scariest, scaliest and slimiest, bug-eyed, blood-sucking beasts.

First, you apply the pieces. Then you work on the edges till they melt away. Finally, as you add the colour, there's that moment when it all comes together. Dick Smith used to call it The Frankenstein Effect. It's when the make-up comes to life and really that's just the greatest thrill.

Pamela Goldammer

Previous pages: Rick Baker slimes up one of his nightmarish Nazi Demons from *An American Werewolf in London* (1982).

Below: Stan (left) and Karen (right) Winston take a family photo with their greatest creations: Debbie and Matt Winston.

Opposite: In the top photo, young Stan Winston models a couple of his earliest make-up creations, ample proof of his growing mastery in the field. In the bottom photo, Matt and Stan Winston in unused prototype make-ups for Tim Burton's *Planet of the Apes* (2001).

"THERE'S THAT MOMENT WHEN IT ALL COMES TOGETHER."

Stan [Winston] never got tired of scaring me and my sister Debbie. If he was home, any time you'd enter a room, you'd have to check behind the door because 90 per cent of the time he'd be hiding behind it, ready to jump out and scare you. This went on until the end of his life.

Here are two horrifying examples from my childhood that encapsulate this side of Dad.

I must have been about seven or so when, late one night in the darkness, something woke me up. I heard a low kind of growling, heavy-breathing sound. Then the sound of shuffling feet. And the sounds were getting closer. I quickly rolled over in bed and turned my back to the door thinking that if I didn't look, it would go away. But instead, it's getting closer and closer until I'm feeling its breath on me. I spin around in horror to find my dad, in full werewolf make-up, blood dripping from his fangs.

I never slept with my door open again.

A little while later, I was eight or nine, I remember I was doing my homework one night when a face slowly rose up outside my window. It was a death ghoul, ghostly white with white eyes – no pupils.

I freaked out and ran to another room, but this nightmare ghoul slowly came up in that window, too. So I screamed and ran to another room, but no matter where I went, the face followed me.

Finally, I ran to my mum and dad's bedroom, absolutely terrified, "Mum, you've got to make Dad stop. He keeps... it's awful... I can't..."

And she goes, very calmly, "You know I can't help you. It's what he does."

Truly, Stan's greatest joy was scaring not only audiences, but his children, too!

Matt Winston

"I NEVER SLEPT WITH MY DOOR OPEN AGAIN."

John: I wrote the script for *An American Werewolf in London* in 1969. Though I didn't end up making the movie till 1981, it's almost word for word what I wrote when I was nineteen. It just wasn't originally set in the UK.

Rick: John first told me about *American Werewolf* while I was making him up for *Schlock* (1973). Before I ever read the script, he basically acted out the whole movie for me.

We talked about David's transformation scene. John said it made no sense that Lon Chaney Jr sat still in a chair until he'd finished changing into the Wolf Man. He told me, "I think he'd be in pain. I want to show the pain. I want to see him move around. And I want to do it in a way that's never been done before."

John: The whole thing was blocked out in my original screenplay. An entire page of description that clearly indicated it was a long and agonising process. I asked Rick how he'd do it.

Rick: I told John, "I have no idea. But I'd so love to try."

John: Rick's original idea was to try to do it in one shot, which proved impractical and impossible. Also it wouldn't have been as dramatic. You know, cutting is what gives a scene drama. It's fine to see a car go off a cliff and explode in one shot, but if you cut to the tyres, then the people inside, do a point-of-view shot… It's more violent. More exciting. Montage is how movies are made, and it turned out Rick was very grateful for that.

Rick: We storyboarded the whole transformation.

John: This was back around 1973, but the finished scene is pretty much what we came up with then. I just added the cutaway to the Mickey Mouse toy!

Rick set about designing different pieces for every shot, and so years before we made the movie, Rick already came up with all this great stuff: the Change-O head, the stretching hand… It was all planned.

Then all through the Seventies, I'd tell Rick, "We're gonna make this movie."

Eventually, Joe Dante approached Rick to do *The Howling* (1981), and he signed on to do that instead as he had all these great ideas and thought we'd never get around to making *American Werewolf*. But then, finally, I got the money for it, and when I called Rick to tell him, as innocently as he could manage, he told me he'd gone to work for Joe.

I went a little crazy. Joe had seen the Change-O head and everything. But as they were still quite early in pre-production on *The Howling*, Rick convinced Joe that Rob Bottin, who was his assistant at the time, could handle the job instead – and he was terrific – and then Rick came to work on *American Werewolf*. That's why the effects in the two movies are quite similar.

The concept was very different, though. *The Howling* metamorphosis was shot in the dark, which is much more

"I THINK HE'D BE IN PAIN. I WANT TO SHOW THE PAIN."

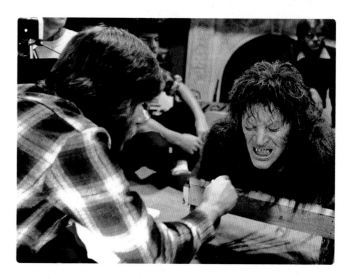

forgiving of make-up. On *Werewolf*, originally I wanted David's scene to be shot in fluorescent light, although we didn't end up going quite that far.

Rick made certain demands. One was that he have six months to prepare everything before we started shooting. Another was that we film the metamorphosis last. That way he'd have another month on top to prepare. So that's what we did. At the end of the shoot, after we'd finished everything else, we kept that one living room set, had it lit and ready for Rick, with only essential crew remaining.

Rick: It definitely spoiled me, but really, that's the way things should be done. You should have a plan, and the time to do it right.

So many times, the stuff we do, the money shots are the last thing the director wants to deal with. They leave it till the end of the day and give us just forty-five minutes to get it done. So, obviously, it was a great experience, working with John.

He'd say, "You can spend ten hours doing a make-up and then we'll shoot that shot, and if we get just that, or maybe a couple more shots a day, that's OK."

John: Rick and David [Naughton] would get to Twickenham Studios in London at, like, 2 a.m. They'd get the make-up done, show up on set at 7 a.m., we'd get our first shot at 8 a.m., and then they'd disappear back into the make-up trailer for at least a couple of hours. Meanwhile the rest of us are standing around, whistling and twiddling our thumbs as we had nothing else to do. It was wild!

Everything Rick did, though, was incredible, and always worth the wait. Take that shot of the hair growing on David. People love that! All Rick did was take a piece of skin and punch hair all the way through. On one side, it looked like natural, curly hair, but on the other, the hairs were all tied to a stick. We shot a close-up of the hair being pulled down, out through the skin, and then all we had to do was play the film backwards to make the hair look like it was growing.

So many people asked how we did that, but I didn't want to tell them, because it was actually so simple!

Rick: The funny thing was…

John: Though he didn't think it was funny at the time…

Rick: I spent months making all that stuff. But it took so little time to film.

John: We're shooting the Change-O head where David's mouth stretches into a snout. I shot it from one angle, three or four takes. Then another angle, three or four takes… Ten minutes of filming and we're done. I said, "Next!"

Rick went, "NEXT?!"

John: I said, "Rick, does it do anything else? Does it sing?"

He said, "No."

I said, "Well, then. NEXT!"

Rick was really frustrated. It wasn't until he saw the movie that he calmed down.

Rick: The payoff came when the FX boys and I went to see the movie. It was the day it came out, and when the transformation happened, people stood up and cheered! I was like, "OK, yeah. We did it!"

When I was nominated for the Academy Award, the first year they gave an Oscar for Best Make-up, I didn't think it was going to happen.

I mean, it was a monster movie. It had nudity in it. It had swearing. It was an honour to be nominated, but I figured Stan [Winston] would probably win it for *Heartbeeps* (1981).

But to my surprise, when Kim Hunter announced the winner, she said my name!

John Landis and Rick Baker

Opposite: Rick Baker tweaks one of the David Naughton Werewolf Change-O head puppets for *An American Werewolf in London* (1981).

Below: The dreamers of the dream, Rick Baker (left) and director John Landis (right), flank David Naughton in one of the many stages of werewolf transformation that Rick created for *An American Werewolf in London* (1981).

I'd never done an animatronic creature before Fluffy. That was my pet name for the monster in the crate I created for *Creepshow* (1982).

I called Rob Bottin, and for two-and-half hours on the phone he explained, step by step, how to do it.

Later, I was in LA for the premiere of *Knightriders* (1981) and Rob came. He took me to his house and tore the skins off his Howling heads. And I'm screaming, like, "NOOOOOOOO!"

But he says, "I don't save the skins. Just the mechanics."

Then he showed me the intricate mechanics involved in the Carradine head. And I saw first-hand what he'd explained to me on the phone. Really, if it wasn't for Rob, Fluffy might never have been born.

How thrilling it was to give life to something that didn't exist before! To make a creature that looked around and salivated and took bites out of people… That was incredible.

Tom Savini

"HOW THRILLING IT WAS TO GIVE LIFE TO SOMETHING THAT DIDN'T EXIST BEFORE!"

Opposite: Rick Baker and his crew, including Steve Johnson (left), Elaine Baker (centre) and Bill Sturgeon (right), ready the insert transformation back with syringes, air bladders and innovation, on the set of *An American Werewolf in London* (1981).

Above, left: Tom Savini sculpts the Arctic terror – nicknamed Fluffy – for *The Crate* chapter of George A. Romero's *Creepshow* (1982).

Above, right: Darryl Ferrucci shows the friendlier side of Fluffy, behind the scenes on *Creepshow* (1982). Darryl was Tom Savini's assistant on the movie, and willing to don the suit and mechanical head for the role.

The Fly (1986) turned out so much better than we all expected. In the shop, the body parts we sculpted looked a little bit like meatloaf. Pretty formless, until we got all the pieces together. I learned a lot from Chris [Walas] and our crew. It was a big family of crazy artisans.

Mike Smithson

I've been very lucky. I could die tomorrow and I've done it all. Monsters, creatures, aliens, vampires… I mean, look at *The Lost Boys* (1987). Who knew that was going to become such a big deal?

I had a picture from an old newspaper of this really good-looking blond guy, with chiselled features. It was so faded, though, it gave him these weird cheekbones and bone structures on his forehead. It was kind of cool, and that's what I used as my basic concept for the vampires in *The Lost Boys*.

Something I never liked in films and shows is if you're going to do a forehead, you need cheek pieces to match. Like, the Klingons in *Star Trek* were all just forehead and that never felt right to me.

So even though Kiefer [Sutherland] had a beard, I still did these little tiny cheekbone pieces to go with the forehead.

Joel [Schumacher] loved the design, but said it was too subtle for Kiefer. That he wanted him to be a little more extreme than everyone else. So I used that make-up on Jason Patric at the end of the film, and created a more sculpted one for Kiefer in really no time at all.

On set, Joel came up to me and said, "We we're only going to shoot everyone from the waist up, but because these make-ups are so good, now we can shoot extreme close-ups!"

I was so pleased with how those make-ups worked out, and for years, people copied that look. Like, every season on *Buffy the Vampire Slayer* (1997–2003), I'd be like, "Where's my Emmy?"

Greg Cannom

Below, left: Kiefer Sutherland was fangful for Greg Cannom's archetypal vampire make-up for *The Lost Boys* (1987).

Below, right: Nicholas Brendon models his *Buffy the Vampire Slayer* (1997–2011) vamp look, designed and created by John Vulich at Optic Nerve, and executed on set by Todd McIntosh.

"FOR YEARS, PEOPLE COPIED THAT LOOK."

Working with John Buechler, all those years in his shop, it got to the point where I'd call him father and he'd call me son. I wouldn't trade those days for anything.

Cellar Dweller (1987) was a big film for us. I built one of my first mechanical heads for the demon in it. It took nine puppeteers to do all the facial stuff, and with all those cables tugging at the head, it was horrible for Michael Deak to wear. But Buechler was so excited, really just over the moon when that thing came to life. He couldn't shoot it enough. "Make him growl," he'd say. "Make him do this, make him do that…" He loved it!

It was a big thrill for me to see him so happy, and it's that reaction, that delighted response to my mechanics, that keeps me doing it. Digital effects are fine, of course, but when you walk on set with an actual mechanical head, a puppet or an animal, and you see how people respond to it, there's something there, something real that touches them. And when that comes across on the screen, it's magic.

I'll never get tired of what I do and plan on never stopping. I'm gonna do this till my fingers just can't do it any more.

John Criswell

Above: Michael Deak as the title terror of John Carl Buechler's *Cellar Dweller* (1987).

Below: Director and special effects wizard John Carl Buechler is blatantly unterrified of Jason (Kane Hodder) on the set of *Friday the 13th Part VII: The New Blood* (1988).

Following pages: Under the supervision of Spectral Motion's Mike Elizalde, Norman Cabrera brought this werewolf to life for *Blade: Trinity* (2004).

Though I hate wearing make-up, playing a vampire with a dick nose in *From Dusk Till Dawn* (1996) was fun for three or four hours. You know, sneaking up on people and scaring them!

But after twelve hours, please, somebody save me. Somebody take this off. Because I hate being sticky and it never stopped being sticky.

Just horribly, horribly sticky.

Tom Savini

"I HATE BEING STICKY AND IT NEVER STOPPED BEING STICKY."

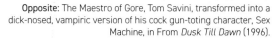

Opposite: The Maestro of Gore, Tom Savini, transformed into a dick-nosed, vampiric version of his cock gun-toting character, Sex Machine, in From *Dusk Till Dawn* (1996).

Top: Quentin Tarantino is out for blood in his KNB EFX-designed vampire make-up for From *Dusk Till Dawn* (1996).

Above: Salma Hayek is startlingly snaked out as Santanico Pandemonium for *Dusk Till Dawn* (1996).

Right: The entire make-up team on *From Dusk Till Dawn* (1996) cameoed as vampires in the film. Wayne Toth was transformed into this handsome demon.

During the six years I did on *Buffy the Vampire Slayer* (1997–2003), every day was an interesting challenge. When you're doing prosthetics for a TV series, the schedules are incredibly tight. For example, actors cast on Friday would turn up for work the following Monday, and you had to be prepared to create art on just a few pennies.

Optic Nerve did their damnedest to keep up the quality and did amazing work through the whole run – everyone from design and sculpting to the foam runners worked at their highest level under great pressure and turned out film-quality products for a TV budget. Often, though, I'd get a box on my doorstep at 3 a.m., full of prosthetics that had to go on an actor that morning. Only I'd never seen the pieces before and sometimes they wouldn't fit. So it became a game of how do I connect this? How am I supposed to anchor that? And where the hell does this go?

I loved when Joss [Whedon] redid the Universal Monsters, but one of the toughest make-ups we ever had to figure out was Adam, *Buffy*'s Frankenstein character.

"I USED MY ENTIRE BAG OF TRICKS TO GET US THROUGH THOSE TIMES."

The first time I did the Adam make-up on George Hertzberg, it took eight hours. Eventually, we got it down to six. If Optic Nerve had been given the time to work it all out in advance, though, it would probably have been easier and the application faster.

There were just an enormous number of zips and seams and each one had to be hidden with a blender, then painted into the suit's colours. Then there were things like the metal headpiece, which had been designed without any way to attach it. The hairdresser ended up pinning Velcro into George's hair so we could just stick it on his head, but that pulled George's hair and was uncomfortable. Then Joss decided the headpiece should open up and the weight of that hinged door must have been excruciating. We never did solve that issue…

As a department head, it was my job to solve problems and make things work, which is why an experienced department head is so crucial – especially in TV where things happen on the fly. I used my entire bag of tricks to get us through those times. It was exciting, stimulating work, but on the other hand, the stress could make you go grey – and it did.

Todd McIntosh

Matt Rose had an idea that I thought was clever for *Hellboy* (2004), and it required the skills of Mitch Devane. The Hellboy make-up was designed to fit Ron Perlman, but obviously the stuntmen had to wear it, too. And they kept hiring different stuntmen. There was a wire gag guy, a fight gag guy... It was a revolving door.

Matt's idea, then, was to sculpt a Ron Perlman likeness for all the different stuntmen to wear underneath the Hellboy appliance. That way it would universally fit all the different faces. It was a far simpler and less costly alternative to sculpting a hero Hellboy make-up for every one of the stuntmen.

So, every time there was a new guy, they'd snap a lifecast of his face, Mitch would sculpt a Ron likeness and often they'd put the Hellboy on it first so both could be put on the stuntman together.

I remember one day Ron came into the shop for a make-up test, and there was a stuntman wearing his face. He's like, "What the hell?!"

Rob Freitas

Creature from the Black Lagoon is both my favourite Universal Monster and my favourite Universal Monsters movie. Back when the remake was going to happen, working at Spectral Motion with my friend Mark 'Crash' McCreery, I sculpted and painted a design maquette and I'm still pretty happy with how it came out.

Breck Eisner, the director, originally wanted the Creature to be CG. But every time he came to see how the sculpt was going, we'd tell him how great it would work as a suit instead. And by the time I was finished, we'd pretty much convinced him to go that way.

Unfortunately, the production was shut down by a threatened actors strike, but at least I got to sculpt my dream maquette!

David Grasso

"I'M STILL PRETTY HAPPY WITH HOW IT CAME OUT."

Opposite, bottom left: George Hertzberg's make-up as Adam for *Buffy the Vampire Slayer* (1997–2003) was a play on Jack Pierce's iconic Monster make-up for *Frankenstein* (1931). Designed by Optic Nerve, the make-up was painstakingly applied over eight hours by Todd McIntosh.

Opposite, top right: For *Buffy the Vampire Slayer* (1997–2003), Optic Nerve and Todd McIntosh rose to the task of creating legions of vampires and demons, including Mark Deakins' monstrous Moloch the Corruptor.

Above: David Grasso's outstanding study maquette for a potential remake of *Creature From the Black Lagoon* (1954), at Mike Elizalde's Spectral Motion studio.

One day, on *Dark Shadows* (2012), I'm taking off Johnny Depp's make-up and he says, "Leave the nose on."

It was this weird little prosthetic bridge. I was like, "Really?"

He goes, "Yeah. I'm doing a *Vanity Fair* shoot later. Just paint it skin-coloured and let's see if anyone notices!"

So he goes to the shoot, no one suspects a thing and the next thing I know, there he is on the cover with Barnabas Collins' nose!

Joel Harlow

"I'M TAKING OFF JOHNNY DEPP'S MAKE-UP AND HE SAYS, 'LEAVE THE NOSE ON.'"

Below: Johnny Depp in Joel Harlow's brilliant Barnabas Collins make-up for Tim Burton's *Dark Shadows* (2012).

On *Chilling Adventures of Sabrina* (2018–2020), all the monster make-ups I did for the women were also beauty make-ups!

I'd apply their prosthetics, but then I'm like, "Now I'm giving you lashes! And here's some cute eye make-up."

And they'd go, "Wow! I don't know how I can look so pretty with all this on."

And I'd say, "See. Being a monster doesn't mean you have to be ugly."

Mike Fields

"BEING A MONSTER DOESN'T MEAN YOU HAVE TO BE UGLY."

Left: Vanessa Rubio as Nagaina on *Chilling Adventures of Sabrina* (2018–2020). The make-up was designed and created at Amazing Ape Studios by Werner Pretorius, and later executed on set by Mike Fields.

Above: Another gorgeous monster make-up from *Chilling Adventures of Sabrina* (2018–2020), designed and created by Amazing Ape Studios and applied by marvellous Mike Fields.

FEATURED CREATURES

Those pursuing proof of extraterrestrial life, rest assured, the truth is out there. It's just not in the night skies, nor in the guarded bowels of Area 57. Likewise, if it's angels or demons you're seeking to summon, turn not to your Bible, nor skin-bound Necronomicon. No . . .

You want fantastic beasts? We'll tell you where to find them. It's not at the end of a wand, nor in galaxies far, far away, but in the workshops of our practically magical make-up masters.

I always got on very well with Stuart Freeborn. Most of my memories of him are of the two of us roaring with laughter. Stuart brought me on to *Star Wars* (1977) to co-chief the cantina sequence. That's all I did on the film.

The aliens I built were my own designs. One of the main creatures I created was a sort of brown-headed walrus-like type with two lobes underneath his bottom jaw. I later discovered he'd been named Ponda Baba.

Honestly, though, nothing much was ever drawn, design-wise. We didn't have the time to do things that way. We just made things up as we went along, like this praying mantis thing I was on for quite a while. I used to take pieces of it home to work on there as I had better materials. Unfortunately, I didn't get time to finish it, so it didn't have claws on the end of its arms, which looked a bit daft. And there wasn't time to mechanise it, so they tied cords to it and moved it like a puppet. But it was in the background, in the shadows, so I don't suppose anyone noticed any of that.

We just tried various things and, with the right costumes, they all just seemed to come together.

Chewbacca was a bigger job. Because he was introduced in the cantina sequence, I was partly responsible for creating him, too. It was me, Stuart and Stuart's son Graham.

He wasn't described in the original script, so we had no idea what Chewbacca was supposed to look like. I remember trying to get information out of George [Lucas] during one of his rare visits to the workshop. That wasn't easy, because he was very vague.

When I say vague, I mean George was the epitome of vagueness. He just didn't know what he wanted. Or, if he did, he was unable to communicate what was in his mind.

We had to fire questions at him, like, "Is he hairy, or do you want him bald?"

And George said, "Hairy will do."

Then we asked him, "Should he be an anthropoid like an ape?"

George said, "Yes, that'll do."

We roughly modelled something up, and asked George, "How about this?"

"GEORGE WAS THE EPITOME OF VAGUENESS."

By then, there wasn't much time and we had to get on with it. So he just said, "Yes, yes. That'll do."

Stuart was stuck with this thing, but I took over the modelling for several days, working on the face and the hands.

When Stuart did *2001: A Space Odyssey* (1968), he came up with a clever way of making the apes a bit more expressive. He built these little toggles into the mask so when the actor moved his jaw, the upper lip got lifted into a sort of snarl. He did the same for Chewbacca.

The suit was the wig maker's responsibility. It involved knotting an entire suit plus backups.

At the time, I don't think any of us were very impressed with the creatures we made. We'd never made a film like this, and honestly didn't know what to think. So after we finished shooting, and we asked George what we should do with everything we'd made, we didn't think anything of it when he said, "I want it all dumped in the skip."

So we just threw it all away. Graham and I did most of that. Went backwards and forwards from the workshop to a giant skip a few yards up the road, and in everything went.

Had we known, in the years to come, that it would all be worth a fortune, I can assure you everything would have gone in the back of our cars. We just couldn't conceive, in our wildest imagination, that anyone outside of an asylum would ever want these things.

"I DON'T THINK ANY OF US WERE VERY IMPRESSED WITH THE CREATURES WE MADE."

When the film came out, it surprised us. While we were making it, we never imagined it would turn out well. But once it was edited and put on the screen, it was actually pretty good.

Christopher Tucker

Previous pages: Sam Raimi's Army of the Dead are ready for combat thanks to the puppets, make-ups and suits created by KNB EFX for the classic horror comedy *Army of Darkness* (1992).

Opposite: Stuart Freeborn takes a lookie at his Wookiee, ensuring Chewie looks perfect in every shot of the original *Star Wars* trilogy (1977–83).

Below: Standing with several cantina aliens that they created for *Star Wars* (1977), Christopher Tucker, Nick Maley, Graham Freeborn and Kay Freeborn were all part of Stuart Freeborn's creature crew.

On *Enemy Mine* (1985), we started as normal, doing the prep, all the sculpts and the make-up for Lou Gossett, then Chris Walas, Stephan Dupuis, Valerie Sofranko and I went to Iceland to shoot it.

After we'd been shooting for about a month, the studio wasn't happy with what they were seeing, so they hired Wolfgang Petersen as the new director. Thankfully, they kept us on, but everything we'd done up to that point was scrapped, and we just started from scratch.

We reset and resculpted with a new design concept, although it wasn't all that different from Drac's original look, which I always thought was cool. He looked more like an iguana, and dark grey, peppered with small, iridescent patches.

Margaret Prentice came on board, and she and Stephan did the majority of the make-ups. There was a scene, though, where a bunch of Dracs are being held prisoner, and for that, we all jumped in. It was my first professional experience of applying prosthetics.

I was eager to get the edges and the painting exactly right, but the guy I had just made everything so much harder. Like, all the guys in make-up were on strict orders to be careful when they ate. To drink with straws and generally take care of their prosthetics. But every time my guy came back from lunch, his whole chin piece was soaked full of soup. He was a real challenge.

Blair Clark

"HIS WHOLE CHIN PIECE WAS SOAKED FULL OF SOUP."

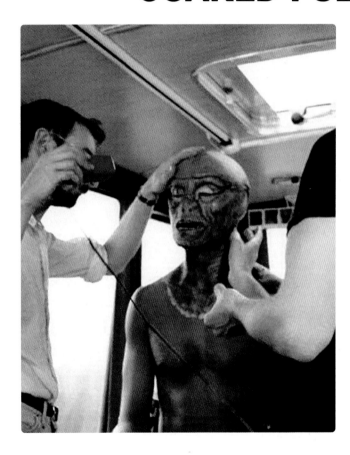

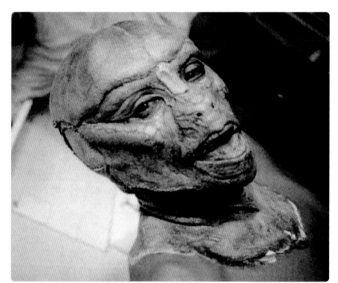

Above: Stephan Dupuis and Chris Walas apply Louis Gossett Jr's original Drac make-up for his role in *Enemy Mine* (1985). After Wolfgang Petersen came aboard as the new director, the design was revisited by Walas and his team.

Right, top: A better view of Louis Gossett Jr's original Drac make-up for *Enemy Mine* (1985).

Right: An early test make-up for Drac from *Enemy Mine* (1985).

Opposite: Shane Rangi as Asterius in *The Chronicles of Narnia: Prince Caspian* (2008). Shane played a different Minotaur in each film of the trilogy.

I flew to London to join Stan [Winston] and the guys on *Aliens* (1986). They'd already started shooting the live action by the time I got there. I remember walking into Pinewood Studios, jet-lagged, in an almost dream state, wandering around.

When I got to the Hadley's Hope set, there's [Jim] Cameron in a Hawaiian shirt, standing by himself with a shot list. He looks up at me and says, "Who'd have thunk it?"

That was a good summation of where we were, and what we were doing, because he and I saw *Alien* together at the Brea Mall in 1979. And just five years later he's written and directing the sequel to that perfect film. It was pretty amazing.

Jim's the best. He's a perfect combo of all the abuse and flattery and charm and terror that we experience in the movie business.

One time, we were filming the Queen. There was some lull in the action, and Jim was commenting about someone who'd complained that he had kind of a rough personality. And he says, "I know I can be an asshole…"

We're standing around him and there's this pause. Then he looks at me and says, "You're supposed to disagree with me!"

And I'm like, "I'm waiting to hear something I disagree with!"

He's charming, though, in his way. Particularly when you're done shooting. He's so grateful that people participate and try their best to get his vision across. And there was definitely a sense, on *Aliens*, that something amazing was happening.

Alec Gillis

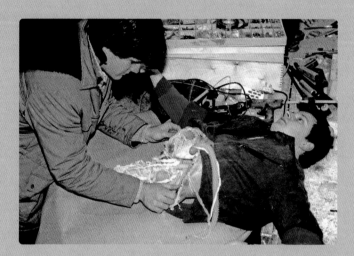

Right: Alec Gillis test fits Lance Henriksen's severed torso rig on a fellow crew mate for *Aliens* (1986).

Below: Stan Winston adds a finishing splash of ultra-slime to the Queen Alien before filming a scene for *Aliens* (1986).

"IT WAS NEVER DULL AT STAN'S!"

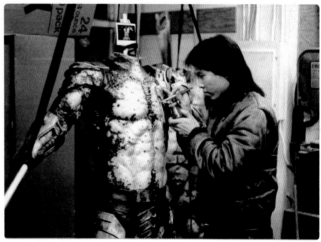

Stan [Winston] called me into his office. He gave me a big smile and said, "I'm doing this film called *Predator* (1987) next and I want you to help me design and build it!"

I was like, "Er, OK!"

Later, when the suit was built, I tried to show Stan my paint job design, but he wouldn't look at it. He said, "I don't want to see it. You've already far exceeded my expectations. Just do whatever you want and I'm sure that'll exceed my expectations, too."

So I painted it, it's what you see in the movie, and he loved it. But I wasn't done yet. I told him, "I still have to put the netting on the body, though."

He asked me, "What netting?"

I said, "The netting in my drawings."

He's like, "Oh no, no, no. This is a great paint job. Don't cover it up with anything."

But I was determined to keep the netting. I explained it was tied to its culture and technology, that it made it intelligent, but Stan said, "NO. Do not cover this paint job. NO NETTING."

The next morning, when Stan arrived back in the shop, I'd already stuck half the netting on with Krazy Glue. So he walks up behind me, and I could feel the heat on the back of my head. I'm thinking I'm fired, but then he says, "That looks great!"

He walks away and comes back a while later with Joel Silver, the producer. He's showing him the creature and when he gets to the body, he's like, "Look at the netting! It shows he's intelligent and gives him culture…"

It was never dull at Stan's!

Steve Wang

Above, left: Steve Wang's original concept drawing for the *Predator* (1987).

Above, top right: Kevin Peter Hall in a test fitting for his role in *Predator* (1987).

Above, bottom right: At Stan Winston Studios, Steve Wang painstakingly airbrushes colour on top of colour on to a Predator body suit for *Predator* (1987).

141

I've been obsessed with UFOs since *Close Encounters of the Third Kind* (1977). That movie really blew my mind as a kid. So when The *X-Files* (1993–2018) started on TV, I was like, "I'm gonna work on The *X-Files*, and I'm gonna make monsters for *The X-Files*, and I'm gonna play aliens on *The X-Files*, NO MATTER WHAT."

I saw on the end credits that it was filmed in Vancouver. Literally one week later, I packed my bags and moved to Vancouver. By the middle of season 2, I was on the show, and then, late in season 3, there was an episode with a ton of aliens in it, and I was like, "This is my chance."

I ended up being one of the most famous aliens in the show: the cigarette-smoking alien in *Jose Chung's From Outer Space* (S03E20). They even made action figures of it!

Even though I was on the show that week, I still had to apply the other make-ups. So I'd be made up as an alien as far as my neck, then I'd do all the other guys as aliens, and then right at the last second, I'd get my head put on.

After that, I played a lot of monsters on the show. If ever someone couldn't be there and they needed a guy in a suit, I would always volunteer. I was just so happy to be there!

Mike Fields

Below: Mike Fields applies the Glenstorm Centaur make-up to Cornell John for *The Chronicles of Narnia: Prince Caspian* (2008).

"I ENDED UP BEING ONE OF THE MOST FAMOUS ALIENS IN THE SHOW."

For *Harry Potter and the Prisoner of Azkaban* (2004), we built a completely computer-controlled Hippogriff that didn't walk, but it moved, and it was beautiful. It was bloody huge!

It had just one set of cables coming out of one hoof, and when they were buried in the ground, it looked absolutely real and alive. It was controlled by Matt Denton, who built BB-8. He was a very clever man, and he'd programmed this thing with umpteen layers of performance.

I love a great, mechanical creature because of the way people react to them. In the woods, our Hippogriff would catch the eyes of passers-by and they'd be like, "Oh my God!"

When they'd come closer, I'd say, "Be careful! You have to bow. I won't be responsible for what it'll do if you don't bow. I remember one guy walking towards it, going, "Oh for God's sake…"

And this thing's head just shot towards him. It really made him jump. He was like, "OK, I'll bow!"

Once a group of Japanese publicity people came to take a look. They bowed, because they knew they should, and it bowed back. So they bowed back. Then it bowed back. And this went on until their interpreter lady asked us, "Please, will you stop it?"

It could have just gone on forever!

Nick Dudman

Above: Feeding time for Nick Dudman's incredible Hippogriff puppet, on location for *Harry Potter and the Prisoner of Azkaban* (2004).

Above, inset: Two Hippogriff puppets mill around in Nick Dudman's workshop, waiting to be called to duty on *Harry Potter and the Prisoner of Azkaban* (2004).

Sitting in front of the TV on a Saturday night, with a bag of crisps, watching *Doctor Who* with my family, was my childhood.

I grew up in Liverpool in the Seventies, and every year we'd spend a few days in Blackpool, a working man's holiday town up the coast. One year, there was a *Doctor Who* exhibition full of props and models from the programme. I was six, maybe seven, when we went, and it all just fascinated me.

Spaceships that were huge on TV were actually more like toy-sized. And there was a Dalek with a place for a man to sit. I put two and two together – people made this stuff!

When I heard *Doctor Who* was coming back in 2005, I desperately wanted to be a part of it. I had a meeting with Russell T. Davies and Phil Collinson, the producer, and after I showed them my portfolio, I went, "Gents, I don't know if this is what I should be saying, but honest to God, I REALLY WANT THIS JOB."

Happily, they gave it to me! And almost as soon as the show started airing, suddenly everyone's sitting around the TV again, watching it as a family on a Saturday night. I loved being a part of that.

For the second series we brought back Davros, a character I always loved. I remember sitting in a meeting where they were discussing him, thinking, "Please get a good actor for this. Someone who's up for the prosthetics."

Because, you now, not all actors want to be under that stuff.

I'd just worked with an actor called Julian Bleach on another show, and he'd been amazing. I thought I should mention him, so I was like, "Have you got someone in mind?"

And they went, "Yes, we're talking to a guy. His name's Julian Bleach."

It was one of those moments where you're like, "YES! There IS a God!"

Not only is Julian a phenomenal performer, but also he'll go through endless tortures and come up smiling. Like being virtually blind in the make-up. And although everyone thinks his chair's controlled by motors, it's actually just Julian walking around under there. And beyond all that, he delivers that juicy Davros performance. He's just brilliant!

The Weeping Angels were new to *Doctor Who*, statue-like beings that only moved when no one was looking at them. Their first appearance was in a standalone episode, *Blink* (2007), and I remember Phil saying, "We just don't want them to look like those people painted like statues on the high street."

The art department calculated how many different poses were required, and said, "There's no way we can build fifty bloody statues in different positions."

The visual effects guys said they could do it, but it meant a lot of complicated shots and would be expensive to produce.

Above: It was a dream come true for lifelong *Doctor Who* fan Neill Gorton to work on the show when it returned in 2005, and a particular thrill to resurrect Davros, described by actor Julian Bleach as a cross between Stephen Hawking and Adolf Hitler.

Eventually, all eyes are on me, and they asked me, "Do you honestly think you can make someone look like a convincing statue?"

And I'm like, "Yeah! I promise we can pull this off."

It was only when I got back to the workshop and looked at the schedule that I realised we only had two weeks to make them.

Lisa Parker, a great fabricator who sadly isn't with us any more, suggested we start by making the costumes for real. So we did that, then dipped them in polyester resin, and once they'd set, we pulled the moulds off those. So they were never sculpted.

We made the skirt the same way. After we hired dancers to play the Weeping Angels, underneath their skirts we hid poles with bicycle seats, as even when you're standing very still, you can't help rocking back and forth a little, but when you're sitting, you're much more static.

The face and hair were separate pieces, and once they were in position, we'd pop these little plastic things over their eyes as, of course, they only ever stood still, so we didn't have to worry about them tripping over anything.

They looked great! As we didn't have time to design anything more complex, we opted for simple solutions and it worked out brilliantly.

Neill Gorton

"IT WAS ONE OF THOSE MOMENTS WHERE YOU'RE LIKE, 'YES! THERE IS A GOD!'"

Right: One of several Weeping Angel masks created by Neill Gorton and his team for the consummately creepy *Blink* episode (S03E10) of *Doctor Who* (2005-Present).

Below: Claire Folkard tries not to blink while applying make-up on a Weeping Angel, designed and created by Neill Gorton and his talented team for *Doctor Who* (2005-Present).

Following pages: Proud father Neill Gorton with his robot creations from the *Dinosaurs on a Spaceship* (S07E02) episode of *Doctor Who* (2005-Present).

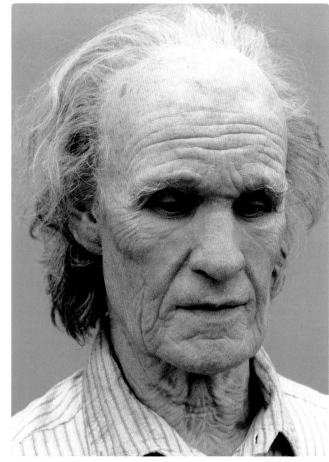

Top, left: Matt Smith in a bald head application by Neill Gorton for
Doctor Who (2005–Present).

Top, right: Matt Smith dons Neill Gorton's outstanding age
make-up for *The Time of the Doctor* (2013), a *Doctor Who* (2005–Present)
Christmas special.

Above: Neill Gorton's updated Cybermen from *Doctor Who* (2005–Present).

Right: Neve McIntosh in a remarkable Silurian test make-up, by Neill Gorton
and the team at Millennium FX, for *Doctor Who* (2005–Present).

Alien (1979) isn't scary because of the creature. It's because the movie is genius. Because it used the monster sparingly, and lit it beautifully, preserving the illusion. Filmmakers today often forget the lessons of that movie, showing too much of their monsters, and for too long. But no matter how great a creature you make, it's not going to be scary unless it's filmed right.

Guillermo del Toro understands that. When you create a creature for him, you know it's in good hands.

I headed up the design and sculpted The Angel of Death for *Hellboy II: The Golden Army* (2008). Guillermo said, "Think of all the Angel of Death characters that you've seen in other movies and don't do anything like that. Like, there's that great Angel of Death in *Monty Python's The Meaning of Life* (1983), and it's beautiful and amazing. But I don't want that. Give me something I haven't seen."

Guillermo showed me a very loose thumbnail sketch of what he had in mind. And he mentioned he wanted eyes in its wings. That still left a lot open for interpretation, which is what you want when you're designing something: For it to be a collaboration, not a directive. And I found a lot of inspiration in Byzantine sculpture and ornate statues of saints and angels in European churches.

Ultimately, I held up my end of the bargain by helping to make Guillermo a cool monster. Then he held up his by shooting it beautifully. I wish things always worked out that way.

Norman Cabrera

"GIVE ME SOMETHING I HAVEN'T SEEN."

The toughest suit I ever had to wear was the Angel of Death from *Hellboy II: The Golden Army* (2008).

Part of that beautiful design were these huge wings. They were practical – not CG – and flapped up mechanically, puppeteered off camera by a couple of people. So not even counting the finger-extension hands, body-conforming suit and five-hour make-up I had to endure, there was this heavy pack strapped to my back that held the wing contraption. It was 40 pounds [18kg], and it had corners, too. Hard ones that dug into me.

For the scene, I had to go from a crouching to a standing position – gracefully. After about the third take, my legs were getting wobbly and I lost my sense of humour. I make the mistake of being a hero sometimes, so even though I was getting visibly worn out, I was telling everyone I was OK.

But I could hear Guillermo del Toro and Mike Elizalde, from Spectral Motion, whispering behind me, "We've got to get some assistance here."

Apparently there was a dribble of blood coming from somewhere… So they added a wire assist to help with the weight and that changed my life within minutes. I could stand! I felt the love again. Had they kept things as they were, though, there's no way I could have finished the day.

Other than that brief, light-headed interlude, nothing's ever stopped me. I can hardly believe it, but honestly, in thirty-five years, nothing's been too much.

Doug Jones

Top: Norman Cabrera sculpts away on a lifecast of Doug Jones, as the Angel of Death comes to life for *Hellboy II: The Golden Army* (2008).

Bottom: Doug Jones as the Angel of Death in *Hellboy II: The Golden Army* (2008).

I'll never forget the day a couple of guys turned up at the shop with Steve Johnson's prototype creature suit for *Where the Wild Things Are* (2009). It took them a while to get suited up. Once they were done, whoever was in the suit could barely stand in it. They certainly couldn't walk around, and within a minute or two, had to sit down and take the head off. Later we weighed the suit and it came in at 200 pounds [90kg]!

I've found, over the years, if you go over 20 pounds [9kg] on a mechanical head, you're doomed. I try to keep them around 12 or 13 pounds [5–6kg], and that's fully loaded with servos. I'd be comfortable asking someone to put that on, provided they're well trained. If they're not ready, though, if they don't take care of themselves, eat right, and exercise, they're doomed. The human body just can't take it. You can't put a suit on just anyone.

John Criswell

"YOU CAN'T PUT A SUIT ON JUST ANYONE."

Left: Carey Jones is fitted into one of several Demon character suits that he wore for Seth Rogen's apocalypse comedy, *This Is the End* (2013).

Below: Carey Jones in monster mode on the set of *This Is the End* (2013).

Opposite: Carey Jones as the climactic Demon from *This Is the End* (2013).

Guardians of the Galaxy (2014) was mad. Absolutely massive. A brilliant opportunity to stir the pot and create lots of very cool things.

You start with all this great concept art, but, of course, once you have your cast, you have to translate those designs into looks that work for each actor. So you start again, get their lifecasts made, keep refining and testing new make-ups until you get there. For everyone. First the main cast and their doubles, then the background characters.

All through production, the more confident we got, the more characters we created. James [Gunn] was very encouraging. He didn't mind what we came up with, as long as it looked real, and we were on a mission to honour that. I had my own concept team, constantly delivering new material. I'd twist and change and adapt it to suit the show. I utilised colours and textures from the ocean bed to outer space and everything in between. It was a massive team effort. A fantastic melting pot.

Of all the characters we created, personally, Nebula was my favourite. Rather than cover Karen [Gillan] totally in rubber or silicone, I was desperate to utilise her real skin as much as possible. I fought with James a while on that but eventually convinced him it would work. That if she was painted and stencilled in areas that had maximum motion, and we combined that with silicon appliances, she'd still look beautiful.

I asked Karen if she'd shave her head and she agreed, so we didn't have to use a bald cap. It created that incredible shape, and seriously cut down her time in the chair every morning. We added an eyepiece and some other silicone details, but it was her

"I UTILISED COLOURS AND TEXTURES FROM THE OCEAN BED TO OUTER SPACE AND EVERYTHING IN BETWEEN."

neck, her mouth, and we got the balance just right. Everything bled into everything else seamlessly and there weren't any wrinkles. I just loved how she turned out.

David White

Below: Dave Bautista in his complex Drax make-up, created and applied by David White and his team for *Guardians of the Galaxy* (2014).

Opposite, top left and right: The sculpture for Nebula's prosthetics on a head cast of Karen Gillan for *Guardians of the Galaxy* (2014).

Opposite, bottom left: An early test make-up of Nebula for *Guardians of the Galaxy* (2014).

Opposite, bottom Right: Karen Gillan in her final prosthetics and make-up as Nebula for *Guardians of the Galaxy* (2014).

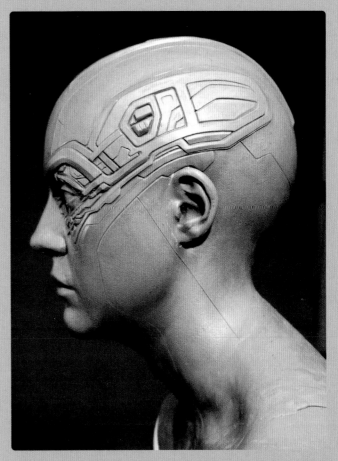

When *Star Trek Beyond* (2016) was crewing up, I hit Joel Harlow up on Facebook and I asked him, "If you need anything, I'd love to come by, even do a couple of background masks."

That's how I always get in. I'll do some background masks. Everybody needs background masks, right? Couple of aliens here and there. And he said, "Sure! I like your stuff. Come on in."

When I get there, it's Norman Cabrera, Joey Orosco, Richie Alonzo, Matt Rose, Miles Teves, Don Lanning and Joel, all sitting there, blasting out sculptures. And I remember thinking, "This is insane!"

So I'm freaking out, working with these bad asses. Guys I've followed since I was a kid. And not only are they throwing criticism at me, and helping me, but also I could feel my skill level jumping, just being around those guys. Like an osmosis type of thing.

The crazy thing was they were handing me stuff they'd been working on and asking me to finish. Like Matt would say, "I got too much going on here, so throw this kind of texture on this."

And of course I'd do it, but I'm shitting bricks, because I'm obsessed with this guy. And now I've got to try to replicate his style. I didn't want to screw his piece up. And that was happening all the time.

Then Norman's handing me tentacles for this big monster that he's doing. And I'm finishing them off, thinking, "This is real trial-by-fire stuff."

But at the same time, this was the most fun I've ever had. Here I was, working with all these legends, and I find out they're just cool, down-to-earth nerds like me. And we're watching stuff like *Prophecy* (1979) and *C.H.U.D.* (1984) while we're working. It was nuts! I couldn't believe I was getting paid for this.

It's what I always hoped working in creature effects was going to be like.

Mike Rotella

"I COULDN'T BELIEVE I WAS GETTING PAID FOR THIS."

If you'd looked through our portfolio prior to *Star Trek: Picard* (2020-Present), there was maybe only one alien in the entire thing. So when I initially got the call about working on the show, I was like, "Are you sure you've called the right guy?"

But they explained they were going for this realistic vibe. That they were downplaying the fantasy and planned to make the aliens a little more believable. So I was like, "OK, now you're speaking my language."

In terms of design, we just toned everything down. Made everything feel less sculptural. We finessed and we softened until everything felt more organic. That was really all it took to push it towards believability.

Ultimately, the greatest challenge on *Picard* was the sheer magnitude of the project. There were times when we had fifty-plus Romulans on set, and we'd have to produce those prosthetics with just a few days' notice. The night before the shoot we'd get the names of the background actors playing them, so we'd list what size pieces each would need, what shade they should be and so on. Then we'd head over to our Picard shop and, one by one, we'd go, "Right, so, James Roy is a medium skin tone with number three ears and a number six forehead."

We basically made grocery lists and then went into storage and packed these orders. That's fifty-plus boxes of prosthetics with lace brows and ears and foreheads, making sure they're all the right size and colour, and labelled specifically for each actor.

It was a huge undertaking.

Vincent Van Dyke

Left: Marti Matulis in a prosthetic Romulan make-up, designed and created by James MacKinnon and Vincent Van Dyke, for *Star Trek: Picard* (2020-Present).

Opposite: Ashley Edner as a crustation-inspired Joel Harlow alien from *Star Trek Beyond* (2016).

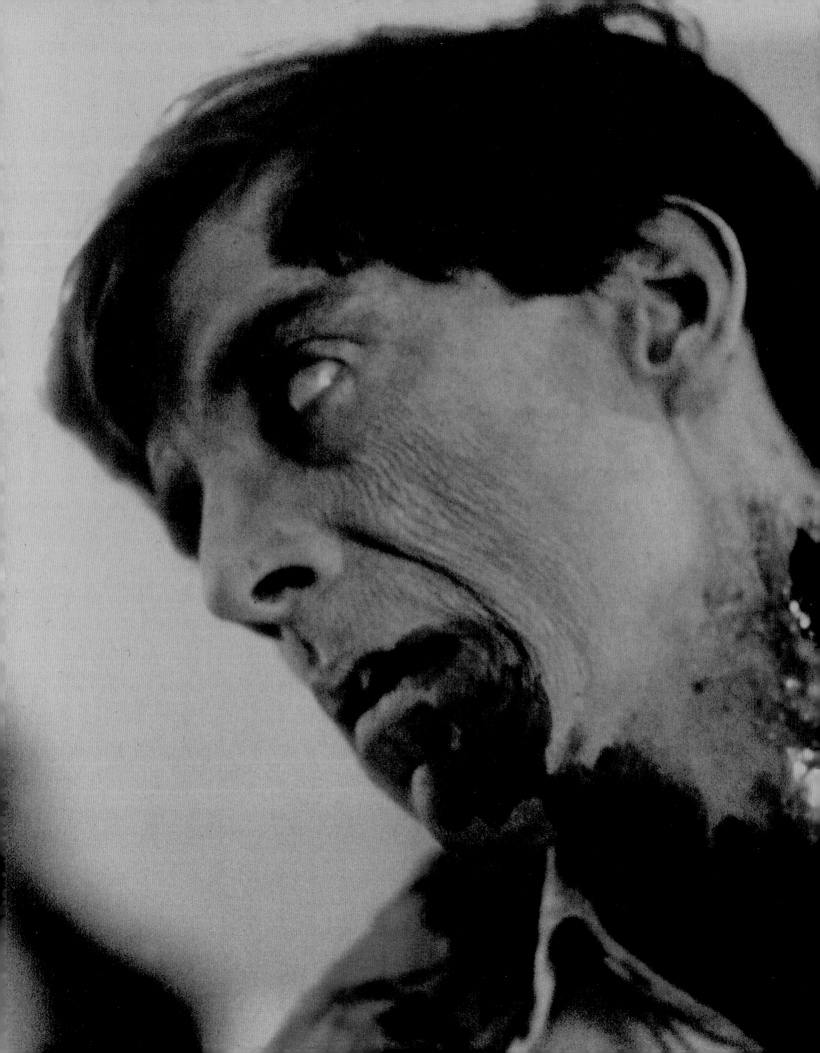

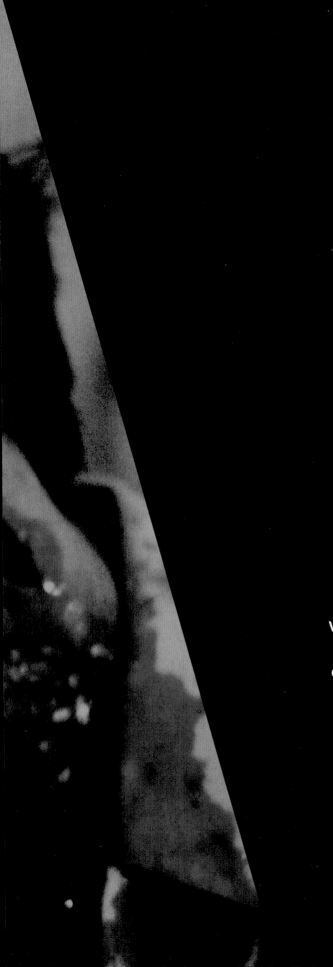

7

THE GORE THE MERRIER

Vampires have to drink. Zombies have to eat. Werewolves love to play with their food. That's how they get the red on them. And we're not just talking a splash, but gushing, crimson torrents of the stuff. Premium, iron-rich vein juice, fresh from the source and swimming with yummy chunks of fleshy, brainy, gristly goodness.

Feeling queasy yet? Because our make-up masters won't rest until they've fed the insatiable blood lust of the greatest monster of them all: the horror film fan.

It started with the neck bite at the beginning. That's the first effect I did on *Dawn of the Dead* (1978), and the crew and the actors applauded! So, of course, we had to keep topping ourselves.

Making that film was like Halloween every day for three months!

So I'd made a cast of Gaylen Ross's head, because the ending was going to be depressing. Everyone was going to die. Ken Foree shoots himself and Gaylen jumps up into the helicopter blades. Then George changed the ending.

But we still had her head! So that was the first time I ever blew a head apart. We put an Afro wig on it with dark make-up and I just blew it to pieces with a shotgun!

In cinemas, the gag that got the most applause was the helicopter zombie. He walks into the rotor blades and the top of his head comes off. It worked out so much better than killing Gaylen that way. Everyone screamed! They loved it. And you know why? Because it was a magic trick.

It's the same when a magician fools you. He makes you believe that what you're seeing is really happening. By misdirecting you, or using hidden mechanical devices, he does something incredible. We did our trick by yanking off a prosthetic head with a fishing line, then using a pump to squirt out the blood.

Sometimes you have to teach the director that it's a magic trick, because he's not the magician. You are! So you tell him what

shots you need, and from which angle, to work. Eventually, it was in my contract that I'd direct the scenes my effects were in to maintain the magic.

Tom Savini

Previous Pages: David Emge lurches towards horror movie immortality in Tom Savini's iconic Flyboy make-up for George A. Romero's zombie masterpiece, *Dawn of the Dead* (1978).

Above: George A. Romero and Tom Savini's creative relationship spawned several great films that championed the art of make-up effects.

Below: Dick Smith's revolutionary blood formula, once sent to twelve-year-old Howard Berger. KNB EFX still uses the same formula, with just a few tweaks.

914 TE 4-7098 • 209 MURRAY AVENUE, LARCHMONT, NEW YORK, 10538 • DICK SMITH

5 Gallons Thin-KARO Blood
for pumping through effects

1. Weigh 42.5 gr. Methyl Paraben in a large paper cup (9 to 12 oz.). Add 2 to 3 oz. Karo and beat to a smooth cream. Stir in more Karo from the quantity in step 4.

2. Weigh 38 gr. Red #33.
   Weigh 52 gr. Yellow #5.

3. Add these colors to 2 quarts of distilled water (or bottled drinking water).

4. Measure 2½ gallons of Karo (minus the amount used in step 1) into a 5 gallon pail.

5. Stir in the Paraben mixture.
   Stir in the colors.
   Stir in 15 oz. Kodak Photo-Flo.

6. Store in a 5 gallon container. When ready to use, add 2 gallons of distilled water. It is easier to do the mixing in a pail and then return it to the container. The reason for not adding the water earlier is that bacteria in the water may cause the mixture to ferment in spite of the Paraben preservative.

DO NOT USE THIS MIXTURE IN THE MOUTH

Notice: The information in this bulletin is presented in good faith but no warranty, express or implied, is given and Dick Smith assumes no liability for the use of this material.

1 quart
2.475

1 Gallon KARO Blood

1. Weigh 9.9 gr. Methyl Paraben in a 5 oz. paper cup. .75 Add ½ oz. Karo and beat to a smooth cream. Stir in more Karo from the quantity in step 3.

1.9 2. Weigh 7.6 gr. Red #33.
2.6 Weigh 10.4 gr. Yellow # 5.
   Add these colors to 1 pint of distilled water.

3. Measure out 3½ qts. (7 pts.) Karo in 1½ gallon pail; 1 pint

4. Stir Paraben mixture into the Karo in the pail.
   Stir in the colors.

1.5 5. Add 6 oz. Kodak Photo Flo.

DO NOT USE THIS MIXTURE IN THE MOUTH

To make one gallon of diluted blood for pumping through effects: .75

Substitute 4 pints of Karo and 3 pints of distilled water for the 7 pints of Karo in step 3 above.

Notice: The information in this bulletin is presented in good faith but no warranty, express or implied, is given and Dick Smith assumes no liability for the use of this material.

Lee ben Color + Chemical Co Inc. for:
111 Eight Ave
N.Y., N.Y. 10011   D+C Red #53
212-924-1901   FD+C Yel #5

"THAT WAS THE FIRST TIME I EVER BLEW A HEAD APART."

I wasn't aware when we shot *Dawn of the Dead* (1978) that the blood was going to look so fake. It looks like melted crayons – just horrible. It looked great in the bottle and on the set. But on film, boy, it sucked.

Because of that, before I did *Friday the 13th* (1980), I stopped by Dick Smith's house and he gave me his blood formula. That changed everything!

The colour of the zombies in *Dawn of the Dead* surprised me, too. Because *Night of the Living Dead* (1968) was in black and white, my intention for Dawn was to make them grey – only, the lighting mostly turned them blue and green.

By *Day of the Dead* (1985), I'd decided that it actually made sense for there to be all different kinds of zombies, and that what each one looked like depended on a great many things. Like, what colour were they? What nationality? How long had they been dead for? And how did they die, because someone who died in an attic with the sun beating down on them would look very different than someone who died in a damp basement.

By *Day of the Dead*, then, the blood looked right and the zombies were realistic. The best I've ever done.

Tom Savini

Top: Michael Trcic as the Operation Table Zombie in *Day of the Dead* (1986). Everyone on Tom Savini's crew, including Michael, had the opportunity to live a childhood dream by becoming a zombie in a Romero film.

Above: Tom Savini's innovative gore effects from *Dawn of the Dead* (1978) blew the minds of horror fans and zombies alike.

I was working on the Chest Chomp scene for *The Thing* (1982). The one where Richard Dysart gets his hands bitten off. I took an impression of his arms and pre-scored them where they were going to be torn. Although Rob [Bottin] said the bones were made out of wax, it was dental acrylic. I added layers of muscle on the inside, hand-laid the hair and pre-painted them.

Dysart's double for that scene was a double amputee. I sculpted up little tear patterns to match what I'd done on the gelatine arms and made those out of foam. Then Jeff Kennemore took a lifecast of Dysart to make a mask for the double.

So now we're shooting the scene. The jaws open up in the chest and bite the amputee double's hands clean off. What you see in the film was that first take, but we actually shot a second. For the second take, I suggested that when the arms get bitten, we keep the jaws closed longer so we could twist and get more of a tearing action. It was way more brutal!

Anyway, [John] Carpenter was on B-Camera and, after he said "Cut!", he comes over to me and says, "Oh, my goodness! That first take was a hard R. But this one's an X!"

I said, "John, even if we use the first take, I don't know how we're going to get this in the film…"

You see, the year before I had created some incredible gore effects for *My Bloody Valentine* (1981). I felt like we'd set a new bar for this type of work. That we were going to blow [Tom] Savini away! I was going to be the new king!

But the censors cut 90 per cent of what I did. When the film came out and I saw how much they'd cut out, I was so upset. I went home and beat on my heavy bag for like, twenty minutes, until my knuckles were bleeding and there were blood splatters on the wall. I was so furious!

I never made that mistake again, though. I never got that attached to my work. I realised that once you've done your final touches and you're happy with your work, it's out of your hands. So, I said, "John, I don't see how we're going to get this in the film, because of what the censor did to *My Bloody Valentine*."

But he said, "I'll get it in the film."

And he did!

I didn't see John again until I was with him on the set of *They Live* (1988). I'd been curious for years, so I asked him, "How did you get that scene in *The Thing*?"

He said, "Oh, the cut I sent the censor just had the jaws clamping down on the arms, but not the ripping."

They'd given the film its rating without ever seeing that part of the scene, and then he added it afterwards. That's what he told me!

I have no idea how he got away with it!

Ken Diaz

"THAT FIRST TAKE WAS A HARD R. BUT THIS ONE'S AN X!"

Top: Rob Bottin's nightmarish Norris-Thing creation for John Carpenter's *The Thing* (1982).

Above: A twisted and terrifying transformation from John Carpenter's *The Thing* (1982).

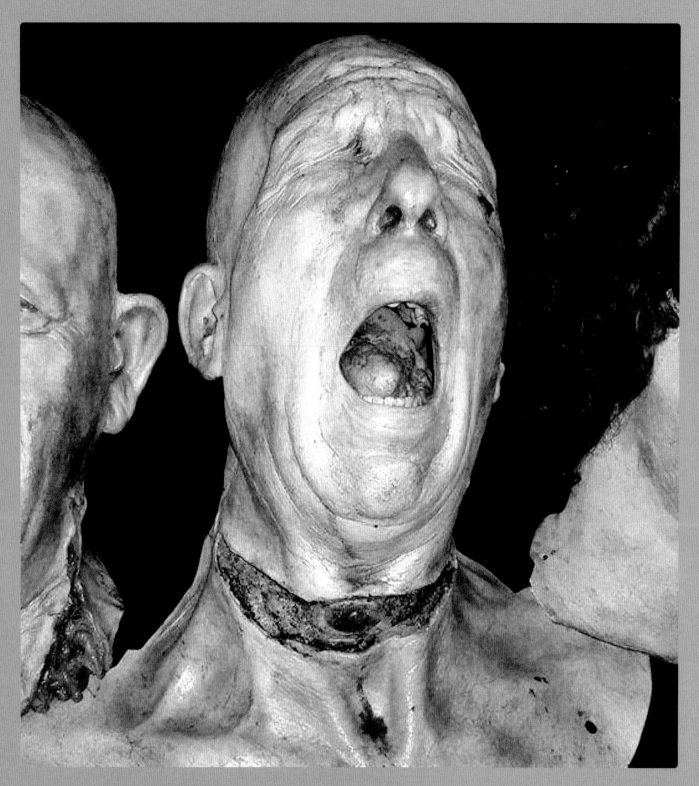

A rt Pimentel made a cast of Gunnar Ferdinandsen's head for *The Thing* (1982). That was Gunnar's head with the slit throat at the burnt-out Norwegian camp. He was such a sweetie!

When Art took the cast off, he saw it went right down to Gunnar's tonsils. He'd swallowed the alginate but kept his mouth open,

didn't move or complain while it set, and it was only after Art got it off him, and saw a cast of Gunnar's tonsils, that he realised what he must have gone through.

That was a great face!

Margaret Prentice

Above: Mould maker Gunnar Ferdinandsen endured an intrusive casting to make a memorable face for John Carpenter's *The Thing* (1982).

There's a sequence in *Cat People* (1982) where John Heard cuts open a dead leopard and an arm falls out. Tom Burman says to me, "Look at the hand. It's my answer to the Universal accounting department for holding up my money so often."

So I'm watching closely, and when the arm bursts out, sure enough, the hand's giving the finger!

Leonard Engelman

"THEY SAID THERE'D BE WAY MORE BLOOD."

Right: Neal Martz and Carl Fullerton's ghastly, gutted guard from *The Silence of the Lambs* (1991).

Below: Margaret Prentice works her magic on the set of *Oz the Great and Powerful* (2013).

For *RoboCop* (1987), I worked on the sequence where Murphy's all shot up and they're operating on him in ER. Peter Weller had a bullet hit on his forehead, shot-up pieces on his chest and arms, and I'm using latex and tissue to make extra wounds.

I'm dressing it all with blood, but I was on orders from Rob [Bottin] not to use too much. He didn't want me to cover everything up.

He told me, "I want to see the sculpture!'"

[Paul] Verhoeven used real doctors and nurses, so everyone's doing exactly what they'd do in real life. And they're really into it. They thought everything looked real and cool. But they said there'd be way more blood. That it would be solid blood.

Margaret Prentice

For me, the standout make-up effect in *The Silence of the Lambs* (1991) was Charles Napier's strung-up, gutted body. Neal Martz was mostly responsible for that. He had a magnificent way of crafting the viscera you see in Napier's belly.

Rather than using moulds, he free-formed the organs using hot, melted candy glass, the material used for breakaway glass. Once it was coloured, I'd never seen bloody guts look better or more organic. His approach was brilliant: fast, realistic and cost-effective.

With the exception of Napier's body, no dummies were used in the film. I'd heard that most people assumed we used dummies for the autopsy scenes, but those were also real people in make-ups.

Having studied cadavers during actual autopsies – like how the striations of colour appear in the skin where the blood settles, and how the body conforms to its resting place – I learned that you can't realistically replicate a corpse on a table using a dummy.

Gravity determines the way that muscle, fat and skin find its own resting position, especially with a heavy person. You can take a lifecast and make an excellent body replica of an actor, but it's not going to conform to its resting place the way a real cadaver would. Corners, edges and sides of a table can very quickly break the desired illusion, so when possible, the first choice is always to use a real actor.

Carl Fullerton

Below: Carl Fullerton and Neal Martz go for the gore as they ready one of Buffalo Bill's victims for *The Silence of the Lambs* (1991).

Bottom: A chillingly realistic tableau from *The Silence of the Lambs* (1991), courtesy of Carl Fullerton and his talented team.

"I'D NEVER SEEN BLOODY GUTS LOOK BETTER OR MORE ORGANIC."

Left: Director John Landis is cheerfully encircled by the undead victims of David Kessler's lycanthropic activities, as detailed in *An American Werewolf in London* (1981).

Above: Dean Cameron and Gary Riley flank Greg Nelson on the set of *Summer School* (1987), a breezy comedy in which the pair play make-up effects aficionados dedicated to the teachings of Rick Baker and other Legends of Gore.

Below left: "Thanks for the ride, lady!" Tom Wright in his stage four make-up as the vengeful Hitchhiker from *Creepshow 2* (1987).

Below right: The eye-catching mechanical puppet used for the Hitchhiker's final freaky look in *Creepshow 2* (1987).

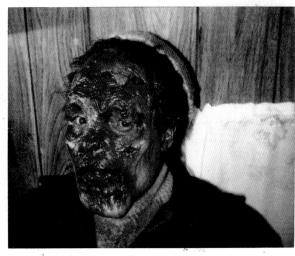

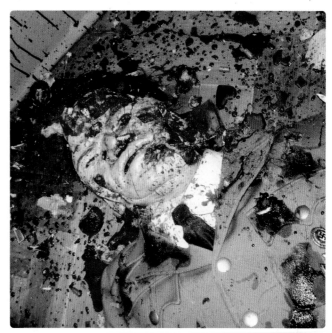

Above left: Because he's worth it: Tom Savini styles Dr. Tongue's flowing locks for *Day of the Dead* (1985).

Above: Hitler never looked so good thanks to the gorgeously gory handiwork of Greg Nicotero and KNB EFX for Quentin Tarantino's *Inglourious Basterds* (2009).

Left: Howard Berger risks a squishing between the crushing glass walls of the haunted house set from Thir13en Ghosts (2001).

Below left: Craig Olejnik as the icky Torn Prince from *Thir13en Ghosts* (2001).

Below right: Spray it again, Tam: Queen of Splatter Tami Lane dresses the set of *Patriots Day* (2016).

Ⓞne time, on *Army of Darkness* (1992), my armour dug into my face and cut my chin open. I looked down and my breastplate was covered with blood.

I'm waiting in the emergency room, in full Ash costume, with a new real wound, surrounded by lots of fake ones. And the doctor comes in, looks puzzled and goes, "Which one do I stitch up?"

I was like, "Ha!"

He couldn't tell. That was a big thumbs-up for the make-up.

Bruce Campbell

Above: Pick an Ash, any Ash! Bruce Campbell (centre) flanked by a pair of (not so) Mini-Ashes from Sam Raimi's *Army of Darkness* (1992).

Left: KNB's *Army of Darkness* report for duty ahead of leaving the effects studio to go shoot Sam Raimi's third *Evil Dead* movie.

Below: Richard Taylor preps the nurse puppet for Peter Jackson's bonkers zom-com, *Braindead* (1992).

"FOR A NUMBER OF WEEKS, I WAS STAINED RED FROM THE ARMS DOWN."

Ⓦe filmed *Braindead* (1992) out at Avalon, which is a government-owned film studio [in New Zealand]. Most of our small effects team of nine would drive out together at the crack of dawn and then [my wife] Tania and I often wouldn't leave for home until the wee hours. It can be so tiring, trying to achieve the maximum for the minimum. Yet they were beyond joyful times and I was in this almost drunk state of euphoria every day working with Peter [Jackson], with Tania, the amazing crew, the actors and the chance to work on such a crazy and special film.

For a number of weeks, I was stained red from the arms down. I couldn't get the blood off! On the way home we'd occasionally stop for petrol, never thinking about having blood speckled or splattered all over us. Often, we'd load up the van with stuff to keep working on from home, stuff for the next day's shoot, and by stuff I mean severed limbs and bodies and body parts. One day we accelerated, and the back door flapped open on the van, spilling limbs out on the street!

Richard Taylor

When you're working on a big, important project like *The Iron Lady* (2011), it's sort of fun, but also stressful and intense, with lots riding on your work.

When I think back on *Hellraiser III* (1992), though, that was nothing but fun, because there was no money, there were no expectations, and so the producers were thrilled with anything we could pull out of the hat.

It was our boss Bob Keen, myself, Steve Painter, Dave Keen and Paul Jones, flying out to America with zero prep and just making things up as we went along. Like making Pinhead's tools from pieces of plywood and shit that was just lying around.

Then there was this big, bloody sequence coming up, a scene in a discotheque where fifty people get killed. And we asked Bob, "How are we going to make all these bodies?"

So Bob threw down a bunch of old newspapers, a few bags of old clothes, a couple of old foam heads, and we literally made a pile of scarecrows! It was all so basic, but honestly, it worked out fine, and we had such a laugh doing it.

Mark Coulier

Above: Team Cenobite gather in the make-up trailer for *Hellraiser III: Hell on Earth* (1992). Top (left to right): Paula Marshall (Dreamer), Mark Coulier, Steve Painter and Kevin Bernhardt (Pistonhead); Centre: Doug Bradley (Pinhead); Bottom: Paul Jones and Ken Carpenter (Camerahead).

Below: The Barbie (screenwriter Peter Atkins), CD (Eric Willhelm) and Dreamer (Paula Marshall) Cenobites from *Hellraiser III: Hell on Earth* (1992).

On *Shaun of the Dead* (2004), there was a team of maybe twenty of us, just doing crowd zombies. It was pretty much out-of-the-kit stuff as well. Besides a few little generic appliances, most of the zombies were made with just artwork, lenses and blood.

Elaborate prosthetics aren't always the way to go. You have to be smart about achieving the result you want, because honestly, so much can be achieved with a great three-dimensional make-up. It's a true art.

Barrie Gower

Right: One of the many great undead make-ups from Edgar Wright's *Shaun of the Dead* (2004).

Below: When there is no more room in hell, the dead will go to the Winchester Tavern in *Shaun of the Dead* (2004).

Bottom: Not only is Stephen Prouty a great make-up artist, but also he makes one hell of a zombie in Ruben Fleischer's *Zombieland* (2009).

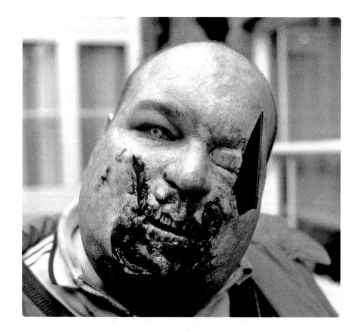

I'll tell you what makes a good zombie: it's the actor.

We could put someone through a three-hour zombie make-up with limbs hanging off them, and tons of other cool stuff, but if they plod through the scene like Bigfoot through the Patterson-Gimlin film, it just doesn't do it for me.

If, on the other hand, you find someone who's into it and really wants to embody the role, all they need are a couple of wounds, and they're a zombie.

I remember we had a few guys on *Zombieland* (2009) who literally had no more than, like, three or four wounds on them. But they were just so into it, you'd have to pull them off people. Like, the director would yell "CUT!", but they'd keep on going.

They really made it much more interesting!

Stephen Prouty

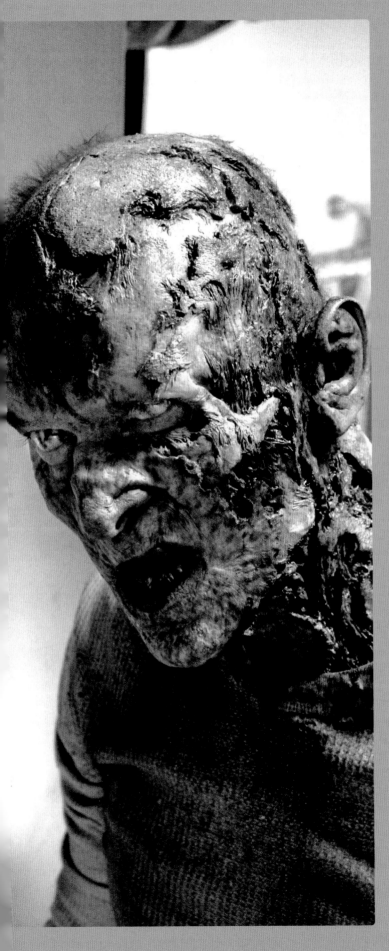

"AS MUCH AS I LIKE FRESH ZOMBIES, THE MORE THEY ROT, THE MORE FUN THEY ARE!"

On season one of *The Walking Dead* (2010–22), as it had been only six weeks since the apocalypse, and most of the kills were quite fresh, most of the make-ups we did were three-dimensional transfers and paint, contact lenses and mouth stain.

As much as I like fresh zombies, the more they rot, the more fun they are! So with each new season, we'd push the make-ups further.

Like, building dentures on the outside of the performers' mouths so we could play with the shape of the lips and show the decomposition. And building the faces out so we could remove the nose.

We never stopped challenging ourselves, and as a result our zombies got scarier and more interesting with each passing season.

Greg Nicotero

Left: Make-up whizz Gino Crognale rises from the grave as one of the many zombies he played in *The Walking Dead* (2010–22).

Above: Greg Nicotero and a large circle of zombie friends from *The Walking Dead* (2010–22).

Following pages: Alex Diaz (left), Andy Schoenberg (centre) and Greg Nicotero (right) operate one of the Walker puppets designed and created at KNB EFX for *The Walking Dead* (2010–22).

Bone Tomahawk (2015) was directed by one of my college classmates, S. Craig Zahler. It was definitely a labour of love.

There's a scene about two-thirds of the way into the film, in the cave, where Deputy Nick's stripped, scalped, dangled upside down and hacked in half. When you work on a scene like that, watching the dailies, appreciating the effects work and editing the footage, you're far enough removed from it that you don't find the sequence too disturbing to watch.

Obviously, that's not the experience of someone who's never seen it. I remember when the film screened at the Beyond Fest in LA, the audience was so horrified by that sequence, when it finally came to an end, they applauded from relief!

The next day, Quentin [Tarantino] told me, "That was easily the best scene in the movie!"

Fred Raskin

Above: Sofie Fatale (Julie Dreyfus) proves relatively armless following her brush with The Bride's (Uma Thurman) Hanzō blade in Quentin Tarantino's action masterpiece, *Kill Bill: Volume 1* (2003).

Below: Howard Berger demonstrates how to get a head in the make-up business on the set of *Kill Bill: Volume 1* (2003).

"STRIPPED, SCALPED, DANGLED UPSIDE DOWN AND HACKED IN HALF."

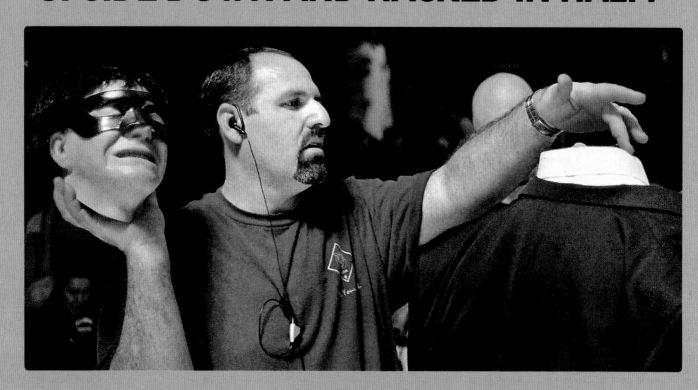

On *Kill Bill: Volume 1* (2003), the first blood effect we shot for the House of Blue Leaves sequence was Uma Thurman cutting off Julie Dreyfus's arm.

Two fire extinguishers, each filled with 5 gallons [19 litres] of fake blood, were charged to [a pressure of] 100PSI and hooked up to a shoulder piece worn by Julie.

On Quentin Tarantino's cue, Uma brought her sword down on the dummy arm and I hit the blood pumps, triggering a 30-foot [9m] explosion of blood that completely covered the crew.

Quentin started laughing, which was a sign you'd done a good job, and we had our first blood gag in the can, with 500 gallons [1,900 litres] more blood and endless strewn bodies to come!

Howard Berger

One of the greatest compliments I've ever gotten was from Sally Menke, the editor of Quentin Tarantino's *Death Proof* (2007).

We built a dummy body of Monica Staggs, who played the blonde driver of the car rammed by Kurt Russell's character. There's an overhead shot of her head jolting back from the crash. It's in slow motion and at one point the head tilts right up to the lens.

Apparently Sally couldn't tell, in that shot, if it was the actress or

the dummy. So Quentin calls me and said, "Dude, our editor doesn't know the difference!"

It felt so great to have fooled an editor who studies footage, every day and frame by frame!

Greg Nicotero

Below, left: Jungle Julia's (Sydney Tamiia Poitier) bloodied and crushed, car-crash body, created by KNB EFX for Quentin Tarantino's *Death Proof* (2007).

Top, right: KNB EFX went out on a limb to create life-like, gory effects for *Death Proof* (2007).

Above: KNB EFX's bloody make-up effects take a fair bit of beating, as does Mikey Madison, in *Once Upon a Time... In Hollywood* (2019).

Quentin [Tarantino] usually makes a point of not letting me know what music he's intending to use in any particular sequence. So my first assembly, as I'm cutting his stuff together, is almost entirely dry.

So I'm cutting the home invasion scene near the end of *Once Upon a Time... In Hollywood* (2019), specifically the part where Cliff takes Katy and bashes her head into the wall, the mantelpiece, and the coffee table. It was as long as it could possibly be in terms of head bashes, with twelve.

Then Quentin brought in the Vanilla Fudge cover of 'You Keep Me Hangin' On', and cutting the bashes in time to that, we had to lose two of the hits. But it just wasn't the same to me after that, so I added one more phrase of the song so we could restore all twelve hits. And Quentin's instant response was, "Oh, this is much better."

This wasn't purely out of respect for the artists involved in creating the blood and gore effects. I just wanted the sequence to be as awesome as it could be. And when Cliff was bashing her head against the mantelpiece, with each successive hit, there was more blood splatter. It seemed very well thought out, and I didn't want to spoil that.

Taking out those two hits kept the splatter from ratcheting up the way it should have. To maintain the progression of the assault, we needed every bash.

Fred Raskin

On *The Shallows* (2016), Blake Lively had to transform from beautiful to ravaged by the elements while being chased by a shark. We didn't shoot anything in sequence so it was quite a challenge.

I'd broken down the script and identified thirty-eight make-up changes that I'd colour-coded into the screenplay, so I knew, no matter where in the story we shot from day to day, exactly how messed up she was. Like, how badly sunburned she was, how chapped her lips were, what state her wounds were in from the shark, and the [Portuguese] man o' war.

Sometimes the director, Jaume Collet-Serra, would say, "Let's cut her arm here on the buoy", but I'd have to jump in and remind him that we couldn't add anything new as we'd already shot the ending! Which was another challenge.

In the end, I felt like I'd gotten to tell the story through make-up, which was incredibly satisfying.

Tami Lane

Above: Beaten, bloody and bruised, Blake Lively's nasty injuries in *The Shallows* (2019) were created by resourceful Tami Lane.

Below: Tami Lane's handiwork on *The Shallows* (2019) enabled Blake Lively to suture her own leg following a savage shark attack.

"I FELT LIKE I'D GOTTEN TO TELL THE STORY THROUGH MAKE-UP."

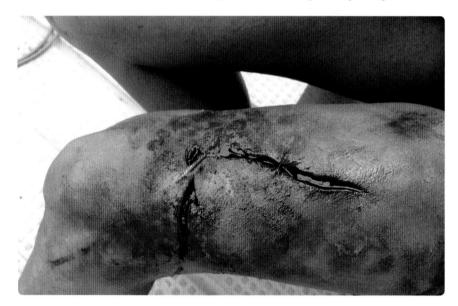

Though blood gags are usually my least favourite thing to do, ironically, a last-minute blood gag of mine turned out to be one of my proudest achievements.

There's a scene in *The Shallows* (2016) where Blake Lively's character is sitting on a rock, 200 yards [180m] from shore, sewing up a wound on her thigh. The director, Jaume Collet-Serra, tells me for the close-ups, he wants the wound to bleed constantly. That every time she pushes it to add another stitch, it should bleed more. Not just be dressed with blood, which was the effect we'd planned for. The effect that was called for in the script. And although the make-up was already finished, and I didn't have bladders on set or anything prepped, Jaume asks me, "How much time do you need?"

So I went, "Give me twenty-five minutes."

I ran back to the trailer and made a bladder using tape and a plastic Ziploc bag. I found some tubing and ran back to the set to apply it. I undid the top seam of Blake's appliance and carefully shoved the bladder down to where the wound was, cutting it along the length of the gash. Then I glued and blended everything, which wasn't too difficult as there was a lot of bruising, so I could disguise some stuff.

When we filmed the scene, because the camera was so tight on Blake's leg, I was able to sit on the rock beside her, with a 3-foot [90cm] hose and a syringe of blood. Every time she pushed down on the silicone wound I gave the syringe a squeeze, the wound would bleed, and then the waves from the wave machine came and washed the blood away. It was a great effect and really added to the scene. I love that I was able to do it in no time at all.

Tami Lane

There are lots of different bloods: eye blood, mouth blood, dressing blood…

So I'm working on *Deepwater Horizon* (2016), doing Mark Wahlberg's make-up. Now there's a guy I love working with. Near the end of the film, his character's pretty messed up from everything he's gone through, and so right before shooting a scene, Mark tells me, "I'm going to squirt some blood in my mouth."

Before I can stop him, he grabs a bottle out of my bag and takes a swig. Only it wasn't mouth blood. Obviously, it wasn't toxic or anything, but it did have Photo-Flo in it, which is just the most bitter, horrible-tasting thing.

Pete Berg, the director, is already shooting when suddenly Mark spits out the blood and starts coughing, tearing up and dry retching… It was quite a scene.

Afterwards, Pete comes up to Mark and says, "Oh, my God – that was GREAT!"

It was a happy accident. Not so much for Mark, I guess, but it ended up in the movie, so it worked out fine!

Howard Berger

"MARK TELLS ME, 'I'M GOING TO SQUIRT SOME BLOOD IN MY MOUTH.'"

Above: Mark Wahlberg and Gina Rodriguez struggle to survive Peter Berg's disaster epic, *Deepwater Horizon* (2016).

Left: Mark Wahlberg, ready for action in *Deepwater Horizon* (2016).

THEY'RE ALIVE!

If you've ever wondered how it feels to get up in the middle of the night to go sit in a make-up chair and be slowly entombed in prosthetics...

To only then join your cast mates for a full working day, and somehow deliver your performance from behind a hot, uncomfortable and claustrophobic mass of silicone, paint and hair...

And then finally, to endure a painstaking removal process, knowing it'll all be back on in just a few hours... Read on!

Actors are inherently vain. It comes with the territory. We age. Things sag. We worry about how our hair looks, or if you can see our bald spot. We get spots. And wrinkles!

One of the great gifts that effects make-up gives you is you no longer have to worry about all that. When I'm Freddy, I'm not worried about what Robert Englund looks like because I'm not Robert Englund.

When those worries are taken off the table, any energy that you'd previously devoted to compensating for all your perceived flaws can now be channelled into your character, into the dialogue, into the scene you're playing…

It's liberating.

Robert Englund

"WHEN I'M FREDDY, I'M NOT WORRIED ABOUT WHAT ROBERT ENGLUND LOOKS LIKE."

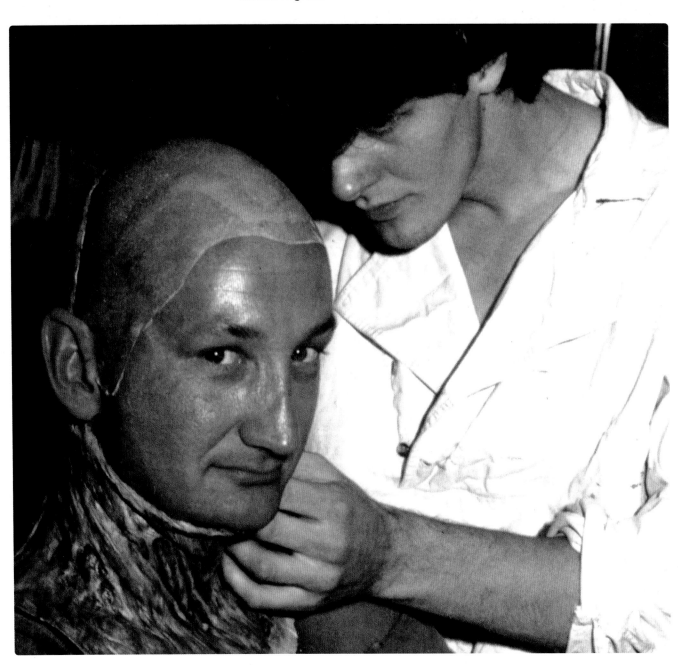

Stuart [Freeborn] rarely spent much time on set. He preferred to be in his workshop. On *Return of the Jedi* (1983), one of the things I assisted him with was Ian McDiarmid's Emperor make-up. After a successful test, Stuart left it to me to apply and maintain.

On Ian's first day of filming, I applied the make-up exactly as Stuart told me: spirit gum, stipple, lenses, lovely! I remember Ian was very hot. Anyway, his first scene involved the Emperor, having just arrived at the new Death Star, walking down a ramp out of a spacecraft, and then there's this long tracking shot where he walks and talks with Darth Vader.

They rehearsed it and everything was fine. Then Ian walks up the ramp and back into the spacecraft, where I'm hiding in the dark with my make-up box, just to quickly check him over before they shoot the scene for real. And we're a minute away from shooting when I hear this mighty sneeze.

I spin around and Ian's whole make-up is in his hands. He'd put his hands over his mouth to try and stifle the sneeze, but ended up literally inflating it off his face. And just outside there were hundreds of stormtroopers, Darth Vader and George Lucas, poised for action.

I grabbed a bottle of Kryolan spirit gum, the kind with the big brush inside, and told Ian, "Close your eyes and hold your breath!"

I plastered his face with spirit gum, took the make-up and smooshed it into position. Stuck some pins in and almost immediately after, they yelled, "Action!"

He walked down the ramp and that shot is in the film! You can see as he's walking along, at least it's clear to me, that the make-up's just about holding on around his eyes and his lips. But it held.

We got away with it!

Nick Dudman

"I SPIN AROUND AND IAN'S WHOLE MAKE-UP IS IN HIS HANDS."

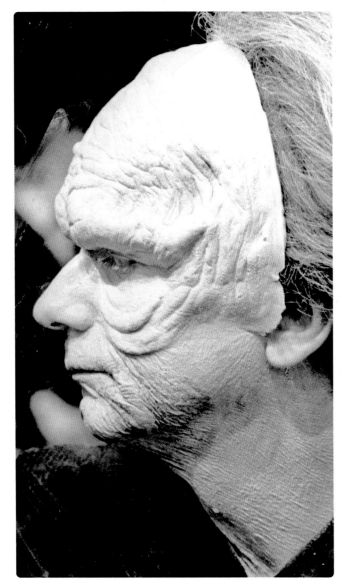

Previous pages: Gloriously gory Kathleen Kinmont in *Bride of Re-Animator* (1990).

Opposite: Kevin Yagher applies his iconic Freddy Krueger make-up to Robert Englund for *A Nightmare on Elm Street 2: Freddy's Revenge* (1985).

Left: Ian McDiarmid from the dark side, mid-transformation as the Emperor in a make-up created by Nick Dudman, under the supervision of Stuart Freeborn, for *Star Wars: Episode VI – Return of the Jedi* (1983).

Above: Witness the power of Ian McDiarmid's fully armed and operational Emperor make-up for *Star Wars: Episode VI – Return of the Jedi* (1983)!

I was just a kid, really, when I designed and applied Woody Allen's make-ups for *Zelig* (1983). He didn't like a lot of people around him back then, and I was this big, hairy Italian guy, but we got along fine. First, I needed to take a cast of his face, which I did in his penthouse on Fifth Avenue. So it's just me and him, and I'd given him a little piece of paper and a pencil so he could let me know how he was feeling, and he just wrote, "HURRY!"

The first thing I did was turn him into a black, 1920s jazz musician. I did this foam latex make-up and everyone liked it, but when we did a test, Gordon Willis, the cinematographer, said, "I love it, but I don't see Woody. I think we should take it back a bit."

That's when I learned that, in make-up, less is more. The best make-ups often just gild the lily rather than shout, "HELLO! I'M A Make-up! LOOK HOW GREAT I AM!"

We call those The Invisibles, like Max von Sydow in *The Exorcist* (1973). Everyone focused on Linda Blair without realising von Sydow was in his early forties. That Dick Smith had turned him into a grey old man. It flew under the radar. It didn't grandstand. It was about creating a character.

For *Zelig*, you had to see Woody Allen through all those famous characters, so completely transforming him was not the way to go. Like William Tuttle's make-ups on *7 Faces of Dr. Lao* (1964), transforming Tony Randall into all those characters, but you could still see Tony in all of them. So I cut back and it worked out great.

John Caglione Jr

"THAT'S WHEN I LEARNED THAT, IN MAKE-UP, LESS IS MORE."

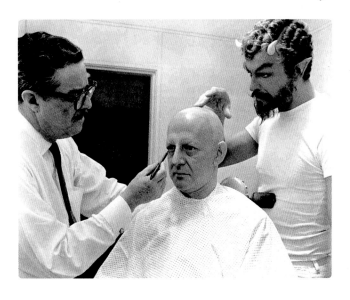

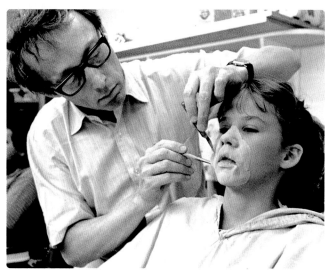

Opposite, top left: Stephen Prouty, Bart Mixon and Will Huff glue the years on to Johnny Knoxville for *Bad Grandpa* (2013).

Opposite, top right: John Rosengrant and Stan Winston co-apply a Penguin test make-up on Danny DeVito for *Batman Returns* (1992).

Opposite, bottom left: William Tuttle applies one of the many amazing make-ups that he created for Tony Randall, enabling him to play multiple roles in *7 Faces of Dr. Lao* (1964).

Opposite, bottom right: In the hands of make-up maestro Dick Smith, Linda Blair becomes a girl possessed for *The Exorcist* (1973).

Left: Tony Randall in William Tuttle's elegant Medusa make-up for *7 Faces of Dr. Lao* (1964).

Above: As well as being a skilled make-up artist, William Tuttle was also a talented illustrator. His drawing of Tony Randall as the Abominable Snowman for *7 Faces of Dr. Lao* (1964) is one of many beautiful concept pieces that he created for the film.

Below: William Tuttle's concept for The Medusa is virtually a mirror image of the final make-up that he created for *7 Faces of Dr. Lao* (1964).

Growing up around make-up effects gave me a lot of patience and respect for the process. As an actor, whenever I'd have to wear prosthetics, I would always try to be on my best behaviour in the chair. Not moving or talking too much during the application. And I was really good at maintaining my make-up throughout the shoot day. Never gabbing too much on set, but sitting quietly in my trailer. And when I'd eat, I'd always take little bites and use a straw to drink.

I have to say, though, as much as I enjoy occasionally being in prosthetics, the joy usually wears off for me by day three. You're in earlier than everyone, you're out later than everyone, and it's no fun being in heavy prosthetics for an extended period of time. You have to get into a zen state, otherwise you can get claustrophobic and freak out.

I have great respect for those people who can do it, day in, day out. Folks like Doug Jones. But it's not for me.

When Stan [Winston] produced the film *Wrong Turn* (2003), he asked if I wanted to play one of the cannibalistic mountain men. I said, "Dad, I love you, but I'm not going to be in full prosthetics for a month. But thank you for thinking of me. I love you."

Matt Winston

Below: Stan (left) and Matt Winston (right) enjoy some father-and-son bonding time on set. Beyond his legacy as one of the greatest make-up effects artists in film history, Stan is fondly remembered as being both a loving father to his children and a caring father figure to the people in his studio.

"I JUST GAINED ALL THIS WEIGHT, AND I HAVE SCARS YOU CAN WORK WITH, TOO."

It's not easy when you're creating a character, and at the same time, you're expected to make them sexy, too. That happened with Helena Bonham Carter's character, Ari, on *Planet of the Apes* (2001). When you're creating an ape but the producers say she's got to be kissable, too, that sure she has hair on her face, but it should be soft and pretty… It's a tricky balance.

Not long after, I started preparing for *Monster* (2003), which was going to star Charlize Theron as the serial killer Aileen Wuornos. I remember we were at the Chateau Marmont and I asked her, "Do you want to be messed up, but really kind of sexy?"

But she's like, "No, dude! I just gained all this weight, and I have scars you can work with, too."

She was so ready to go for it.

She'd grown her eyebrows out, because she thought they'd look terrible, all untweezed and rough, but it's Charlize, so she looked really beautiful. In the end, on top of everything else we did to her, she let me remove most of her eyebrows. We created this really angry face!

After the first test make-up, she walked out of the trailer and I got chills from my heels to the top of my head. It was like she was channelling Aileen. She was incredible. You know, you can do a decent make-up on someone, but it's up to them to bring it to life.

Even on that movie, though, there was a moment when one of the producers asked me, "Does she have to look that bad? Can't we get a little of her back?"

And I was like, "Talk to Charlize."

They didn't ask me again, because they knew she was up for anything, and thank God for that.

Toni G

Above: Helena Bonham Carter monkeys around in Rick Baker's Ari make-up for Tim Burton's *Planet of the Apes* (2001).

Below: Tony G – could be, the "G" stands for GREAT! – applies make-up to one of the Tinkers for *Oz the Great and Powerful* (2013).

You can't just put anyone in a creature suit. We've tried. Most people have no idea how to move in one, and God, some never stop complaining.

When you work with Doug Jones, though, he gives so much, he's like 50 per cent of every creature we create. Put a suit on Doug, and it becomes a living, breathing character.

Besides being very smart, kind and up for anything, Doug's just so very, very patient. And it's interesting: when you put a make-up on him, you can see he's analysing it. Staring at it in the mirror and thinking about what he can do with it. Would you believe, some actors don't even look in the mirror?

And if there's, say, a wrinkle in the foam latex, something we can't remove, he'll find poses that stretch it out and hide it. He really helps the make-up.

Doug is an actor who plays with you, not against you, and we just love working with him.

David Martí

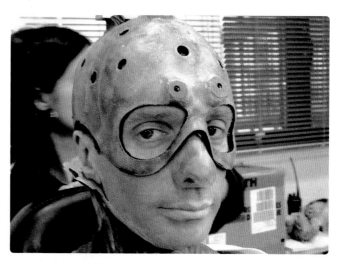

Above: Doug Jones prepares for a lengthy transformation process after being strapped into his Fauno head gear for Guillermo del Toro's *Pan's Labyrinth* (2006).

Below: Not even a broken hand can stop David Martí from working his magic as he adds a few finishing touches to Doug Jones' Fauno for *Pan's Labyrinth* (2006).

"PUT A SUIT ON DOUG, AND IT BECOMES A LIVING, BREATHING CHARACTER."

After David [Martí] and I agreed to create Young Hellboy for *Hellboy II: The Golden Army* (2008), Guillermo [del Toro] asked me to play him in the movie. As I'm small, he said, I was perfect for the role.

At first, I thought it was a crazy idea. I'm no actress! But the idea of designing and building a suit, and then performing in it, was amazing to me.

At the time, they were still writing the script. Guillermo reassured me, "There's no dialogue. You won't have to say anything. It's just flashbacks of Young Hellboy and his dad. You'll be taking a bath, sleeping in bed…"

I said, "OK, I can do that!"

It was my job to sculpt the head, and it turned out to be a challenging process. The design was actually really hard to find. At first, he just looked like a child, but it was too simple. He had no character.

So Guillermo's like, "No, no, no. Do it more like the comic."

Then, "No, no, no. Make it look more like Ron Perlman."

I was making all these changes, but right up until the end, nothing ever looked quite right. Even the last one we did, it looked good, but honestly, we weren't super happy with it. And neither was Guillermo. But we told him there was no time left. That we had to make the moulds now, or they wouldn't be ready in time. So he said, "OK."

Everything changed, though, when we did the test make-up. When Guillermo saw me, he was like, "WOW! THAT'S FANTASTIC!"

He said, "Honestly, based on the sculpture, I didn't give a damn about the make-up. I was actually going to replace it with CG. But now I see it on you, it's alive! I LOVE IT!"

With the make-up finished, we arrived in Budapest, where they were shooting the movie, and they gave us the finished script. And I'm reading it. And I'm like, What's this? I have dialogue now! Oh, my God."

What could I do, though? I couldn't back out now. I just had to be brave. And on the first day, sure, I was nervous, but actually wearing the make-up helped a lot. It was like I was someone else!

The first time I ever met John Hurt, I was already made up as Young Hellboy. He was super nice, but he talked to me like I was a kid. Then I realised: he thought I was a little boy! Eventually, I plucked up the courage to tell him that actually, I was a woman, and he just roared with laughter!

We shot for five days straight, and those were very long days.

Above: As well as creating Young Hellboy for *Hellboy II: The Golden Army* (2008), multitalented Montse Ribé also rose to the unexpected challenge of playing the character.

David did my make-up all by himself. It took six hours to apply. Then we shot for twelve hours, and at the end of the day, it took another hour to remove the make-up.

One night, I was so tired, all I wanted to do was sleep. So we removed the face and the hands and drove to the hotel. I walked into the lobby, bright red with horns and a tail, but the staff were so professional, they just pretended not to notice!

It was a tough week but an amazing experience, and I'd do it again in a heartbeat. In fact, I discovered I love being inside make-ups! And beyond that, I have more empathy now for actors in big creature suits and try to help them through the process, however I can.

Montse Ribé

Tom Cruise is very professional and friendly but, man, he stares in the mirror at every little move you make. And he keeps an eye on his watch, too. So if you've got him, say, for two-and-a-half hours, he'll be counting the time down. "One hour… Half an hour…"

He's kind of having fun with it, but at the same time, he's totally serious.

I helped apply Tom's make-up on *Tropic Thunder* (2008). Barney Burman did a nice job on the design. When the movie came out, most people didn't even realise it was Tom under all that silicone. And he really impressed me.

A lot of actors would have struggled to pull a performance out of that make-up, but Tom really had a lot of fun with it. He took it and had a good time.

Margaret Prentice

Since the beginning, the aliens on *Star Trek* have mostly been head and hand make-ups. The show rarely ventured from that aesthetic, and, for J.J.'s first movie, I wanted to respect that. To update the techniques and the sculptures, but keep their silhouettes humanoid.

Working with Leonard Nimoy was particularly amazing. Even if you don't know *Star Trek*, Spock's so iconic, you'd recognise his silhouette in a second.

Leonard had very specific notes on Spock's ears, like how far in they went, how far forward they went and even how thick they were. Getting them just right took sculpting five different pairs of ears, but it was a fascinating process.

The night we won the Academy Award for *Star Trek* (2009), my parents were there to see me accept the award with Barney Burman and Mindy Hall. I kept my Oscar for the night, then gave it to my parents.

After destroying my mom's oven, dumping plaster all over my dad's library carpet and almost burning their garage down, giving them my Oscar was their payoff.

Joel Harlow

"SPOCK'S SO ICONIC, YOU'D RECOGNISE HIS SILHOUETTE IN A SECOND."

Top: While watching *Tropic Thunder* (2008), few folks realised that deep inside Les Grossman hid Tom Cruise, in a make-up created by Barney Burman, under the supervision of Michèle Burke.

Above, left: Leonard Nimoy as Spock Prime in a make-up created by Joel Harlow and his team for J.J. Abrams' *Star Trek* (2009).

Opposite, left: Johnny Depp in Joel Harlow's detailed old-age Tonto make-up for *The Lone Ranger* (2013).

Opposite, right: Joel Harlow applies the multi-piece prosthetic make-up required to turn Johnny Depp into old-age Tonto for *The Lone Ranger* (2013).

My husband Joe [Dunckley] is a speciality costumer, props maker, armourer and overall creative dynamo. Our first big show representing WETA Workshop together as on-set supervisors was *District 9* (2009). I handled the prosthetic make-ups and Joe handled the rest of our kit, including all the make-up effects gags.

Sharlto Copley was cast as Wikus in the eleventh hour. He was a long-time friend of director Neill Blomkamp and actually producing at the time. Sharlto was helping out with auditions by reading alongside prospective actors. He caught the eye of Peter Jackson, who was one of the D9 producers, and suggested that actually HE should be cast in the role of Wikus!

The make-up time took anywhere from forty-five minutes for normal nerdy Wikus, to almost six hours in the chair for when his alien transformation was furthest along. Though Sharlto had never acted before, let alone worn prosthetics, he was spectacular to work with! He'd just sit in the make-up chair and go to his happy zen place.

Because Sharlto was cast so late in the game, the appliances had not been customised or generated off his body form, so it took a lot of improvising to make them fit seamlessly and work in accordance with one another.

Thank God he handled it like a pro and was super patient and friendly all the way through. If not, it would have been a total disaster!

Sarah Rubano

"HE'D JUST SIT IN THE MAKE-UP CHAIR AND GO TO HIS HAPPY ZEN PLACE."

There's a long scene in *The Lone Ranger* (2013) where Johnny Depp's all muddy. I could have used fake mud but it would never have held up. He goes in and out of the water, he's on top of a train, and continuity would have been a nightmare.

I did prosthetics instead and it worked great. At the end of the first day, Johnny didn't want it removed. He just wore it home, and kept it on, like, three or four days. And the longer he wore it, as it got all ingrained and dirty, the better it looked!

When we finally took it off him, you couldn't tell he'd been wearing prosthetics at all, let alone for days. That man has amazing skin.

Joel Harlow

ngie [Angelina Jolie] takes appliances really well. Of course, we take extra good care of her, but still, it makes such a difference when you're working with someone who understands and has patience for the process. And beyond that, even collaborates on the design, like she did with *Maleficent* (2014).

She knew exactly what she wanted.

Toni G

"SHE KNEW EXACTLY WHAT SHE WANTED."

hen you walk on screen in make-up and costume, before you've even opened your mouth, you've already told 75 per cent of your story.

James McAvoy

ho better to play a monster than a monster guy?

Howard Berger

Above: Howard Berger (left) was always playing the monster, be it Halloween or any other day. Here he is with his family, including his father in the gorilla suit.

Opposite: Angelina Jolie in Arjen Tuiten and Toni G's exquisitely executed make-up for *Maleficent: Mistress of Evil* (2019).

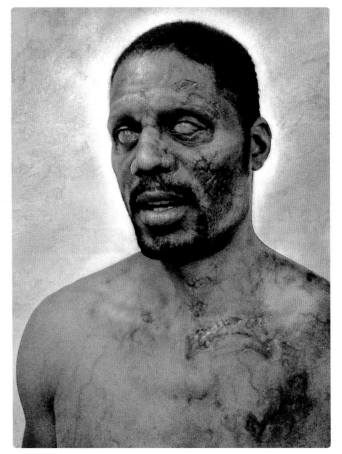

The many creatures of Carey Jones:

Top, left: A werewolf by KNB EFX for the series pilot of *Teen Wolf* (2011–17).

Top, right: Carey brings all creatures great and small to life. His portrayal of UNK, however, was definitely a biggie for Seth MacFarlane's sci-fi series *The Orville* (2017–22).

Above: Wayne Toth and Mike O'Brien dress Carey as the River Ghost for *Predators* (2010).

Right: When Greg Nicotero began designing Walker make-ups for *The Walking Dead* (2010–22), he used Carey as a leaping-off point, as seen here in John Wheaton's concept art.

We were working in the shop on the first *Narnia* film and Howard [Berger] asked me if I was up for being their fit model. I was like, "I don't know what that is, but fine."

Turns out that meant things like walking back and forth in the minotaur suit, moving my arms around. I'm 6 feet 7 inches [200cm], so built like a suit performer, and me being around to try things on was a lot more convenient than calling someone in.

Besides, it's fun wearing creature suits! And that's when I first thought, "There's people who do this for a living…"

Five years on, Greg [Nicotero] told a bunch of us about this thing coming up. A pilot for a new show. It sounded cool: *The Walking Dead* (2010–22)!

A while later, Greg asked me and a couple other guys if we could model the new make-ups. He told me they'd be shooting in Atlanta, and that a lot of the extras would be African-American, so they wanted to test different skin tones on camera.

I was down to be a zombie, so I said, "Cool!"

We went over to Panavision and Andy Schoneberg did me up. We spent the day walking towards camera, away from camera, inside, outside… Just lots of different scenarios.

Then Greg's like, "We're doing *Predators* (2010) next, and we're going to need more than just Derek [Mears] and Brian [Steele] in the suits, so would you be up for doing it?"

I said, "Yes!"

Honestly, though, I didn't think I'd spend more than a day in the suit. But they were like, "Actually, we need you to do this scene now, and that scene, and then all these other scenes…"

The amount of work I did for that movie just grew and grew. At the end, the director was so grateful. He told me, "You should do this all the time…"

So I'm out in Atlanta on an episode of *The Walking Dead*, applying make-ups, and Greg's like, "You've been on the show since the beginning, but you haven't played a zombie yet. You wanna play a zombie?"

I said, "Cool!"

So Gino Crognale does my make-up and I'm walking out to set but they're like, "Dude, you're the biggest zombie we ever had! We don't want the actors to see you until we shoot the scene."

When the scene starts shooting, I'm supposed to burst out of this garage door. And when I do, the actress spins around, screams, and runs away.

So they're like, "CUT!"

And they say to her, "You're not supposed to leave camera."

But she was genuinely freaked out by me! She wasn't acting. When she saw me, she just instinctively ran away! And even after we'd

"THEY'RE LIKE, 'DUDE, YOU'RE THE BIGGEST ZOMBIE WE EVER HAD!'"

finished shooting, she wouldn't come anywhere near me.

Although suit performing was always something I did on the side, it had grown into something I realised I really liked doing. But it's not for everyone, you know.

Like, on *This Is the End* (2013), I'm standing on a rooftop in New Orleans, it's summer, 92 degrees Fahrenheit [33.3°C] with 89 per cent humidity, and I'm in a hot, heavy demon suit. I felt like I might pass out any second, but I was in the middle of a take and that wasn't an option. You just have to force yourself to keep going.

I guess I have a unique point of view, since I'm also on the other side, designing and building the suits. Certainly, I treat them with a lot more respect than many other performers.

A lot of people who wear suits, as soon as they think they're done for the day, they'll just rip the head or arms off. They're tired and uncomfortable, so they're rough with it, and they end up doing more damage to the suit than they did while they were wearing it.

Me, no matter what, when they yell "Cut!," I just wait. I'll wait for whoever's there from fabrication to take the head and gloves off. When they unzip the rest, I know what to grab, and what not to grab, so that when they're taking it off, I won't tear the armpits, the crotch or the sides.

I'm definitely more patient than most suit performers, because I appreciate the artistry and the time it took to make those pieces. Of course, you want to rip them off when you're tired and overheated. But the more damage you do, the later someone's going to have to work to repair it for the next day, and I don't want that on my conscience.

I'll never quit working on the make-up side of the business, no matter how much work I get as a suit performer. But the kid in me is definitely most excited about the job I just finished…

The first film I ever saw at the cinema was *The Empire Strikes Back* (1980). It blew my mind. Walking out after seeing that film, I knew I had to do something to do with filmmaking and creature effects. I never imagined for a second, though, that I'd be a part of the *Star Wars* universe. For me, it was on, just, too high a pedestal.

But, like, dude: I'm Black Krrsantan in *The Book of Boba Fett* (2021)!

OH MY GOD!

Carey Jones

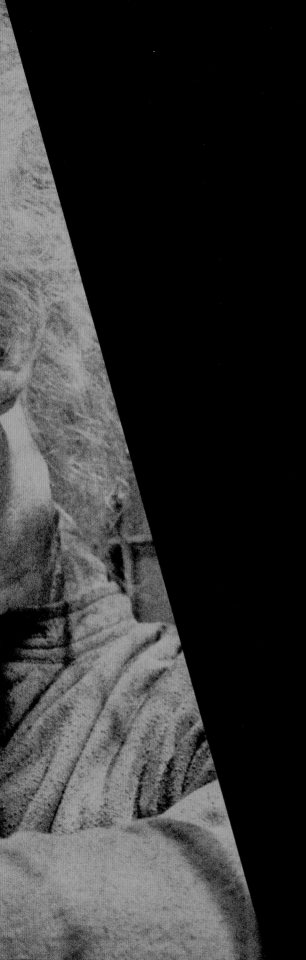

MAKING
FACES

Here we observe our make-up masters in their natural
habitat: The Shop. Whether at home, alone, or in sprawling,
shared facilities, they're all essentially occupying
professional versions of the bedroom labs they set up
as kids. Safe, fun, creative spaces, limited sometimes by
budgets and schedules, but never by imagination.

It is in these shops, both big and small, that dreams
become reality via three key qualities: artistic ability,
technical prowess and unrelenting force of will.

Dick Smith told me once, "If they ever do a film of the Elephant Man, I'd love to do the make-up."

A couple of years later, he rang me to say they were making one here in England, and could I find out who was doing it? I asked around, but no one seemed to know anything.

Then a month or so later, I got a call from a production manager, asking where he could buy some silicone foam for a film he'd just started working on called *The Elephant Man* (1980).

That pricked up my ears. I asked, "Who's doing the make-up?"

He said, "Well, the director, David Lynch."

That was certainly a surprise. Anyway, I told him where to find the foam and asked him what he was planning to do with it.

He said they were going to make feet with it, and I told him, "That won't work!"

A few days later he calls me back: "That didn't work!"

Then he asked me about some other material they wanted to try, and I told him where to find it, but that didn't work either. I told Dick what was going on and he said, "If the director's doing it, they don't need us."

Eventually, they asked if they could come to see me, straight away. I was very busy, and I told them so, "But if you insist," I said, "come round."

Next thing I know, round comes David Lynch, John Hurt, Terence Clegg and the producer, Jonathan Sanger. After testing his make-up, David admitted he'd bitten off more than he could chew. "For one millionth of a second I thought I had a film," he said. "But then I knew I hadn't!"

They wanted me to do the Elephant Man make-up. I said I couldn't possibly. Then John got down on bended knee and said, "Please... PLEASE!"

I told them I had two films on the go already, and that designing and building a make-up that complicated would take weeks.

They asked, "How many weeks?"

I said, "At least five."

I agreed to think about it, as one does, and off they went. Then a few hours later, a hand-delivered letter arrived stating I'd guaranteed to deliver the make-up in five weeks.

A bit like Vesuvius, I exploded with incandescent rage. How could they be so rude? I called them and said, "NO", in no uncertain terms.

They said, "Well, even if you don't do the film, we've arranged for you to see Joseph [John in the film] Merrick's remains in the London Hospital Museum, so would you be interested in that?"

It's not open to the public, so I could hardly refuse and, of course, I found it fascinating. They knew if anything would hook me, it would be that, and they were right. Also, I'd started feeling sorry for them and felt I should probably rescue them, so I agreed to do it.

Filming had already begun. Anthony Hopkins could only work in the country for so many months a year. It was November and he had to be gone by the end of January, so time was expiring rapidly.

At the time, I was supposed to be applying make-ups on *Reds* (1981), but they paid for make-up people to take my place. Then they insured me for $3 million in case I got run over by a bus. Not that there was the slightest chance of that, as I'd be entombed at home the whole time, working on the Elephant Man.

In the end, it took me eight weeks to deliver. My wife and an assistant helped with menial tasks like mixing plaster, but aside from that, as usual, I did everything myself: design, sculpting, moulds, teeth, punching hair... Everything.

Nothing was to be approved. I was given carte blanche to produce the make-up exactly as I saw fit, and I gave them strict instructions not to visit or even telephone me.

The one exception was John Hurt, who I needed throughout the process, and since he wasn't doing much on set, he'd come to the workshop every day. He almost lived with us, then.

We'd discuss how he wanted to play the part of John Merrick. Though we wanted to capture all his essential characteristics, it would have been impossible to replicate the Elephant Man

"A BIT LIKE VESUVIUS, I EXPLODED WITH INCANDESCENT RAGE.'"

"I GAVE THEM STRICT INSTRUCTIONS NOT TO VISIT OR EVEN TELEPHONE ME."

exactly without making a very heavy, immobile mask. That would have severely restricted John's performance, so it was never really an option.

Ultimately, I built the head out of fifteen thin overlapping sections, and it took a lot of time because every time I altered one bit, I'd have to alter the next, and the next, like a chain reaction down the line, as everything fit together like a jigsaw.

When the day came that I deemed everything was ready, John came to the house and it took about seven hours to stick all the bits on him correctly. After that, we drove to the studio.

Everyone was waiting for us there, the entire cast and crew, anxious to see how things turned out because production had ground to a halt by then. They'd run out of material to shoot without John, and were nervously twiddling their thumbs, wondering if they even had a film a not.

When we arrived at the studio, everyone was so quiet. They seemed so nervous! So we just walked over to this little set they'd built, the attic room, and filmed the 23rd Psalm scene.

When it was finished, there was a noise that you wouldn't believe as everybody in the building applauded. I thought, "Thank God for that! They bought it. They liked it!"

David Lynch was over the moon. He kept telling me, over and over, "You've saved my life."

Christopher Tucker

Previous pages: John Hurt was heartbreaking as John Merrick in Christopher Tucker's pioneering prosthetics for David Lynch's iconic period biopic, *The Elephant Man* (1980).

Below: John Hurt sits patiently while Christopher Tucker works his magic, transforming him into John Merrick for *The Elephant Man* (1980).

Following pages: Two of the only colour photographs of the spectacular make-up on John Hurt for *The Elephant Man* (1980), taken by Christopher Tucker himself.

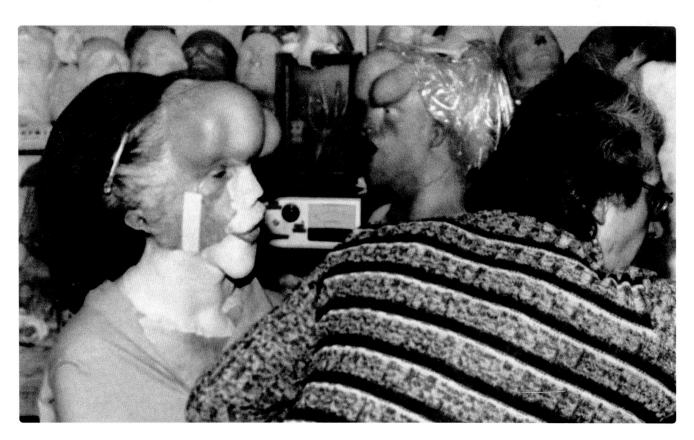

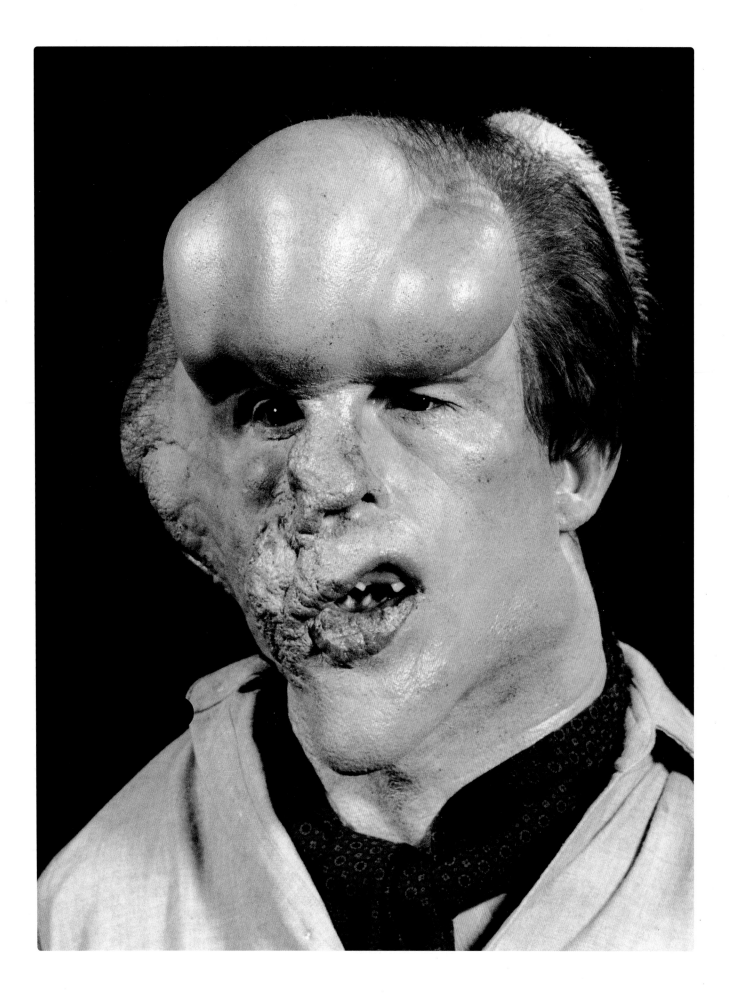

*H*ighlander (1986) was the toughest shoot of my life, in many ways. We shot seven days a week for the first six weeks, with long hours, often in inclement weather. Twenty-hour night shoots were not uncommon, so the rate of attrition among the crew was high. By the end, I was one of the last men standing, and after completing that shoot I felt I'd never have to prove myself again.

One time, we were preparing for a night shoot. Clancy Brown had already shot his scene, been cleaned off and headed home. Suddenly a stunt person comes in and we're told he's going to be playing the Kurgan for the rest of the night shoot. Only we didn't have the pieces to create the character.

So Graham Freeborn, a lovely man who was my second on the film, digs out a bald cap that was really more a swimming hat. We stick it down but we needed ears. Then I spy a powder puff… We cut it in half, whipstitch the pieces into an ear shape and glue them on. Done.

Then out goes the stunt man with powder-puff ears. I'm sure you can spot them if you look close enough! Graham and I certainly did at the cast and crew screening.

Lois Burwell

Below, left: Clancy Brown in his Kurgan make-up for *Highlander* (1986).

Below, right: The Kurgan (Clancy Brown) on the battlefield during the filming of *Highlander* (1986). There can be only one!

"THEN OUT GOES THE STUNT MAN WITH POWDER-PUFF EARS."

"I'M GOING TO BE WEARING PROSTHETICS?"

Gene Hackman was originally cast to play Lips Manlis in *Dick Tracy* (1990). I remember him turning up to the lab, and John Caglione explaining we'd need to take a lifecast.

"Lifecast? What's the lifecast for?"

"Well, you're going to be wearing prosthetics."

"I'm going to be wearing prosthetics?"

"Yeah."

"OK, then. Let me make a phone call."

Hackman walks out and later John gets a call.

"Gene's not doing the movie."

They hired Paul Sorvino to replace him.

After Hackman, I understood that some actors are claustrophobic, and not big fans of having their heads completely encased in plaster.

Kevin Haney

Top: Paul Sorvino as Lips Manlis from *Dick Tracy* (1990). John Caglione Jr and Doug Drexler won an Oscar each for their work on the film.

Above: Kevin Haney's beautiful Steve the Tramp make-up on Tony Epper for *Dick Tracy* (1990).

Stan [Winston] stepped back from doing the effects work on *Pumpkinhead* (1988) so he could focus on directing. He put me, Tom Woodruff, Shane Mahan and John Rosengrant in a room together, and left it to us to design the creature.

He said, "I want you guys to be inspired by each other."

There wasn't a lot of description of the creature in the screenplay. It might have said something like, "With its claw, it carves an X on her forehead," but a lot of monsters have claws. So there was no real blueprint, except for the fact that it was called Pumpkinhead, of course, so we had somewhere to start. Though, even there, Stan told us not to take the name too literally.

He put us in this room and told us, "Leave your ego at the door."

I'd always sneak a little bit of ego in, though, in my pockets.

At the end of every day, Stan would sit and review what we'd designed. Shane's ideas were compelling, but a little bit out of left field. There was a head of his I really liked, kind of like a lemur with giant, night-vision eyes.

With buggy eyes, though, there's not much you can do with brows, so that design would have required committing to a more static, expressionless face. I thought it was terrifying, but Stan wanted something more expressive and alive.

So I'm thinking, I'm going to make sure there are shapes on his face that can be pushed around via animatronics. And then John designed something that Stan quite liked, so I tried a riff on that. Eventually, I came up with the design that Stan picked for the head.

So it was kind of a collaborative process, because everyone contributed ideas. But it was also kind of a competition to see

"IT WAS FUN, BECAUSE I WON!"

whose design Stan liked best. And it was fun.

It was fun, because I won! Well, I designed the head, and Tom designed the body.

When it came to painting the creature, there was a lot of disagreement. Tom and John were very much of the idea that it was a corpse and therefore should have no warm tones. John even used black, which I'm not a fan of, as I think it looks a little one dimensional. Me, I thought it should look diseased, inflamed and tumorous, so my head had lots of red.

We disagreed and couldn't come to a compromise, so we didn't compromise. John used lots of black on the body, and the head and neck, which I painted, had lots of red. And you know what? It worked out fine.

It's not like anyone could argue what a Pumpkinhead's supposed to look like.

Alec Gillis

Above: Richard Landon, John Rosengrant, Richard Weinman, Stan Winston and Alec Gillis stand shoulder to shoulder with the Pumpkinhead Demon (Tom Woodruff Jr) from Stan's directorial debut, *Pumpkinhead* (1988).

Opposite: Tom Woodruff Jr is steadied on the challenging leg extensions he wore playing the Demon in *Pumpkinhead* (1988).

I have a huge collection of head casts, a lot of great actors, and they're all so different. I often use parts of them to create new make-ups.

On *White Chicks* (2004), I found the one thing that made the Wayans brothers look like women was Angelina Jolie's top lip. That really rounded everything off!

Greg Cannom

Below: Marlon Wayans and his *White Chicks* (2004) alter ego, a feat of transformational magic conjured up by Greg Cannom.

Opposite: Stellan Skarsgård as Bootstrap Bill in Joel Harlow's innovative prosthetic make-up for *Pirates of the Caribbean: Dead Man's Chest* (2006).

Stellan Skarsgård's barnacle-encrusted make-ups for the second and third *Pirates of the Caribbean* movies are real favourites of mine. It was a five-stage transformation and, though the last three stages were originally supposed to be digital, Stellan pushed for all five to be done practically.

Stellan's a real champion of make-up effects, and kudos to him, because that final stage, in particular, was brutal. The first test application took eight hours, but that's hardly surprising since it was a 250-piece make-up! Fortunately, for all our sakes, we got it down to three hours.

It was worth the effort and a wonderful effect, but still, I think for the rest of our lives, Stellan and I have had our fill of barnacles.

Joel Harlow

Stan [Winston], my father, like so many in the make-up effects industry, was hugely inspired by *Planet of the Apes* (1968). In fact, that was the movie that convinced him to pursue a career in the field. In the early Seventies, as part of a show-and-tell for my kindergarten class, he made me up as an ape using some leftover Roddy McDowall appliances he had saved from one of the sequels! When there was talk, then, in the early Nineties, of a reboot, he wanted that job so bad.

Oliver Stone was briefly attached, I think, and Jim Cameron, but it was when Chris Columbus came on board that Fox finally approved a make-up test. Stan asked me if I'd act with him in the test and I was thrilled.

The first make-up my dad considered using was traditional from the eyes up, with an animatronic muzzle, which looked and moved well, but with all the servos inside, it was noisy and fairly bulky. Stan wanted to create something that would be a little less intrusive to the filming process and more actor driven.

One night he had a dream about a linkage system that would allow the actors' lip motions to be translated to the lips of a prosthetic muzzle. He went into the shop the next day and explained his idea to SWS mechanical designer Richard Landon.

He said, "Here's kind of what I'm envisioning. You know, I'm not a technical person…"

But then he went ahead and described EXACTLY what he wanted. Richard did the initial R&D, which was further developed with the assistance of other members of the mechanical team, and that's what we used for the test.

It was incredibly innovative and completely actor driven. We wore these dentures that connected to a muzzle further out. Tabs connected our lips to the foam make-up lips and it was incredible. You could get all kinds of articulation out of those lips, which a typical make-up wouldn't allow.

And it was fun, too! We spent a lot of time rehearsing the scenes together. Stan initially came out to Hollywood to become an actor so, for him, it was a dream come true. And for me, running lines with him, rehearsing with him and acting with him was priceless. Absolutely priceless.

Shooting that test with my dad at 20th Century Fox is one of my fondest memories. Unfortunately, the project died. A few years later, Tim Burton did it with Rick Baker, and, of course, Stan was disappointed that he didn't get that job. But at least we had done that test, and a version of the linkage system developed for it was eventually used for the Sarris character in *Galaxy Quest* (1999).

Matt Winston

"IT WAS INCREDIBLY INNOVATIVE AND COMPLETELY ACTOR DRIVEN."

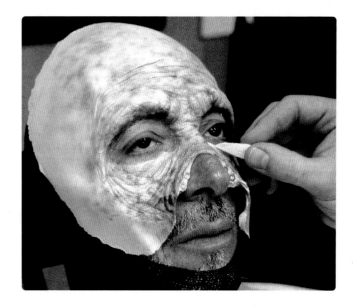

Above: The actor-driven ape make-up that Stan Winston originally conceived in a dream is applied to the make-up master.

Above, left: Stan Winston in the final test of his ape make-up, though Rick Baker was ultimately awarded *Planet of the Apes* (2001).

Opposite, top: Shane Mahan and Mike Hill ready Doug Jones as the Amphibian Man, aka The Asset, for *The Shape of Water* (2017).

Opposite, bottom: Designer Mike Hill makes sure Doug Jones is ready for action in *The Shape of Water* (2017).

The first time I visited Legacy Effects to talk about the Amphibian Man, they took me to a secret room in another building to see a life-size clay sculpture of the design, as it was then.

The secrecy and security around the creature for *The Shape of Water* (2017) was so tight, it was like getting into a bank vault. I did a 360 around the sculpture just marvelling at it. The proportions were perfect. It was so beautiful, so athletic, and it had an organic monster look that didn't come from a comic book. It came from nature.

And its ass was the most gorgeous thing I'd ever seen. I was like, "I get to wear that?!"

Guillermo [del Toro] told me that his wife at the time, Lorenza, was very particular about the Amphibian Man's ass. She said it had to be grabbable or the character wouldn't work. So they spent a lot of time getting the dimensions and shape down perfect. And I'll tell you what – they did!

When I was wearing the costume and make-up on set, if I was sitting with my co-stars, every time I got up and walked away, Octavia Spencer would go, "Mmmm!"

So I knew the ass was working.

Doug Jones

"ITS ASS WAS THE MOST GORGEOUS THING I'D EVER SEEN."

Love: *Dune* (2021) was the biggest job we ever did, not least because of the literally enormous character make-up we did on Stellan Skarsgård as Baron Vladimir Harkonnen. Donald Mowat brought us on board and we love him for that.

Eva: When Love told me about the job, I was like, "This is not for me. This is not what we do. We have a small shop. We create small characters. And now you want to do this really huge man, all covered in prosthetics? I don't want to do it!"

Anyway, we agreed to do it, but we were totally terrified!

Denis [Villeneuve] wanted the Baron to look like Stellan, but at the same time, something else. Originally, the plan was for him to mostly wear a big suit of armour, but for the first test make-up we had to have him naked as there's a scene when he's in this big mud bath.

Love: We designed a giant, naked foam suit with huge silicone pieces. The legs, belly and arms were foam. The hands, bald cap, cheeks, chin and this big, weird neck piece were all silicone.

Eva: The only thing that wasn't going to be covered in some sort of prosthetic was Stellan's nose and upper lip.

Love: We had to build an oven in the workshop that could fit the full-body mould. It was so big, it filled the entire space. Before we built it, then, we had to prepare everything else as once we installed it, there was no room to do anything other than run foam.

We went to Budapest to do that first test make-up. It took seven hours to apply. And when Denis first saw Stellan, huge and naked, he was like, "I LOVE THIS MAKE-UP!"

So they told us, "Right, so, now we want him to be naked, like, most of the time."

Or if not always entirely naked, then with just this thin see-through dress on top. We'd only planned to do one suit for Stellan and one for the stunt double. But then they said, "Also, now we want six more suits."

And we're like, "Six more suits?!"

We'd just about managed to make one, and we only had, like, a month before shooting. But when you work on films like that, you can't say, "Oh, we can't do that."

We just had to manage.

Eva: It's fantastic, though, that we actually got to do something like that. That they didn't do it digitally.

Love: Yes, I think, originally, the plan from the studio was to create the character digitally, but Denis didn't want that, and neither did Stellan. Even though he's seventy years old and obviously a make-up like that takes quite a toll.

It took seven hours to apply, and we did it, maybe, thirteen times. They were long days on set, but Denis shot around Stellan in the mornings.

Eva: Then as soon as we were done and Stellan was ready, they'd shoot his scenes. And he'd rest a day between make-ups as it would have just been too much to manage without a break.

When they finally wrapped Stellan, the whole crew stood up and applauded us. I felt like, "God, I'm going to start crying. This hell is finally ending!"

Love: *Dune* was a huge experience for us. Horrifying, but also fun!

Eva Von Bahr and Love Larson

"WE WANT HIM TO BE NAKED, LIKE, MOST OF THE TIME."

Rick Baker's make-ups for *Coming to America* (1988) played such an important part in its success. The sequel's producer, Michele Imperato, understood that.

I told them, "Before I say yes to *Coming 2 America* (2021), I have to ask Rick for his permission."

Rick was like, "Mike, I understand what it's like to have a studio and wages to pay. I will not hold it against you if you do this job, but if you win an Oscar, you'd better fucking thank me."

Mike Marino

Left: Eddie Murphy in *Coming 2 America* (2021) as Saul, a character first created by Rick Baker, respectfully revisited as a much older man by Mike Marino and Mike Fontaine.

Opposite: Under the supervision of make-up department head Donald Mowat, Eva Von Bahr blends the neck prosthetic on to Stellan Skarsgård's body suit as he prepares to play Baron Harkonnen in Denis Villeneuve's *Dune* (2021).

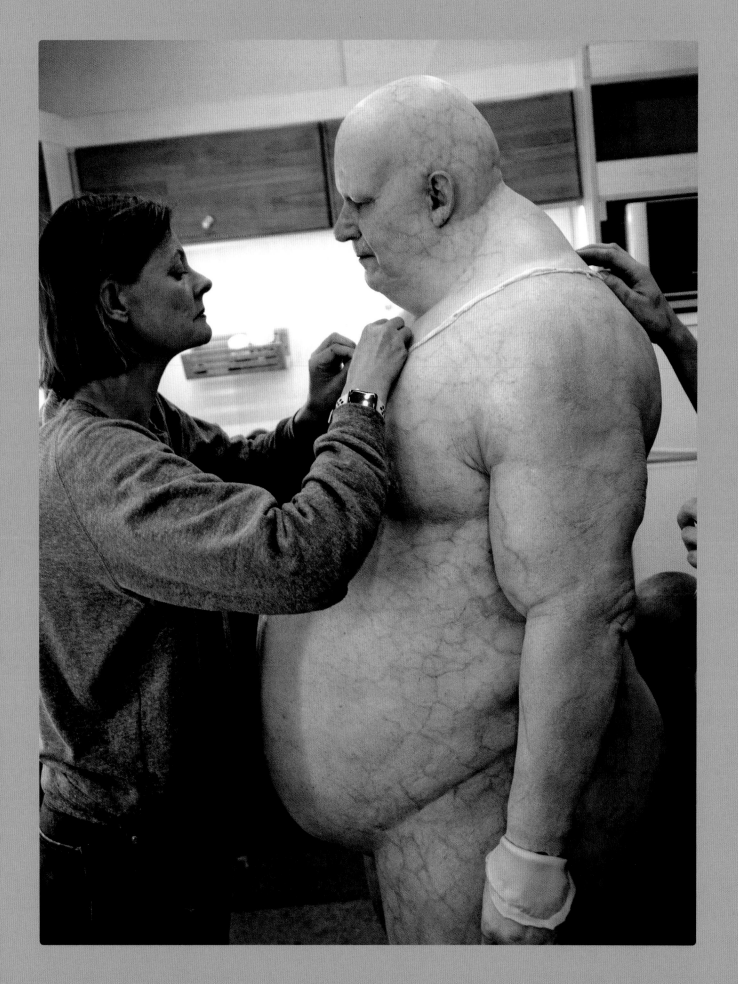

TO GLUE
OR NOT
TO GLUE

Give any one of our masters a chair, a mirror, a box of tricks and a movie star, and we'll show you their home away from home: the make-up trailer. That's where the party starts every morning, and where it ends every night.

It's where friendships are forged, battles fought, and where, after months of thinking, talking, designing, planning and building, the magic finally happens. Because that's where the actor and their make-up finally merge, creating a living, breathing, third magnificent thing.

From start to finish, a make-up is like a relay race. It starts with a concept artist, then a sculptor, then a mould maker, and by the time I'm handed the baton, it's my job to go for the finish line. I have to take those designs and the manufactured pieces and actually try to make it all work.

Tami Lane

Robert [Englund] was the best training ground anyone could have wished for because he never stops talking! Applying his Freddy make-ups, I felt like I was in sniper school, learning to hit a moving target. His father once told me he'd been hyper like that since he was a kid.

I mean, usually when you tell an actor to hold still for a second, they'll freeze because they want their make-up to look good. But not Robert! He's always telling one amazing story or another, and constantly looking around. I love him though! And once you've made up Robert, you can make up anyone.

Kevin Yagher

Previous pages: Joel Harlow applies his take on Uncle Creepy, the horrible host of Warren Publishing's *Creepy* magazine, to actor Marti Matulis.

Above: Tami Lane applies the final version of Colin Farrell's Vampire Jerry make-up for director Craig Gillespie's remake of *Fright Night* (2011).

I talk all the time, but it's just my mouth moving, and there's a lot more of me to make up besides that. So tell me to shut up when you get down to my mouth.

If I have to be in your make-up chair from 5 a.m. for eight weeks, I need to shoot the shit. Let's talk about music or a new TV show, a movie we all love, a bad divorce or a girlfriend or whatever. Because that's how I get to know you guys and trust you guys.

Seriously, when somebody has their finger up your nose and in your mouth or eyes, you know, for four hours every morning, you sort of have to joke around with them.

I'm not the sort of actor who can sleep in the chair. I can't read a book. To be honest, I'm a little nervous every morning, not about the make-up, but about that day's work. It's almost like opening night, every day. So I have to funnel that adrenaline somewhere. Then again, sometimes it's just about me being full of coffee and sugar and needing to talk your ears off.

Really, actors are more intimate with their make-up people than anybody else on the set. They're the first person we see in the morning. They're the last person we see at night. It's a unique relationship and something I'd never want to change.

Robert Englund

The first time I ever saw myself as Pinhead was when we screen-tested the make-up.

I loved the idea of being radically transformed. Of sitting in the make-up chair as me, and then at the end of it, looking in the mirror and thinking, "Who the fuck are you?"

And that's exactly what happened.

The process took about five or six hours that first time because Geoff [Portass] and the others were feeling their way with the make-up. Eventually, they got it down to three or four.

When it was done, and I looked in the mirror, I recognised my ears, my eyes and my mouth. But the rest was no longer me. It was a genuinely strange moment.

For fifteen minutes I sat there, staring at myself. Seeing how my new face moved, finding an appropriate voice to say, "I'll tear your soul apart" and really just accepting that I wasn't me any more. I was this new thing.

Ninety-five per cent of my performance came out of those fifteen minutes in front of the mirror.

Doug Bradley

"I LOVED THE IDEA OF BEING RADICALLY TRANSFORMED."

After playing Pinhead a few times, I became aware that, on the first day of filming, I'd do anything to delay getting made up. Suddenly I'd need the toilet, or have to make an important call, or need to check something with the production office.

Because when they finally got me into the make-up trailer, and I'd see all the brushes and bits laid out for me, and my Pinhead make-up staring at me, and then the smell of everything would hit me, I'd feel ill. I'd want to scream, "GOD! Not again! Why me?"

So I'd like to apologise now, unreservedly, if I was ever grumpy with anyone on my first day. Once I was over that hump, though, I was fine. On day two, I'd be like, "We're back in the sandpit! Let's play and build sandcastles!"

Doug Bradley

Opposite, bottom: Kevin Yagher applies blood red colouring to Robert Englund's Freddy Krueger make-up for *A Nightmare on Elm Street 3: Dream Warriors* (1987).

Right: Doug Bradley is ready to tear your soul apart as horror icon Pinhead, from *Hellraiser III: Hell on Earth* (1992).

had three or four days to put together Courteney Cox's Fat Monica make-up for *Friends* (1994–2004). I had my training on *Saturday Night Live* (1975–Present) though, so I'm used to turning things around quickly. Plus I had a fair bit of experience doing fat make-ups as I'd recently done Marty Short's Jiminy Glick show.

So we're doing the test and Courteney says, right in front of me, "I don't know if I like this. Can't we get the guy who did Jiminy Glick?"

So I said, "That would be me."

A while later I did a subtle, heavy make-up for Paul Rudd and he says, again, right in front me, "Can't we get the person who did Fat Monica?"

Kevin Haney

"MY SKIN'S BURNING. IS THAT NORMAL?"

On *Hocus Pocus* (1993), I did Bette Midler's old-age make-up and two other people did Sarah Jessica Parker and Kathy Najimy. But we were all using the same latex formula.

Two hours into the make-up, Sarah Jessica Parker said, "You know, my skin's burning. Is that normal?"

And Kathy Najimy says, "Yeah, my skin's burning, too."

Bette was OK, but I went to the producers and said, "We have to remove everyone's make-up. There's something going on and they're having an allergic reaction. If they go through the day like this, you're going to seriously hurt their skin."

So we took it off.

Later, Kathy Najimy says, "We even did facial peels yesterday…"

I said, "You did what?"

She said, "Yeah, we went and had facials, because we thought, you know, it would help the make-up."

I told her, "You probably should have been cautioned about that, because you stripped all the protective skin off your face, so we were putting all this stuff today on raw skin."

We came back the next day and everything was fine. But there were no more facials until we wrapped.

Kevin Haney

Top: Kevin Haney's prosthetics pile on the pounds as Courteney Cox becomes Fat Monica for *Friends* (1994–2004).

Above: Kathy Najimy, Bette Midler and Sarah Jessica Parker stir up toil and trouble as the wicked, witchy Sanderson Sisters in *Hocus Pocus* (1993).

On *Saturday Night Live* (1975–Present), for the dress and pre-records, I try not to spend more than fifteen or twenty minutes on any of the make-ups. On movies, they'll sit in the chair for hours, but on SNL no one wants to be there for long. It's live, so everyone just wants to get going.

During the show, we have maybe two-and-a-half minutes to put on a make-up. There'll be four of us working at the same time, like some crazy make-up pit crew.

One time, Sarah Michelle Geller hosted and we did this whole Buffy the Vampire Slayer sketch. We got everyone into their make-ups in like five or ten minutes. Later I read an interview with Todd McIntosh saying, every time Sarah comes back from SNL, she asks me, "How come they did it in ten minutes and we take an hour?"

Thing is, for SNL they only have to keep it on for fifteen minutes. It doesn't have to last a whole day!

Pretty much half my life has been spent at SNL, and still the biggest challenge, week after week, is figuring out how to do everything in so short a time. I love figuring things out, though, when we're down to the wire. I just switch to autopilot and power through.

Like Lorne Michaels says, "We don't go on at 11.30 because we're ready. We go on at 11.30 because it's 11.30."

Because the host is in every sketch, often we have almost no time at all to get them ready for the next one. Once we had two minutes to do a full old-age make-up on Adam Driver. He was running to the stage and I kept painting him. They're counting "Five, four, three…" And I'm still at it.

Only when they got to "Two, one…" did I step out of the frame.

And I'm like, "I wish we had just thirty more seconds. Or even ten seconds. Just ten more seconds!"

I thrive on pressure, though. Twenty-five years at SNL and it's never, ever dull.

Louie Zakarian

There was a heavy in *The Rocketeer* (1991), a character who was modelled after the 1940s horror actor Rondo Hatton. It was a tribute make-up, designed and sculpted by Rick Baker, and applied by me.

The actor was Tiny Ron, who was 7 feet [213cm] tall and looked terribly threatening once I'd finished with him every day. I applied that make-up at least thirty-five times, and every time I did, I'd try to improve it. Just subtle little tweaks to the skin texture and things like that, because you should never stop aiming for better.

It was tough to apply, but Tiny was very nice and patient. We laughed a lot! On set, though, he couldn't understand why no one would ever come over to chat with him.

I said, "Tiny, you wanna look in the mirror?"

Greg Nelson

Top, left: Jimmy Fallon as the cereal-craving Count Chocula, another brilliant Louie Zakarian make-up for *Saturday Night Live* (1975–Present).

Top, right: Will Ferrell prepares to suck on *Saturday Night Live* (1975–Present) in a make-up inspired by *Buffy the Vampire Slayer* (1997–2003), which was itself inspired by *The Lost Boys* (1987).

Left: Tiny Ron as Lothar in Rick Baker's Rondo Hatton-inspired make-up, applied by Greg Nelson for *The Rocketeer* (1991).

Following pages: Garrett Immel applies Peter Macon's Bortus prosthetics while Tami Lane works on Heather Forte's alien crew person for Seth MacFarlane's comedy sci-fi show, *The Orville* (2017–2022).

There's an orc character in *The Lord of the Rings: The Fellowship of the Ring* (2001) that I'm very proud of. Usually when you make up an orc, it's a stunt guy and he's going to get killed that day, so there's no continuity to worry about. But we'd been making orcs for three years already and I felt like doing something different.

So this guy, Lee Hartley, came sat in my chair and I came up with this idea that maybe orcs had battle ornaments. Like when [American] football players put stickers on their helmets to mark an amazing play, a tackle, a touchdown or whatever. So the orcs embedded chain mail into their skin. Maybe each link meant a kill, and it became ornamental. So I ended up embedding chain mail down this orc's forehead, nose and chin. It looked sore, and different, and I sent him off to war!

Peter Jackson noticed him on set and loved his look so much, he gave him a line with Christopher Lee! The line was, "The trees are strong my lord, the roots go deep."

Only now they needed him on set, in that make-up, for five days in a row. But like I said, those make-ups were one-offs. I hadn't made a note of what paint I'd used or what colour anything was. We hadn't taken any pictures for reference, either, but somehow I pulled it off.

He was just a stuntman, you know, and a carpenter. Not an actor. But to this day, I still hear from him as he was able to make a career out of going to conventions because he was a very recognisable orc. I took a shitty orc who was supposed to die, did something new with him and now he's able to feed his family because he got a line! How great is that?

Tami Lane

Below: Lee Hartley (right) in prosthetics designed by Richard Taylor and WETA Workshop, ingeniously applied by Tami Lane for *The Lord of the Rings: The Fellowship of the Ring* (2001).

Bottom: Richard Taylor (centre) and Jason Docherty (right) polish off a Goblin for *The Lord of the Rings: The Fellowship of the Ring* (2001).

"IT LOOKED SORE, AND DIFFERENT, AND I SENT HIM OFF TO WAR!"

When it comes to make-up removal, you're way better off if you've acted for twelve hours. By then, your pores have loosened it up and the make-up just falls off. It's worse if they only need you for a couple of hours, because then it feels like you're gonna need a spatula to pry everything off.

Bruce Campbell

If it slips on and zips up the back, it's a suit. If it's glued or painted on, it's make-up. That's how I delineate one from the other.

Abe Sapien from the *Hellboy* movies was probably my longest make-up. If I was wearing just the shorts and a lot of fish guy was showing, it was make-up from head to toe. Nothing slipped on. No suit was involved. Everything was glued on. And it took about seven hours a day.

There were twelve different prosthetic pieces: chest piece, back piece, arm pieces to give me a little more muscle, webbed fingers, fins added every which way, and every bit of it was glued down.

The head was particularly complicated, with not only a face piece and battery-operated gills, but also separate mouthpieces so it would move correctly when I spoke. Lots of glue, then. Lots of moving parts. And taking it off took hours more.

So that was one job where, if I was shooting three, four, five days, I'd leave the legs and arms on. To save us all some sleep and time and effort, I'd knock off for the day with my limbs well hidden in a sweat suit. Because no one could know I was still half Abe.

That's the sort of thing producers take advantage of. If they found out I was willing to wear things home, they'd tighten the schedule even more. But the only reason I did it was to buy us breathing room the next day. Which it always did.

Doug Jones

Above: Doug Jones as Abe Sapien, amphibious agent of the Bureau for Paranormal Research and Defense, from *Hellboy* (2004).

Below: The dreamers of the dreams: Steve Wang, Michael Elizalde, Doug Jones and Maestro Guillermo del Toro at Spectral Motion, testing Abe Sapien for *Hellboy* (2004).

I loved that so much of *The Chronicles of Narnia: The Lion, the Witch and the Wardrobe* (2005) was achieved practically. The artistry in that film really elevated it. When things are real on set, and you can touch them, I think that touches something in the audience as well.

Playing Mr Tumnus was one of the biggest adventures of my career.

On the page he's not scary, but on film he's a man who takes a tiny, little girl back to his house, ultimately kidnaps her, sedates her and gives her away. It's terrifying, dicey territory, and probably one of the reasons why they didn't cast a middle-aged man in the role. Instead they got a twenty-two-year-old man who looked like a sixteen year old.

Mr Tumnus could so easily have been more beast-like, but thanks to Howard [Berger] and the guys at KNB, he was friendly, warm and unthreatening. Even cosy, and not just to look at, but also to live in. That make-up helped me lean into a softer and more comforting performance than I might otherwise have delivered.

The attention paid to every detail of that make-up was incredible. It was that level of finesse that made Mr Tumnus not a make-up, not a monster, not a half-man/half-something else, but a person.

Even though Howard was overseeing the make-up on a production where, on some days, there were 200 creature performers, he was always there, at 4 a.m. every morning, devoting three hours to Mr Tumnus. To focusing just on one person, and getting that character exactly right. It's that level of commitment that fuels the film industry.

There's an endurance element to sitting in one position, trapped in the chair, for hours every day. But Howard and the guys were an example to me, a priceless professionalism workshop for months and months and months, in how to show up at the crack of a

gnat's whatsit, be present, be patient and go, "This is our day. As hard as it is, we're going to be OK. We will smile and do our best to make everyone else smile, too."

Watching movies together, chatting crap and making each other laugh turned what could have been a very hard time into a very good time. I've no doubt it informed my performance, too, as Mr Tumnus is all about good cheer and being pleasant under strenuous circumstances.

When we first saw the film, at the premiere in London, I wasn't particularly focused on how Mr Tumnus came across. I'd spent such a long time looking at Howard's make-up in the mirror that I knew it was good. It just felt like that was my face, and there'd be no surprises. I was more on the edge of my seat about Georgie's reaction to seeing Mr Tumnus for the first time.

Georgie [Henley] was a very young actress, out of her depth in this humongous production, and so Andrew [Adamson], the director, made sure that we spent a lot of time together and had a connection with each other. But he never let her see me as Mr Tumnus. So the first time she sees him in the film, is the first time she saw him on the set. It was just one take, and that was her genuine reaction.

At the time, I think everyone expected her to be like, "Wow!"

And there's an element of that in there, but also fear, because she wasn't quite sure how to react. Neither Georgie, the actress, nor Lucy, the character. There was fear and hesitation and it was a genuine, authentic moment. An added layer of complexity in a film I'm very proud of.

James McAvoy

Above: Lucy (Georgie Henley) and Mr Tumnus (James McAvoy) meet for the first time in *The Chronicles of Narnia: The Lion, The Witch and The Wardrobe* (2005).

God bless David [Martí] and Montse [Ribé] from DDT, my Oscar-winning make-up team on *Pan's Labyrinth* (2006).

They're so meticulous, particular and precise with their artistry. Every shape, every colour, every placement of every piece is exact. They take their time, and I love them for it, because you walk away going, "This is gorgeous!"

Come clean-up time, they're every bit as slow and meticulous.

The Faun character should have left red marks all over me. Most every kind of suit involving mechanics and hard parts leaves red marks on you somewhere, often everywhere, by the end of the day. The Faun, though, is the only thing I've worn in thirty-five years that came off every day with not one red mark on me anywhere.

Nothing rubbed funny. It was that beautifully designed and balanced. And that carefully applied and then removed. I was astounded by that.

Doug Jones

"YOU WALK AWAY GOING, 'THIS IS GORGEOUS!'"

Nicholas Hoult's Beast make-up on the *X-Men* movies was very cool. Some actors feel trapped inside prosthetics, but I think he felt augmented. That he'd been given something new to have fun with. He's such a good, expressive actor. He really embraced that character.

For the third movie, at least make-up-wise, I thought I was going to have an easy time of it. I just had to be bald, so I got my head shaved.

But they were like, "It doesn't look like you've gone bald. It looks like you've shaved. So we're going to have to paint your head."

That ended up taking an hour-and-a-half every day.

Meanwhile, Jennifer Lawrence's make-up, which had originally taken seven-and-a-half hours, had been cut down to an incredibly fast hour-and-a-quarter. Because I don't think she'd have come back otherwise.

So yeah. Jennifer's Mystique make-up was quicker than mine!

James McAvoy

Top: The living embodiment of Guillermo del Toro's imagination, Doug Jones as the Fauno from *Pan's Labyrinth* (2006).

Right: Tyler Mane as Blackstar, in the Netflix series *Jupiter's Legacy* (2020). This was a full make-up and foam rubber suit created by KNB EFX Group, who convinced production to ditch the idea of a digital suit, and go 100 per cent practical, which proved a great success.

There's a Navy SEAL phrase I learned on *Lone Survivor* (2013) that always helps me get into the right headspace, both in the make-up chair and later, when I'm wearing a make-up for long hours on set: "Get comfortable being uncomfortable."

After all, there are worse and harder things to endure than making movies.

Ben Foster

"GET COMFORTABLE BEING UNCOMFORTABLE."

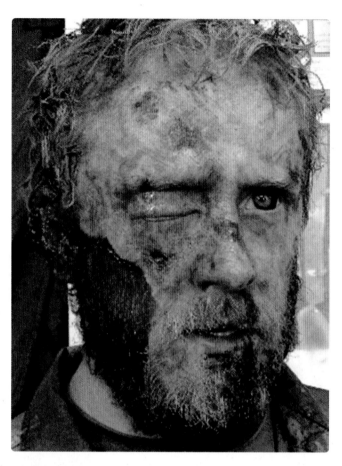

Right: Ben Foster in his final stage make-up for *Lone Survivor* (2013).

Below: Jamie Kelman bloodies up Ben Foster for his final scenes as Matt 'Axe' Axelson in *Lone Survivor* (2013).

Opposite: Göran Lundström's beautiful make-up designs, applied by Pamela Goldammer, transform Eva Melander and Eero Milonoff into Tina and Vore for the unique and magical *Border* (2018).

Göran Lundström designed the brilliant make-ups for *Border* (2018), and I applied them on set. For Eva Melander's Tina make-up, we used silicone for the chin, nose, forehead and eyelids, and gelatine on the cheeks as Eva found that more comfortable.

Although I'm vegan, and would never choose to work with a gelatine prosthetic, because it was part of Göran's design, I worked with it.

The day we shot the love scene between Tina and Vore [Eero Milonoff] was very intense and emotional. It was important not to disturb the flow by running in every five minutes to check the make-up. Also, as the film was shot on a very tight schedule – just thirty-eight days – on a few occasions we had no choice but to let things go.

I noticed at one point that the gelatine prosthetic, which reacted to the cold weather, slightly lifted on the side of Tina's nose, but Ali [Abbasi], the director, didn't let me step in. You work so long and so hard, you want everything to be perfect, so it wasn't easy, holding back. But sometimes the production's priorities differ from your own.

Pamela Goldammer

"YOU WANT EVERYTHING TO BE PERFECT."

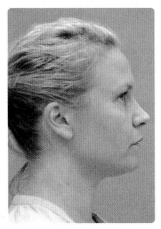

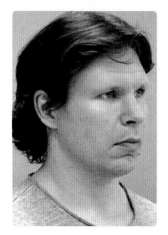

TEAMWORK MAKES THE DREAM WORK

It takes an army to make a movie. Really just a staggering number of people. Anyone who's sat through the voluminous end credits of a film knows that.

And though not every production, of course, can be entirely harmonious – something we'll get to in a later chapter – it's certainly a happier and often more productive experience when folks gets along. When there's trust, and everyone's on the same page.

This next batch of stories covers just such scenarios.

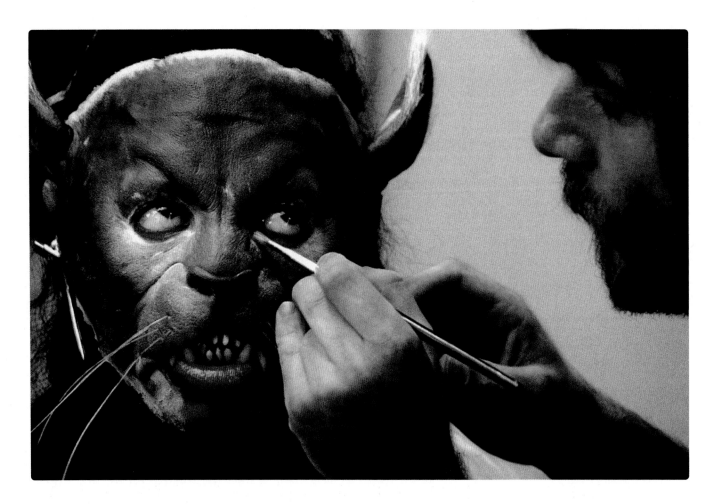

John: *Thriller* had been out for over a year, and was already the number one best-selling album of all time, before Michael Jackson called me. Two important and influential videos had already been made from it – 'Billie Jean' and 'Beat It' – and CBS wanted Michael to focus on his next album. But first, Michael wanted to make a video for his song 'Thriller'.

Michael was a big fan of *An American Werewolf in London* (1981), specifically the metamorphosis, and he wanted to turn into a monster on screen. Clearly, changing his appearance was something that interested Michael.

Rick and I came over with a bunch of books full of monster illustrations. But Michael didn't want to see them. He told us he was too scared to watch most monster movies, and that it taken him, like, fifteen times before he managed to see *Werewolf* all the way through.

We budgeted the video at half a million dollars and CBS literally told us to go fuck ourselves. They considered it a vanity video. Michael offered to pay for it, but I told him, "No. You never use your own money."

It was George Folsey Jr's idea to shoot behind-the-scenes footage and produce a making-of documentary that, along with the video, would give us an hour we could sell. Showtime and MTV ended up giving us the money, and that's how we funded the video.

Rick: Originally, I wanted to recreate every famous monster, but there wasn't the time or the money for that, so we decided to just do zombies.

John: And Michael loved being a zombie. He had these big, beautiful eyes and I'd say, "Michael, I want you to open your eyes as wide as you can and burn the lens!"

Obviously, Rick's make-up was amazing, with those sunken cheeks and everything, but when Michael did his eye thing, that made the make-up fabulous.

Rick: When it came to the other monster that Michael was going to play, I didn't feel he should be a werewolf. I thought something feline would suit him better.

John: However, the first cat creature Rick came up with was terrifying. I told him it had to be attractive and he nailed it with the second design.

Rick: It was only when Michael came into the shop to do his lifecast that I found out about the making-of. John says, "By the way, there's going to be a camera crew here today."

Michael was already kind of uncomfortable. When he first arrived, he had to go sit alone in the restroom to acclimatise. Then when he was in the chair, I had to coax him to take his sunglasses off. So it didn't help that there were two 16mm cameras right in our faces. Once I even had to push one out of the way.

There was this one time, I was being interviewed in the make-up trailer and I had a paper cup with water in it, and another with

isopropyl myristate, which is an oil-based make-up remover. And my voice was getting hoarse, so I grabbed what I thought was the water, but instead I got a mouthful of the isopropyl myristate. Since I was on camera, I tried to be cool about it. I just gradually spat it back into the cup, wiped my mouth and kept talking!

John: Rick was certainly annoyed about the camera crew. He didn't want to do the making-of at all.

Rick: Yeah, at the time it pissed me off, but I'm so glad John did it, because so many people have come up to me over the years to tell me they were inspired to become make-up artists after seeing *The Making of Thriller* (1983). That certainly made it worthwhile.

John: While we were making it, George and I used to call it *The Making of Filler*. When it was released on home video, though, it sold, like, seven million copies!

John Landis and Rick Baker

Below, left: Michael Jackson is soothed by his pet boa constrictor, Muscles, while Rick Baker applies a transformation stage Werecat make-up for *Michael Jackson's Thriller* (1983).

Below: Michael Jackson surrounded by a horde of Rick Baker's undead for *Michael Jackson's Thriller* (1983).

"CHANGING HIS APPEARANCE WAS SOMETHING THAT INTERESTED MICHAEL."

reating a character requires an ecosystem.

You don't just have your make-up artist. You also have your wig-maker. And someone to make your eyebrow pieces and your teeth and your contacts… And every one of them is an authority, a master of what they do.

So you're working together to achieve a common goal. You're testing everything and refining everything until, suddenly, you all feel it. That click. That moment when it all comes together. And it's not about looking like the character. It's about that character stepping out of the chair and moving in the room.

That's the birthing place.

Ben Foster

Above: The many faces of Harry Haft (Ben Foster); make-ups designed, created and applied by Jamie Kelman for heartbreaking Holocaust biopic *The Survivor* (2021).

Opposite, top right: John Caglione Jr and Doug Drexler brought the many villains of Chester Gould's *Dick Tracy* comic strip to life for Warren Beatty's 1990 feature. From left to right: Ed O'Ross as Itchy, Al Pacino as Big Boy Caprice, William Forsythe as Flattop, James Tolkan as Numbers and Henry Silva as Influence. John and Doug won the Academy Award for Best Make-up for their brilliant work.

Opposite, bottom: Al Pacino as Big Boy Caprice in *Dick Tracy* (1990).

I got a call from John [Landis]. "I'm doing this movie. You've got to do it. There's a whole bunch of make-ups. Eddie Murphy's playing an old Jewish man."

Eddie was at the height of his fame when we made *Coming to America* (1988), so I had to fight like crazy to get him in for a test. When he came in, I didn't apply all the pieces. Just enough so that I could see the Saul make-up was going to work.

Throughout the process, Eddie was testing it, too. Moving his face around, making expressions and figuring out what he could do with it. By the end, he seemed surprised, because I think the make-up was better than he'd expected.

He improvised a scene with his friend Fruity, right there in the chair. He started out serious, playing an old Jewish man who'd been beaten up by some black guys, and I remember thinking, "Wow! This guy can really act."

After that, he had some fun with it, explaining how his hands, which I hadn't made up, had gotten so badly sunburnt. That's when I realised that working with Eddie was going to be a great experience, which it was.

Rick Baker

I was working in the lab one night, prepping *Dick Tracy* (1990), and Warren Beatty calls. He says, "We finally cast Big Boy. I'm sending him over." And he hangs up. A few hours later, the doorbell rings. I peek through the window and it's Al Pacino.

AL PACINO!

I had to deal with Al Pacino. My knees went weak and I actually had to hold on to the wall for a second. I don't usually geek out about actors, but I grew up watching the *Godfather* movies and Pacino's up there with Brando, you know. So I'm trying to catch my breath. And I guess a couple of minutes go by before I managed to open the door.

It was hard, in that moment, separating fantasy from reality. Michael Corleone was sitting in my chair! But he was very kind. He got me to relax, like the best actors do. He's like, "Calm down. Take it easy."

And that was it. Thirty years later, we're still working together. It's a bromance! How does something like that even happen?

John Caglione Jr

"IT WAS HARD, IN THAT MOMENT, SEPARATING FANTASY FROM REALITY."

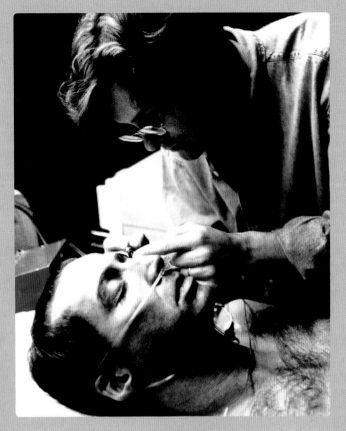

Top: Kevin Yagher touches up the unnervingly authentic Nicolas Cage replica that he created for John Woo's *Face/Off* (1997).

Above: Kevin Yagher's gory Nicolas Cage replica from *Face/Off* (1997).

Face/Off (1997) was one of my favourite things to work on. John Woo is such an amazing, humble and super sweet man. If you showed him something, he'd approve it, then never come back to question me, always showed faith and trust in me. That movie went like clockwork.

There's a shot in the film where Nicholas Cage's skin goes on to John Travolta's face and the doctors massage it into place. Those were my hands, by the way, doing all the close-up work! And they wanted to dissolve from the rubber face we'd made into Nick Cage lying on the table, so they had this whole motion-control set-up and they went ahead and shot it. But to morph the two shots, I think the CGI guys were going to charge over 100,000 dollars to do that one shot. At the dailies, though, Oliver Wood, the DP, goes, "Why are we spending all this money? Look at that. The silicone rubber face is perfect. It looks just like Nick. We should leave it as it is."

And they did. They ditched the real Nick and used our silicone rubber Nick for the whole shot. Then, of course, the visual effects guy comes up to me and says, smiling, "You just cost me 100,000 dollars."

I said, "Good, 'cause you guys always take stuff from us!"

It was great to get one back on that!

Another time, Nick Cage was stuck in make-up but they needed to light the operating theatre set, so they asked if our Nick Cage dummy could stand in for him. So we got the body in, laid it out, hid the puppeteers round the corner and we turned the thing on. It was breathing, twitching, all that stuff. So the ADs head to the set but then stopped at the door, stared at the dummy from about 10 feet [3m] away, maybe even closer, and started whispering. So I walked up to them and said, "What do you think?"

And they're like, "Keep your voice down. Don't wake him up."

They thought it was the real Nick! That he'd gotten out of make-up and come to set early, gone into a zen state or something, to prepare for playing his character in a coma. So I said, "That's our fake body."

And really, they were just amazed. Then John Travolta walks in, and he goes, "Unbelievable! You could make sex toys out of these things…"

They'd been right in the room with it but had no idea. We fooled them, and fooling people is why I got into this business. There's an incredible feeling of excitement when you're able to use your techniques and skills to trick someone that completely.

Like gluing down a mechanical animatronic skin and turning Chucky on for the first time. You're playing with the controls and he's blinking, he's looking back at you and he just looks like he's alive. Honestly, you feel kind of godlike.

Kevin Yagher

My favourite make-up is the one I did for Gary Oldman in *Hannibal* (2001). I wanted to create a nightmarish, disturbing, uncomfortable-looking make-up and it worked far better than I ever thought it would.

Based on Ridley Scott's original concept for the character, I came up with lots of different designs for Mason Verger, but they all looked like zombies. Then Ridley goes, "I've changed my mind: I want him to look like a diseased foetus."

He showed me this weird painting of a diseased baby with a tiny pixie nose.

Gary's got a good-sized nose on him, so I wasn't sure it was possible, but I sat down with some clay, and in one day I basically sculpted the whole thing. Glen Hanz just did a little work on it, then we showed it to Ridley.

He goes, "That's it!"

After that, I made a few quick, minor alterations, but really it was so easy, it was ridiculous! In just two days we had the basic design.

That's the way it is sometimes. Some of my best work has been done at three in the morning, the day before the shoot.

We got so lucky that Gary was cast in the role, because no one else would have gone through what he did. With no concern over

"HE PUSHED THAT MAKE-UP AS FAR AS IT COULD POSSIBLY GO."

how uncomfortable he'd be, he pushed that make-up as far as it could possibly go.

He was like, "Isn't there a way of clamping my eye open?"

And I went, "Oh, yeah."

He also wanted his teeth exposed, so Wes Wofford did these little vacuum-form pieces that glued to his lips so he couldn't move them much. It was a painful make-up for him, and he was in it every day for two weeks. Honestly, he was incredible.

Then to see him act in it, he was so good. So bizarre. Just absolutely unforgettable.

Greg Cannom

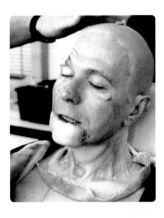
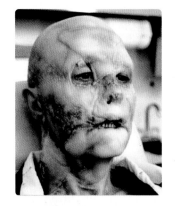

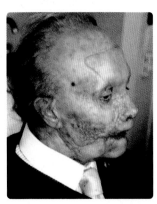
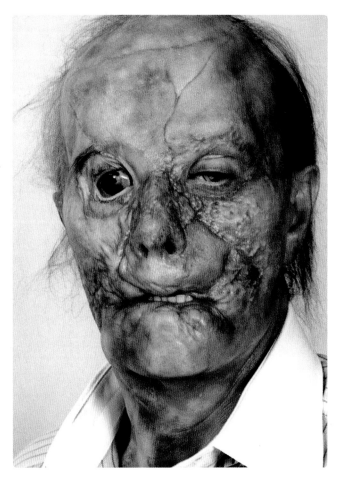

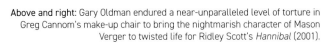
Above and right: Gary Oldman endured a near-unparalleled level of torture in Greg Cannom's make-up chair to bring the nightmarish character of Mason Verger to twisted life for Ridley Scott's *Hannibal* (2001).

We were on a beach in New Zealand, 25 minutes away by helicopter from base camp, and we needed a nose. It was while we were filming *The Chronicles of Narnia: Prince Caspian* (2008). We'd shot a scene with Peter Dinklage, as Trumpkin, being dunked in the water. Just for that one scene, we'd put a foam nose on him, which doesn't look as good as gelatine, but because gelatine dissolves in water, we had no choice.

Suddenly, they decide they want to shoot some additional close-ups of Trumpkin on the beach, but the foam nose was in no fit state after the dunking. I was like, "No, no, no, no, no, no, no. We need to change the nose!"

So, instead of flying Peter and myself back to base camp, someone put a new gelatine nose in a box and they flew it out to us. We replaced the nose right there on the beach and they got their shots. It worked out. But what an expensive nose that turned out to be! Probably 60,000 dollars.

Tami Lane

"WHAT AN EXPENSIVE NOSE THAT TURNED OUT TO BE!"

The first thing we did on *Inglourious Basterds* (2009) was shoot a test scalping. We sent Quentin [Tarantino] the tape and then later in Berlin, when we were making the movie, he told me to go shoot that sequence myself.

"You know what I want," he said. "You already shot it!"

Greg Nicotero

Above: Tami Lane ensures that Peter Dinklage's Trumpkin is ready for his adventures in *The Chronicles of Narnia: Prince Caspian* (2008).

Left: Greg Nicotero shows there's more than one way to skin Jake Garber for his cameo in Quentin Tarantino's *Inglourious Basterds* (2009).

Opposite: Warwick Davis as Nikabrik and Sarah Rubano as herself, in the make-up trailer for *The Chronicles of Narnia: Prince Caspian* (2008).

On *The Chronicles of Narnia: Prince Caspian* (2008), Howard [Berger] assigned me the character of Nikabrik, played by Warwick Davis. Of course, it was a total honour to work with Warwick, because of all the incredible films he's made and the staggering variety of make-ups he's worn over the years.

Every morning Howard would blast out a different theme tune as Warwick entered the trailer. *Star Wars* one day, *Harry Potter* the next, then *Willow* (1988)…

Warwick's a great guy, but more than that, the man really knows how to wear a make-up. He knows what he's in for. He just sits in the chair, puts his head back and lets you get on with it.

Every morning, he'd put his wedding band in a little dish at my station. He'd say, "Rubano, be careful with that. That's my wedding ring. I never take it off, but obviously I can't wear it in character."

So I was in charge of keeping it safe while he was filming. And at the end of the day, after I took off his make-up – a full-face gelatine – he'd grab his ring, put it on and off he'd go.

Only one morning he came in and said, "Rubano, I forgot to put my ring back on last night."

My internal dialogue said "CRAP", but outwardly I was more optimistic and said, "It'll be here somewhere – don't worry."

We looked and looked but it wasn't at my station or anywhere in the trailer. His eyes start welling up. Then we realise it was probably

"THE MAN REALLY KNOWS HOW TO WEAR A MAKE-UP."

cleaned up and thrown away by mistake, so now we're panicking.

He says, "Rubano, we gotta find it, my wife doesn't know I take it off when I'm acting!"

So I say to Howie, "We gotta find the ring!"

We enlist a team of people, Warwick included, to jump into the skip and throw out all the bags. Then we begin tearing them apart, carefully sorting through each and every mushy morsel. It was a hideous task. Finally, after an hour or so, Howard shouts out, "I think I've found Warwick's face!"

So he delicately pulls apart this big ball of gelatine and right in the middle of that sticky mess was Warwick's ring! We'd found it!

Sarah Rubano

After finishing season 3 of *Game of Thrones* (2011–19), the producers were thinking the show had turned into quite a beast. That rather than requiring a few make-up effects, and a couple of make-ups per episode, the series now required a large department to handle everything. And they were basically looking for someone who'd be 100 per cent exclusive and committed to their programme. Someone who wouldn't take anything else on and who'd be basically terrified to screw up as it was their first big show.

We got the call! I was driving at the time and when they told me, I almost crashed. I rang Sarah [Gower] and told her, "We've got *Game of Thrones*!"

And she said, "Oh my god! Amazing!"

And then we're both like, "How are we going to do this?"

We didn't have a workshop, but the producers helped us get started. We hired this little space, not far from Pinewood Studios, and built everything from the ground up over a couple of weeks.

We didn't have a crew, and that was a struggle, because at the time David White was hiring for *Guardians the Galaxy* (2014) and Mark Coulier was hiring for *Dracula Untold* (2014), and it felt like they were nabbing all the best artists. But I called all my friends and managed to assemble this crack, little stealth team of about fourteen guys.

I remember, we were on our way to our first production meeting in Belfast. We didn't really know, back then, that much about the show. The night before our meeting, the Red Wedding episode aired and everyone went nuts. It was all anyone was talking about, or writing about, or posting about. And we're both like, "What have we signed up for here?"

It was a steep learning curve.

By the end of our first season, we had six guys in full body make-ups, and I was wondering how we could keep up the pace. But cut to the following year and we had, like, seventy-five guys in zombie make-ups and a huge crowd marquee. The scale was immense. The quality really ramped up as well. And suddenly everyone's calling me, asking, "Can I come work on *Game of Thrones*?"

That was quite a contrast to the year before.

Barrie Gower

Left: Barrie Gower and his team designed and created the truly terrifying Night King along with his White Walkers and undead minions for *Game of Thrones* (2011–19).

Following pages, left: Hafþór Júlíus Björnsson as Gregor "The Mountain" Clegane in a make-up designed by Barrie Gower for *Game of Thrones* (2011–019).

Following pages, right: Javier Botet as one of Barrie Gower's Night Walkers for *Game of Thrones* (2011–19).

When an actor initially tries on their make-up, it's exciting, but seventy times in, it kind of loses its lustre. It can test you and your actor. On *The Lone Ranger* (2013), Bill Fichtner was a trooper. So committed to his character. So patient and good-humoured in the chair.

There were a lot of parts to that make-up: the cleft lip, silver toothed dentures, age stipple, scarring, skanky hair pieces, plus layers of grime and sweat. It's a lot to endure when you're working long, hot, dusty days.

Johnny Depp was likewise amazing on that film. His Tonto make-up was such a big process, a few times he'd actually sleep in it.

The next morning, we didn't know what we were going to see. Would it be shot? Would we have to start from scratch? But he'd come in and it was almost pristine. I don't know what he did – maybe he slept hanging upside down – but we barely had to touch it up.

Those were easy mornings!

Mike Smithson

"IT'S A LOT TO ENDURE WHEN YOU'RE WORKING LONG, HOT, DUSTY DAYS."

I've designed and applied Heidi Klum's Halloween make-ups for years. She loves make-up. We do all this crazy prosthetics stuff and Heidi shows it to the world. It makes us all look good.

Mike Marino

Right: Heidi Klum is a huge Halloween enthusiast and relies upon the talents and creativity of Mike Marino to bring her elaborate make-ups to life.

Below: Heidi Klum (left) transforms into the Werecat from *Michael Jackson's Thriller* (1983), courtesy of Mike Marino (centre) and Mike Fontaine (right).

I work so closely with creature effects make-up artists, it's genuinely a relationship. Almost like we're dating! I spend more time with them in a production day than I do with anybody else, so we really do have to click.

And it's not just a relationship of artist and applicant. It is a relationship of trust. Because I'm not just an actor and they're not just a make-up artist. I'm also kind of a nursing home patient, and they're my caregiver.

Depending on how extensive a make-up is, I can be completely debilitated and need help with everything: I can't go to the restroom for myself. I can't get snacks for myself. You're just constantly being looked after.

So my favourite make-up people, over the years, have been the ones who not only pay attention to shapes and colours and are really great artists, but also are decent, warm-hearted people who understand what you're going through and will always be there for you.

Doug Jones

When I first met Kevin Peter Hall, right away I could tell he was more than just a big guy. He could really act, and he didn't move awkwardly, like men his size often do. He was great.

On *Harry and the Hendersons* (1987), Kevin and three puppeteers had to synchronise their performances to bring Harry to life. That wasn't easy, because it was a small set full of cameras, crew and the Henderson family.

So we had three puppeteers trying to get a line of sight on the character without getting in the way of the camera. We had no headsets either, so I'd have to run up to Kevin before each take to talk him through how we should all play it.

But after a while, we all became one character. We could follow Kevin's lead and he could follow ours.

It was a magical experience.

Rick Baker

For *Philadelphia* (1993) I was able to do an enormous amount of research. I pestered everybody in production until I got access to doctors and other healthcare workers handling the AIDS crisis, as well as people who had come down with the virus.

The research aspect remains particularly fascinating to me. On several occasions, it has been the most exciting part of my involvement with a production.

Tom [Hanks] was very patient with me, never pushing back against my obsessive need to get every last detail perfect. He was just completely committed to that character and allowed me to do the best work I could.

Carl Fullerton

"AFTER A WHILE, WE ALL BECAME ONE CHARACTER."

Top: Tom Hanks in an unused, test age make-up for *The Green Mile* (1999), as ultimately director Frank Darabont cast Dabbs Greer to play the elderly version of Hanks' character. This is the only photo of that test make-up, designed and created by Garrett Immel under the supervision of KNB EFX Group.

Above, left: Carl Fullerton's brilliant make-up on Tom Hanks for Jonathan Demme's *Philadelphia* (1993). The make-up on the right was a test using subtle prosthetics, though ultimately it was abandoned in favour of a more out-of-the-kit approach.

Talking about Dustin Hoffman once, Dick Smith said something that's informed my whole career: "Your actors are naked up there on the screen, in front of the world, 40 feet [12m] tall. All their flaws. And they're trusting you as their make-up artist to make them look good and not let them have egg on their face."

Ben Foster lives and breathes his craft, as I do. I feel like he appreciates that I'm as serious about my job as he is about his. So when he bears his soul for a role, he trusts I'll make him look exactly right.

Jamie Kelman

"HE'LL GO HEAD-TO-HEAD WITH ANYBODY IN DEFENCE OF THE WORK."

Besides being a calming presence, Jamie Kelman is also a fighter. He'll go head-to-head with anybody in defence of the work, and I love that.

When we first met, it wasn't the first time I'd been blown away by the work of an amazing artist, but it was the first time I'd felt empowered by one. We share the same excitement for opening up a character's potential.

We've done at least four builds together. I'm not talking powder and a speck of blood, but significant builds.

The first character we collaborated on was Matt Axelson for *Lone Survivor* (2013). Jamie created a five-stage make-up for Axe's eye to appear to close in real time. It takes a certain kind of precision and dedication, even obsession, to make effects like that feel real, but I immediately knew I was in good hands.

Our most recent collaboration was on *The Survivor* (2021) and, by then, I felt I was seeing someone at the top of their game.

I so admire what Jamie does.

Ben Foster

Opposite: For *The Survivor* (2021), Ben Foster readies himself for a fight sequence, while Jamie Kelman snaps into action with a few final touches. There's something magical about the working relationship between actors and make-up artists who respect each other's crafts. Ben and Jamie exemplify that ideal.

LET'S DO THE TIME WARP

Old people are everywhere!
Given their familiarity, creating a convincing age
make-up is perhaps the greatest and most appealing
challenge faced by our masters. The trick is being able to
design something so natural, so credible, that audiences
might not even realise it's a make-up.

Here, then, is a swift appreciation of the science, art
and magic it takes to create a convincing senior citizen,
accompanied by a handful of stories that – ahem – will
never get old.

Vincent Van Dyke

I'm a big fan of not completely covering someone. I think if you can use portions of their face, you should. I rarely do a nose in an age make-up, although that's something almost everyone else does. I don't want to lose their likeness so, at most, I'll add a little tip at the end to help drop it. You have to remember, it's not a disguise. It's them. Still them. Just them, plus time and gravity.

Really there's nothing I enjoy more than creating age make-ups. Every time I get a call to do one, I'm like seven inside and giddy!

I could do them every day, and it would never get old for me – no pun intended!

They're the hardest make-ups to pass off as real, because everyone knows what an old person looks like. Even if they can't express exactly why something's wrong with a make-up, they just feel somehow that it's not quite right. It may be a proportional thing. Maybe the colouration is off or the sculpting doesn't look as natural as it should. So getting it right is a tremendous challenge, and that's a big part of why they appeal to me.

Vincent Van Dyke

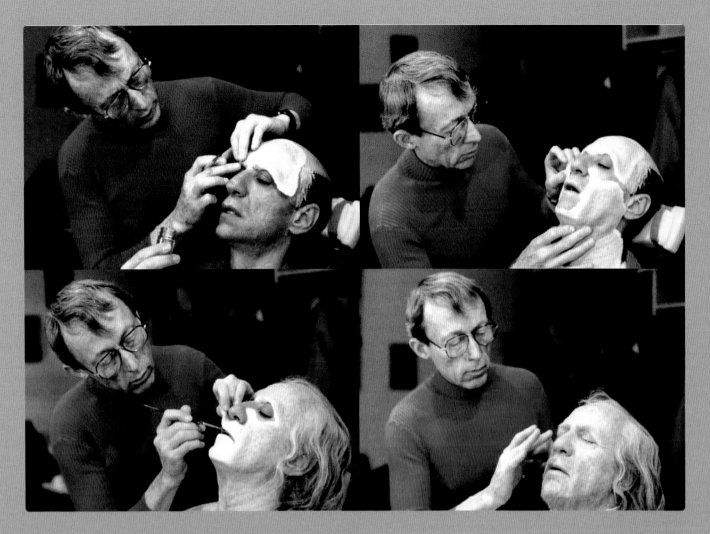

"DICK UNDERSTOOD HOW GRAVITY WAS GOING TO AFFECT PEOPLE'S FACES."

I always felt that Dick Smith was the only person who could really forecast what someone was going to look like when they got older. Just look at Father Merrin in *The Exorcist* (1973), and then see what Max Von Sydow looked like in his seventies.

Dick understood how gravity was going to affect people's faces: I worked with F. Murray Abraham and now he looks just like Salieri.

Howard Berger

Previous pages: Eddie Murphy sits patiently while Mike Marino applies the final touches to his Saul make-up on the set of *Coming 2 America* (2021).

Opposite: The very young and beautiful Sasha Camacho skips ahead a half century or so, courtesy of Vincent Van Dyke, who created and applied this remarkable make-up as a personal project.

Above: Dick Smith ages F. Murray Abraham for his Oscar-winning role as Antonio Salieri in *Amadeus* (1984).

Left: F. Murray Abraham in his final make-up as the vengeful and ultimately tragic Antonio Salieri in Milos Forman's masterful Mozart biopic, *Amadeus* (1984).

243

Above, left: David Morse as real-life American footballer Mike Webster in a make-up designed by KNB EFX and applied by Chris Gallaher for *Concussion* (2015).

Above centre: Johnny Depp as notorious crime boss James 'Whitey' Bulger, made up by Joel Harlow for *Black Mass* (2015).

Above: Stan Winston checks Cicely Tyson's final age make-up for the TV movie *The Autobiography of Miss Jane Pittman* (1974).

Far left: Pete Postlethwaite in a beautifully designed and applied make-up by Kevin Yagher for *Æon Flux* (2005).

Left: Barrie Gower is a master of ageing actors, as evidenced by this demo on Amie Aspden at the International Make-up Artists Trade Show (aka IMATS).

Below: Arsenio Hall can't quite put his finger on what it takes to make a world-class age make-up. So we'll tell you: Bill Corso, Mike Fontaine and Mike Marino, working as a dream team on *Coming 2 America* (2021).

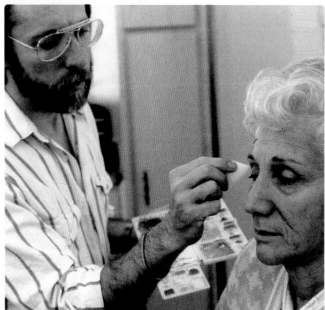

Top, left: Stephen Prouty piled the years on to actor CJ Jones for *Baby Driver* (2017).

Top, centre: Mike Marino and his team aged Stephen Dorff for *True Detective* (2014–19).

Top, right: Barrie Gower delivered this authentic peek into Lee Mack's future.

Left: Kevin Yagher impressed Dick Smith with this personal old-age make-up that he applied to his friend Alec Gillis back in the Eighties. It remains an iconic make-up in the industry, because it's the first time anyone hand-punched facial hair into their prosthetics.

Above: Greg Nelson helped Olympia Dukakis go full grandma in *Dad* (1989).

esigning Mahershala Ali's old-age make-up for *True Detective* (2014–19) was like drawing up engineering plans. You have to identify what's going to fall.

I shone a torch in his face and marked out every line I saw. I took photographs of him bending and turning and looking up and looking down and making faces and squinting…

I printed them all out and studied them. "He's creasing there. He's creasing here. There's a little fat thing…"

I accentuated all that stuff.

Mike Marino

"YOU HAVE TO IDENTIFY WHAT'S GOING TO FALL."

Below, left : A set of silicone age prosthetics, created by Mike Marino for Mahershala Ali on *True Detective* (2014–19).

Below, right: Mahershala Ali in his final aged look as Wayne Hays on *True Detective* (2014–19).

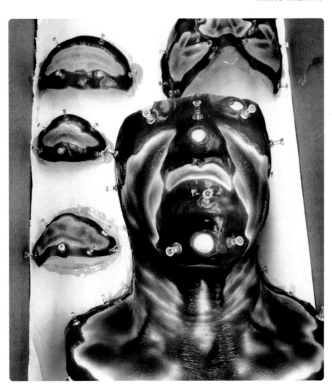

CJ Jones was cast in *Baby Driver* (2017) because he's deaf, and because his audition was great. He was perfect for the role but about twenty years too young for it, so we aged him up.

When I'm designing really any make-up, but especially an age make-up, the tenets I always follow are: be as sheer as possible, as minimal as possible to get the effect on and use as much of the actor as possible.

With CJ, we didn't put anything on his forehead because, honestly, for me, the forehead's a tough sell. Unless it's paper thin, it looks like you're wearing a piece. So we used stipple instead, on his lids and his forehead, and just a few pieces, on his cheeks and elsewhere.

Mitch Devane taught me to sculpt make-ups that allow the actor to be the actor. You're not trying to bury them in a prosthetic. You're just accenting what they need to get the character across.

When the movie came out, because most people weren't that familiar with CJ, no one knew it was a make-up. They just assumed it was a real old guy. And that was actually the biggest compliment.

Thing is, you can make someone up, put horns and weird shit on them, and say, "Here's a demon."

And people are like, "OK, that's a demon."

Because who's to say what a demon looks like? But people know what old looks like. They see it every day. So to emulate that, to create that and have it fool people, that's the ultimate achievement. That's really what I strive for, so you don't want it to be noticed.

It's like when I look back at *The Exorcist* (1973). I had no idea that Max von Sydow was only in his early forties when he played Father Merrin. That was just so well done.

Stephen Prouty

A job I had on *The Irishman* (2019) was to take Domenick Lombardozzi and make him an old gangster: Fat Tony Salerno. So, I did this whole thing: a neck and cheeks, a chin, a nose, eye bags, a brow… I totally went for it, to see if I could get away with something cool, you know?

I try to make everything look as good in person as possible. That's something I learned From Rick Baker. If it looks good in person, it's gonna look good on film.

One day on set, Domenick's shooting a scene, sitting in the middle of the frame with Robert De Niro on one side and Joe Pesci on the other. And between takes I'm going up to him to check on his make-up, not painting or anything, just pushing on his prosthetics to make sure the glue's holding. And De Niro asks him, "Why does the make-up guy keep touching your face like that?"

And Domenick goes, "Oh, this isn't my face – this is a make-up!"

De Niro's like, "What do you mean?"

So Domenick finds a picture of himself on his phone to show them. He says, "I'm this guy!"

I went back over after he'd done that and De Niro grabs me by the arm. And he goes, "You did this? I don't know, I don't know, I don't know… You did some job!"

And Pesci goes, "You did some fucking job on him, man! I don't know who the fuck this is. I thought he was a fucking real guy!"

Oh, God. It was hilarious!

Mike Marino

"THEY JUST ASSUMED IT WAS A REAL OLD GUY."

Below, left: Domenick Lombardozzi takes a breather, mid-transformation into real-life wise guy Fat Tony Salerno, for Martin Scorsese's *The Irishman* (2019).

Below right: While shooting *The Irishman* (2019), Domenick Lombardozzi was unrecognisable to his co-stars, who all assumed he was just a real old guy.

Following pages: Mike Fontaine and Mike Marino ensure Domenick Lombardozzi blends into the crowd while sitting beside Joe Pesci for *The Irishman* (2019).

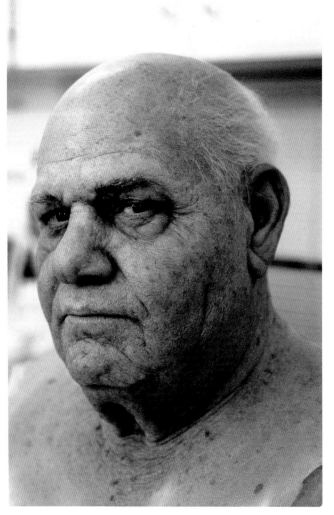

When we shot *Dad* (1989), Jack Lemmon was sixty-two and I aged him up to eighty-two. His son Chris was filming on the lot and he came around to see him.

So Chis looks at his dad and says, "I'm looking at you right up close. You do look a lot older, but I can't see any make-up on you whatsoever."

That really was the ultimate compliment.

Ken Diaz

"YOU DO LOOK A LOT OLDER, BUT I CAN'T SEE ANY MAKE-UP ON YOU WHATSOEVER."

Each one of Dick Smith's age make-ups is unique, because how his character lived affects its design.

In Father Merrin's case, you can see in the sun-bleached, ruddy textures of his face that he spent his life in hot, dusty countries, digging for relics.

Although Dick played a key role in building the characters he worked on, his make-ups were so subtle, most people didn't even realise they were make-ups. Which is exactly how it should be.

David Grasso

Above, left: Jack Lemmon looking dashing as always.

Above, centre: Jack Lemmon in his make-up for *Dad* (1989).

Above, right: Ken Diaz applied layers of age stipple and other out-of-the-kit techniques to Jack Lemmon for his role in *Dad* (1989).

I created a subtle, relatively youthful middle-aged make-up for a young actress on *Warlock* (1989). I was proud of it and felt it worked well for the character. Unfortunately, when I tested it on her at my shop, she seemed to freak out. She looked in the mirror but turned quickly away and refused to discuss the look any further.

I felt the make-up maintained her natural beauty, just adding a few years of elegant maturity. But for her, perhaps, it was an unwelcome preview of that inescapable moment when we teeter on the precipice between youth and middle age, and the downhill slide becomes inevitable.

Some people are fascinated by a preview into their future. Others, not so much.

Carl Fullerton

said I needed six weeks to create a convincing age make-up for Maggie Smith on *Hook* (1991).

I barely had a week!

Christopher Tucker sent me her face cast from England. It arrived on Tuesday night and I showed the sculpture to [Steven] Spielberg Friday morning.

I had no time to think about it, so I just kept it subtle: a wraparound piece and stipple. If I'd had weeks to work on it, I'd probably have oversculpted it, made too many pieces and it would have been too heavy. So it actually worked out very well.

Working with Mitch Devane, I made the mould on Saturday, ran the foam on Sunday and did the make-up test on Monday. The following day they started shooting, and Maggie came up to me and said, "Everyone's saying it's one of the best make-ups they've ever seen!"

I was told I'd only have to apply it five times, but I ended up applying it twenty-six times! And when I asked Spielberg "What would you have done if this didn't work?", he just smiled.

I got so much work from that one job. For ten years, everyone wanted me to do their age make-ups!

Greg Cannom

"EVERYONE'S SAYING IT'S ONE OF THE BEST MAKE-UPS THEY'VE EVER SEEN!"

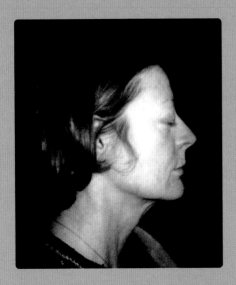  

The make-ups I'm proudest of are often the ones I didn't have a lot of time to work on. Like, the age make-up I did on Robert Downey Jr for *Chaplin* (1992). Specifically, the scenes where he's in his sixties, sailing to Switzerland.

When [Richard] Attenborough called, they were already deep into filming and just a week-and-a-half away from shooting those scenes. I'm a big Chaplin fan, so I was excited to do it. When I met with Sir Richard, he asked if I could create and test the make-up in, like, three or four days. But this was foam latex, we didn't have a mould of Robert yet, and even getting it done in ten days was going to be a rush.

So I said, "If you're game to try this, why don't we just aim for the shoot?"

To skip the test and just go for the shoot. So the first time we ever shot that make-up was on the *Queen Mary* in daylight. That was our test, and you see it in the film.

It was a terrifying way to do things, but I ended up being really happy with it. I mean, sure, I look at it now and wish I could sculpt it again, but for what it was, given the time we had, I was very pleased with how it turned out.

Often, if you have too much time to tinker, you can go past it. I remember at the premiere of *Dick Tracy* (1990), I was talking to Dick Sylbert, the production designer. "Jeez," I said, "I wish I'd had more time."

And he replied, "Caglione, if you'd had any more time you would have fucked it up."

There's something to be said for just going on impulse sometimes.

John Caglione Jr

Above: Maggie Smith becomes Granny Wendy, via Greg Cannom's considerable skills, for *Hook* (1991).

REEL LIVES

Transforming one famous face into another requires a degree of balance that would put all but the most accomplished high-wire acts to shame. Because it's not about hiding the actor behind a mask. The aim is not impersonation.

Like the performance, it's more of a portrait that's the goal, a subtle addition of elements designed to suggest the character to the audience's satisfaction, without completely erasing the actor in the process.

feel I've achieved something when audiences don't realise they're seeing one of my make-ups. They just feel them. It's all about realism for me. Even when the transformation is relatively extreme, like Drew Barrymore in *Grey Gardens* (2009), realism is everything.

Bill Corso designed the prosthetics for that one, and, after the first camera test, I felt we needed to change the sculpt a bit. That we needed a nose to tie all the pieces together. Bill sent me the mould and I'd make the noses in the trailer. Only the director didn't want a nose. Michael Sucsy was adamant about that. But Drew said, "Just do it."

So I did. And we were a couple of weeks into shooting before Drew walked up to Michael in the bright sun, like we're on the beach, and she goes, "Michael, you know, I'm wearing a nose."

But he had no idea! Which, of course, was exactly the effect I was going for. And it really did help us lock everything in.

Vivian Baker

"REALISM IS EVERYTHING."

I got a phone call about doing the Margaret Thatcher make-up for *The Iron Lady* (2011). While I considered it, the terror crept in. "Can I do this?"

It was one of those things that could make or break your career, but sometimes you just have to take the bull by the horns and say, "Yeah," then work out the issues later.

So I said, "Yeah!"

And now I'm thinking, "How do I turn Meryl Streep into Margaret Thatcher?"

With the right wig, the proper costume and Meryl's performance getting her most of the way there, I felt we could do our part and complete the character.

You study the actor's face because that's your canvas. I focused on the younger Thatcher make-up, and Barrie Gower focused on the older. For both, we decided to keep it minimal, to keep as much of Meryl as possible and not bury her under too many prosthetics.

Rather than try too hard to make Meryl look like Margaret, I just nudged the likeness in the right direction but let the actor's features shine through. I made the decision to use Meryl's own eyes and eye shape and to keep the prosthetics from mid-cheek down.

Then it was just a question of how we'd work with J. Roy Helland, Meryl's personal hair and make-up artist. They've been together since the Eighties, and you never know how it'll work out, getting in the middle of that close a working relationship. Of course, I'm happy to collaborate, just as long as we have control over our part of the process.

Fortunately, Roy was great. Really good fun. And he keeps his make-up materials and equipment on the minimal side, like me. So we were on the same page. He was like, "I don't know anything about prosthetics. You do all that, I'll do my wigs and just colour up a little bit afterwards."

We worked together well and both he and Meryl were very gracious the whole time.

I remember the most amazing moment. It was the first time we tested the old-age make-up. Barrie, Roy and I did our thing, then left Meryl to get her costume and padding on. When she came out of the costume room, she'd shrunk down by about 18 inches [45cm] just by stooping. Then she pottered down the corridor towards us, and I thought, "Wow, we might not get fired after all."

After that, it was just a question of refining the design, honing the edges and stuff like that. Still, until you see it on the screen, you're never completely confident you've nailed a make-up. And it certainly doesn't help calm your nerves when someone says to you, like the DP did to me once, "This could be a real career killer for you, couldn't it?"

I was thrilled, then, when Roy and I won the Best Make-up Oscar for our work. So I'd say we pulled it off, and career-wise, I'm still standing!

Mark Coulier

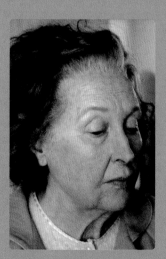

Previous pages: Sir Anthony Hopkins delivers Sir Alfred Hitchcock's signature silhouette for the lively biopic *Hitchcock* (2012).

Opposite, top: Jessica Lange and Drew Barrymore as Big and Little Edie in *Grey Gardens* (2009).

Opposite, bottom: Drew Barrymore and Jessica Lange in make-ups designed by Bill Corso and applied by Vivian Baker and Sean Sansom for *Grey Gardens* (2009).

Above, left to right: Mark Coulier, J. Roy Helland, Barrie Gower and Stephen Murphy collaborated with Meryl Streep to produce this trio of Margaret Thatcher looks for *The Iron Lady* (2011).

We ran a lot of tests for *Hitchcock* (2012).

To start with, I had Richie Alonzo sculpt a make-up that transformed Anthony Hopkins into a likeness of Alfred Hitchcock, and it was great, but we lost Tony. I realised we weren't so much looking for a likeness as we were something more interpretative, like a portrait.

What I needed was to find a combination of Hopkins and Hitchcock.

Hitchcock's defining characteristics were his weight and lower lip, so we designed a multi-piece, silicone make-up that added those elements to Tony without losing him in the process.

Then the night before we started shooting, Tony called to say,

"I don't want the lower lip. Let's lose the lower lip. I'll do the lower lip myself."

I had to quickly readjust the make-up on day one, but actually, it worked out really well with Tony pursing his own lip. The make-up was suddenly much lighter and even less charactery. Plus, I didn't have to bother Tony all day, retouching his lip every time he ate or drank something.

Tony's such a great actor and so much fun. I had a blast applying that make-up on him, thirty-five days in a row, with my cohort, Peter Montagna. And I loved the way the movie turned out, which was an added bonus.

Howard Berger

"WHAT I NEEDED WAS TO FIND A COMBINATION OF HOPKINS AND HITCHCOCK."

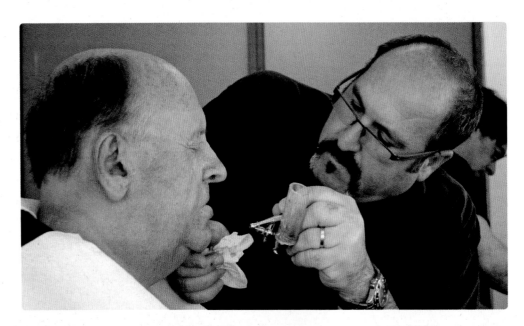

Left: Sir Anthony Hopkins and Howard Berger worked closely to create the perfect balance of Anthony and Alfred for *Hitchcock* (2012).

Below, left and right: John Wheaton's designs for *Hitchcock* (2012) demonstrated how Sir Anthony Hopkins could convincingly become Sir Alfred Hitchcock.

Opposite: Peter Montagna (left), Sir Anthony Hopkins (centre) and Howard Berger (right), dressed to impress for *Hitchcock* (2012).

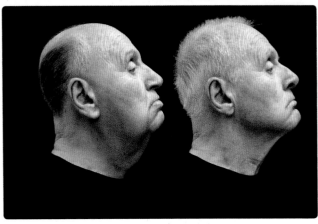

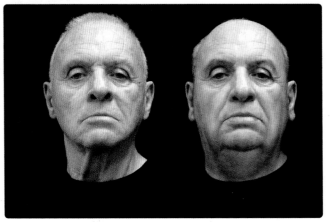

Harrison Ford doesn't like to be fussed with make-up. He's very low maintenance. He prefers five minutes, in and out.

It was different, however, when we did *42* (2013). He was playing a real-life baseball manager, Branch Rickey, and he was excited to go all-in on the make-up. He told me, "I don't want to be Harrison Ford. I want to be this guy. So what can we do?"

We did a nose, a hairpiece and I suggested we cover his scar with a small chin appliance. If he really didn't want to be himself, I thought that was the way to go. And he loved the idea, so we went for it.

At first, all I thought it would take to cover the scar was a quick transfer. And it was fine when it worked, but if the transfer didn't

line up exactly right, there'd be bumps and all sorts of weird deformities. It was just this little thing that I'd suggested, and now every day it was driving me out of my mind.

I tried to take a shortcut and it wound up being a mistake. I eventually built a full silicone chin, which is what I should've done in the first place.

Thing is, you never stop trying to improve your make-ups. All the way through every shoot, I'm always polishing, always trying new things to make it better. That's why I always say to actors in my chair, "Trust me. By the last day of this movie, your make-up is going to be perfect!"

Bill Corso

"YOU NEVER STOP TRYING TO IMPROVE YOUR MAKE-UPS."

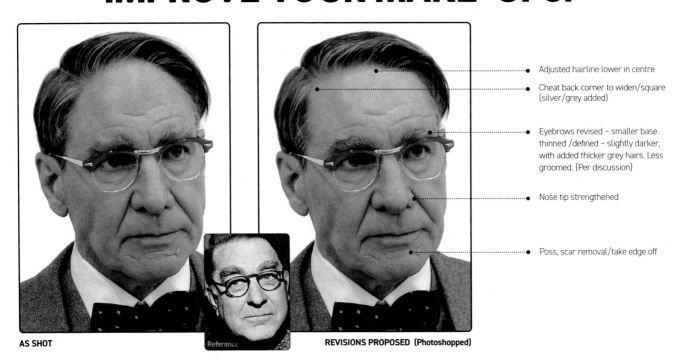

AS SHOT — Reference — REVISIONS PROPOSED (Photoshopped)

- Adjusted hairline lower in centre
- Cheat back corner to widen/square (silver/grey added)
- Eyebrows revised – smaller base thinned /defined – slightly darker, with added thicker grey hairs. Less groomed. {Per discussion}
- Nose tip strengthened
- Poss, scar removal/take edge off

When I first read the script for *Foxcatcher* (2014), I realised the casting of Steve Carell as John du Pont was going to be a real challenge. The real guy looked more like Jeremy Irons, who I thought would be perfect to play such a creepy role.

Bennett Miller, the director, told me he hired Steve Carrell because, with him, you couldn't guess what he was going to do. He didn't want the audience to have any preconceived notions. To take one look at the actor and go, "That's the bad guy."

What worried me though, because I thought Steve would require extensive work, was the make-up might get trashed in the media for drawing attention to itself. I didn't want to be the guy blamed in

every review for ruining a great movie with distracting prosthetics.

But Bennett said, "That's not your problem. If you do your job right and I do my job right and Steve does his job right, they'll forget about the make-up after the first couple of minutes. And for the rest of the movie, he'll be that guy."

So I told him, "All right. I'm putting my faith in you and I'll do my best."

I certainly didn't want to let him or Steve down. Thank goodness we were able to do a lot of tests to really nail the final look.

Sometimes it does you good, I think, to take the scary job.

Bill Corso

"SOMETIMES IT DOES YOU GOOD, I THINK, TO TAKE THE SCARY JOB."

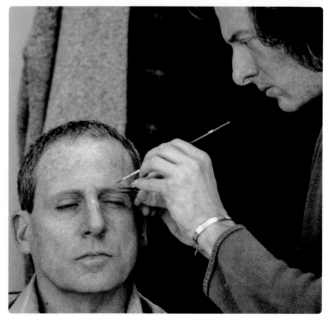

Opposite: Bill Corso's detailed notes on refining Harrison Ford's transformation into baseball manager Branch Rickey for Brian Helgeland's *42* (2013).

Above: Steve Carell as John du Pont in Bill Corso's Oscar-nominated make-up for *Foxcatcher* (2014).

Right: Bill Corso embraced the 'scary job' of turning Steve Carell into philanthropist and murderer John du Pont for *Foxcatcher* (2014).

I first met Gary Oldman during pre-production on *Planet of the Apes* (2001). He was originally cast as Thade, so we did a lifecast, but ultimately he dropped out. Later, he saw the portrait I sculpted of Dick Smith, and was impressed by it. He told me, "Someday I want to work with you."

That was 2002, and although he contacted me several times over the following years, nothing happened until 2016. He said, "There's a movie called *Darkest Hour* (2017) where I'm portraying Winston Churchill. I want you to do the make-up, but if you can't, I won't take the job."

At that time, I'd left the film industry to focus on fine-art portraits, so I asked Gary for a week to consider it.

I thought about my biggest inspiration: Dick Smith's Lincoln make-up. That's really what led me to starting my career in the film industry. But I'd never had the opportunity to create a main character make-up like that. I realised then, that if I didn't take this job, I'd regret it for the rest of my life.

Also, it was a very important film for Gary, and I didn't want to be the reason he passed on it. So I said I'd do it.

I created three different versions of the make-up, from light to heavy, and we tested each one. We chose the lightest one, because that's the easiest for an actor to work with. I refined the design, we tested it in London and, although that was right before filming was due to begin, I decided I wanted to change the cheek pieces. I told the production, "You don't have to pay me. I just have to do this one thing."

Trying to create a human being, to mimic nature with artificial materials, is almost impossible. Because nature is amazing! So nothing is more important to me than doing the best I can to perfect every element.

I resculpted the cheek pieces over the weekend, we did another test on Monday and that's the version we shot with. The version you see on screen, though, is more than just my make-up. It's Gary's performance. It's Joe Wright's direction. It's the lighting and how it was shot by Bruno Delbonnel.

Everything came together beautifully and I felt the experience restored my passion for film. Honestly, watching it reminded me why I got into the industry in the first place.

Kazu Hiro

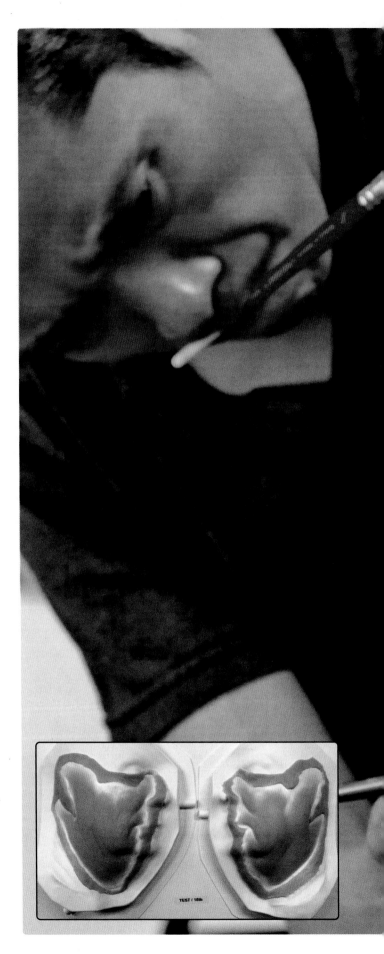

Right: Kazu Hiro carefully applies silicone prosthetics to Gary Oldman for his role as Winston Churchill in *Darkest Hour* (2017).

Inset: Silicone prosthetics on the verge of being applied to the sides of Gary Oldman's face for *Darkest Hour* (2017).

Following pages: Gary Oldman strikes a commanding pose as Winston Churchill in Kazu Hiro's Oscar-winning make-up for *Darkest Hour* (2017).

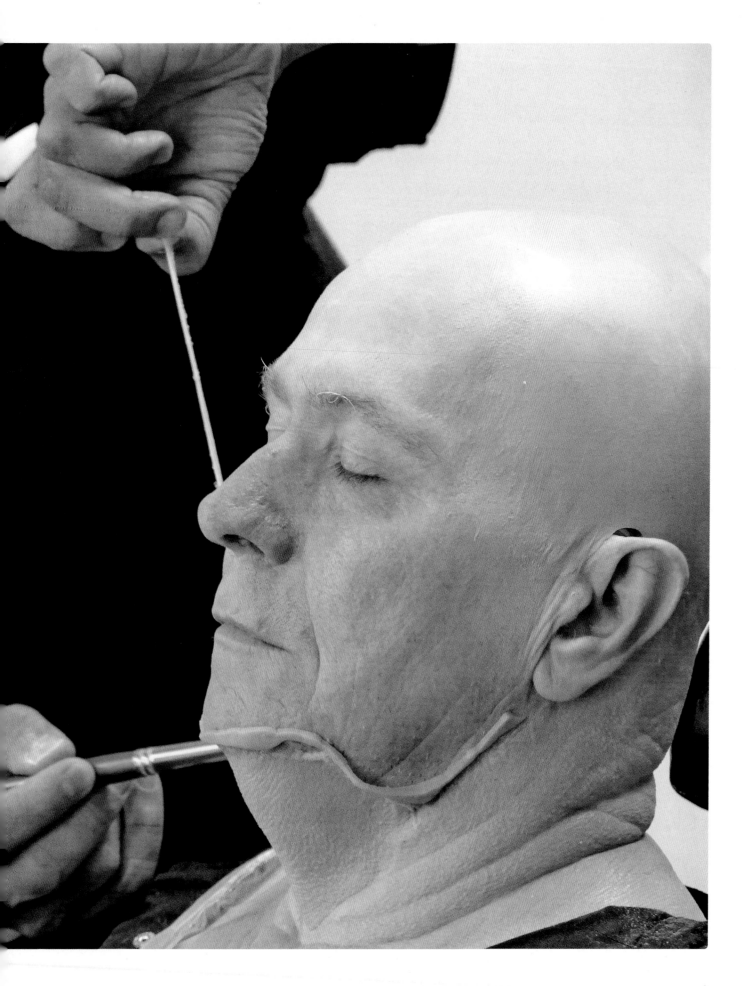

We did a likeness make-up on Evan Peters. Turned him into Andy Warhol. Ryan Murphy loved it so much, I think that's what inspired him to transform Evan into a bunch of different cult leaders for *American Horror Story: Cult* (2017).

Evan's so dedicated, so keen on prosthetics and always so excited to play other people, that you can just keep pushing him. To wear lenses, teeth… I love that part of him! He's an old-school, Tony Randall, *7 Faces of Dr. Lao* (1964) kind of actor.

There was the night Evan played Jim Jones and, the following morning, we had thirty minutes to take him out of that eight-piece prosthetic and turn him into Jesus Christ. There were four of us working on him at once, and, honestly, we didn't know if we were going to be able to do it in time. But like always, we tried our best and, as usual, it worked out.

Eryn Krueger Mekash

I did a Shakespeare make-up on Kenneth Branagh for *All Is True* (2018).

Before we started, he said, "I'm directing the movie, we're doing it on a low budget, and I'm trying to shoot the whole thing in four weeks. I need a make-up that can be done in ninety minutes, as I can't keep going back to the trailer. I don't care if I'm trying to direct and you're crawling all over me, fixing things. That's fine. I'll let you. I just can't leave the set."

So that's how we operated. A ninety-minute make-up every morning, prosthetic forehead, hand-laid beard, the works.

Later, when Ken was cast as Boris Johnson in *This Sceptred Isle* (2022), because he trusted me and I never once set off his bullshit meter, he asked me to do the make-up.

When we started out, because director Michael Winterbottom's all about stripped bare filmmaking, he was like, "Surely Ken can just dye his hair a bit blond and that will do?"

But Ken looks nothing like Boris! So he pushed for a full make-up. His only stipulation was that it take no more than two hours to apply. Eventually we streamlined the process to an hour and fifty minutes.

Ken had a forty-day window to shoot his scenes, and – not including weekends, of course – he was in that make-up every day. We didn't do teeth or lenses, but apart from that, and a little area below his lower lip, Ken was completely covered in prosthetics, fat suit and everything.

And although Michael had fought the idea of make-up right up until the first day of shooting, once Ken was on set in his full Boris Johnson make-up, suddenly he loved it.

And he's like, "Why don't we do some pieces for all these other characters now?"

Neill Gorton

As much as it can create a look, a prosthetic can hinder movement. On *Stan & Ollie* (2018), I worked with Steve Coogan to find the right balance of straight make-up, prosthetics and hair for his role as Stan Laurel.

We started with a nose, but Steve quickly decided against it. He's quite vocal about what he will and won't put up with, but we got the ears through. The chin was touch-and-go for a while but we got that through, too, which was good as it made him look much more like Stan.

Steve used his own hair. We just coloured it. Not many people know that Stan Laurel was a redhead, but we thought if we dyed his hair bright red, it would be too distracting, so we chose a warm mid-brown instead.

Mark Coulier and Josh Weston worked with John C. Reilly to create Oliver Hardy. He showed great patience for the process, and he loved the effect.

Both Steve and John wanted their make-ups to be as close to the real thing as possible and were quite competitive with each other on that score, which might even have added to their characters' on-screen dynamic.

Jeremy Woodhead

Opposite, top: Kenneth Branagh as Boris Johnson in Neill Gorton's outstanding portrait make-up for *This Sceptred Isle* (2022).

Opposite, bottom: Eryn Krueger Mekash applies one of many transformative make-ups to Evan Peters for *American Horror Story: Cult* (2017).

Top: For *Stan & Ollie* (2018), Jeremy Woodhead and Mark Coulier embraced the challenge of turning John C. Reilly (left) and Steve Coogan (right) into vintage comedy legends Oliver Hardy and Stan Laurel.

Above: Steve Coogan as Stan Laurel in *Stan & Ollie* (2018).

The biggest joy of all for me is helping an actor find their character.

On *Judy* (2019), when we started working with Renée Zellweger to create her Judy Garland make-up, we tried every trick on her. I blocked Renée's brows and painted new ones in. Gave her a nosepiece, more pronounced cheekbones and also sunken jowls, as Judy had those towards the end of her life.

We quickly dumped the eyebrow blockers, because they gave Renée an almost Botoxy look. Also the cheeks presented as many problems as they solved. Although they brought her more into the Judy area, they didn't justify the lack of movement in her cheeks. So we dumped those as well.

The nosepiece we kept to turn her nose up, and everything else I ended up doing with paint and shading, bringing things out and shadowing things away in an old-school make-up style.

As their facial structures are so different – Renée's face is oval while Judy's was diamond-shaped – getting the hair right was key to transforming Renée into Judy. So we cheated, opting for Judy's iconic, upswept style, even though she'd actually abandoned that look by the time the movie was set.

We shot the movie in six weeks. Every day, Renée would come sit in the chair. The make-up would go on. The hair would go on. The lenses would go in. The teeth would go in. And as the layers went on, her whole body language changed.

She became Judy, and it felt great to be part of that.

Jeremy Woodhead

Top: Renée Zellweger gets the tip of her nose altered by Jeremy Woodhead for her role in *Judy* (2019).

Above: Jeremy Woodhead (right) adjusts Renée Zellweger's wig for *Judy* (2019).

Below: Renée Zellweger embraced Judy Garland, body and soul, for her Oscar-winning role in *Judy* (2019).

Building a connection with talent is key. From your initial meeting, then lifecasting them, talking about the design and creation of your make-up for them, to eventually applying it, you have to put them at ease and make them feel they're in good hands.

When I met Malcolm McDowell to discuss his Rupert Murdoch make-up for *Bombshell* (2019), he was clearly apprehensive. He said although he wasn't against a little bit of make-up, he didn't want to look in the mirror and see it. He pushed for it to be as subtle as possible, so I only did a partial face cast on him. But he has such a good face! So I took it a little further than he'd asked for, but assured him it would work really well.

After we tested it, he was like, "If I'd known this was possible, I'd have requested prosthetics on other shows I've done. I feel like it's opened this whole other lane of acting for me."

Vincent Van Dyke

"WE ENDED UP HAVING TO BALANCE REALITY WITH ARTISTIC LICENSE."

We were working on the final season of *Game of Thrones* (2011–19) when Daniel Parker came to us with an irresistible pitch. He said, "I've been approached about a project that's going to have a lot of burn and age make-ups in it. It's very technical and will be one of the most complicated jobs you've ever done."

He didn't tell me what it was, but I was in.

When I found out it was the miniseries *Chernobyl* (2019), I started to do my research. Searched high and low for reference images of radiation burns, because there are hardly any from the actual Chernobyl event. No way to see what really happened and how people looked, because the Russian government downplayed the magnitude of the disaster and the only pictures they released were softened propaganda shots.

We found a few images of the fireman whose death is documented in the series, a man called Vasily. We saw various stages of his radiation sickness. And we had a written account by his wife, Lyudmilla, detailing her experiences from the moment her husband was first exposed to the radiation, on the night of the explosion, to the different stages his body went through as he slowly died of it over the next few weeks.

It's something like five different stages. First, the body looks sunburned, then there's swelling, and then almost a period of remission where the body looks like it's recovering but actually the internal organs are melting, and then finally the radiation just comes out of the skin. It was terrible to read but invaluable.

Because film and TV make-ups don't usually aim for the level of realism we wanted for Chernobyl, we ended up having to balance reality with artistic license. If we went too far, if we produced make-up effects that looked absolutely horribly real, most people would think they looked fake, because it's not what they're used to seeing.

It really was the most enormous challenge.

Barrie Gower

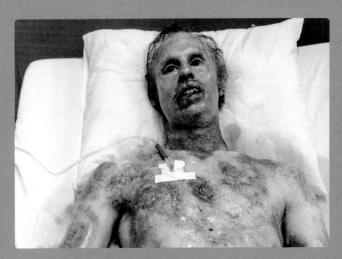

Top: After being cast as Rupert Murdoch in *Bombshell* (2019), Malcolm McDowell overcame his initial misgivings about wearing prosthetics, completely embracing Vincent Van Dyke's make-up process.

Above: One of the horrific radiation make-ups that Daniel Parker, Barrie Gower and the team created and applied for the HBO miniseries *Chernobyl* (2019).

WAR STORIES

We're taking a break, now, from celebrating the world of make-up effects with transcendent tales of talent, teamwork and artistic triumph.

Instead, we're now wilfully picking at the scabs of a whole series of sore points and digging deep into wounds that, to this day, refuse to heal.

Yes, it's not always roses and sunshine in the movie business, so here we've collected stories of stink and sweat, of conflict and calamity, of insult, injury and all sorts of other juicy stuff!

Tippi Hedren and her second husband Noel Marshall were shooting this five-million-dollar home movie called *Roar* (1981), about a family in Africa trapped in a house full of lions. That movie took years to make. Anyway, it was the first day of shooting and they wanted to film something good to get more investors. So they enticed two pairs of male lions from separate prides on to the compound and forced them to fight. The idea being that Noel would run in like King of the Beasts and break them up.

It worked great for the first two shots, but on take three, he got bit through the hand and there was arterial bleeding. People were running around panicking. And I'm screaming from the fence, "Guys, he's gonna bleed out, you need to apply direct pressure!"

I had Boy Scout training and first-aid training, so I knew he was in trouble. But I wasn't allowed on the set once the lions were out. If I went inside the fenced-off area, I was told I'd be immediately terminated. But nobody was listening! I had no choice but to enter the fenced-off set and run over to him.

The wound looked like raw chicken meat. The part that freaked me out the most, though, was I could look through his hand and see the grass. Anyway, I put pads on each side and clamped them down.

I said to him, "Hey, lay down. You're going to go into shock."

But he's screaming and hollering so I just swept his foot out from under him and put him on the ground, yelling, "STAY DOWN!"

That was my first day as a professional make-up artist on my first ever movie.

"THE WOUND LOOKED LIKE RAW CHICKEN MEAT."

Later in the shoot, I rescued the DP, Jan de Bont, as he was getting mauled by a lion. I was the closest one there, so I ran in screaming, waving my cane, chasing a large group of lions away from him.

Some months later, a crew member was trapped in a pen, face down in the dirt, while being attacked by a hormone-enraged ostrich. I ran into the pen and chased that ostrich off of him. I was able to leap up, get my arm around his neck and started punching him, but not before getting a hard kick in the shin.

Even after all that, I got fired after the first AD came into the make-up room, cussing at me, accusing me of something that I didn't do. I told him to quit cussing at me, but he kept it up. So, I told him, "Hey man, where I come from we don't take that shit!"

But he cussed at me again, so I backhanded him.

When I left, I was cheered by the crew as I rode off into the sunset!

Ken Diaz

Previous pages: Greg Nicotero learned the hard way not to mess with Mickey Rourke as Marv from *Sin City* (2005).

Left and above: The cast of *Roar* (1981) eventually learned that there are some lions you just don't cross.

Roger Deakins photographed *The Shawshank Redemption* (1994) brilliantly, except he's what I call a "sourcey" DP, meaning every light has to come from a specific location, with no traditional Hollywood "cheating".

There was one day early on where, for a courtroom scene, I'd done a make-up on Tim Robbins to youthen him up. But there was this huge window and the light was hitting him hard on one side of his face.

I said to Roger, "This light's making him look really old. Is there any way we can put a light on the other side to even him out a little bit?"

And he was like, "Where would the light come from?"

And I went, "I don't know, but we need something there."

Under protest, he ended up adding a slight bounce just to even Tim out a little bit.

Directors of photography are sometimes at odds with make-up, but you have to stand your ground.

Kevin Haney

Working on *Saving Private Ryan* (1998) was like D-Day minus the live bullets. Fast paced and physically demanding, but also thrilling. With Steven Spielberg directing and Tom Hanks in the cast, how could it not be?

It also meant a lot to me personally as my father was part of the D-Day landing with the British Army on Sword Beach.

Steven Spielberg wasn't going to be on set until the day before we started shooting. I kept nagging Ian Bryce, the producer, that we needed more prosthetics than were called for in the script, because it described the principal characters' injuries and demises but not the smaller parts, the background people or the stuntmen.

We needed wounds to dress the soldiers surrounding the principals, and blank face pieces that we could put squibs under. Also, we needed blank faces to change the limited number of stuntmen to create alternative features so it wasn't the same few chaps turning up over and over.

But Ian, at that point, said, "No. We only make the prosthetics as scripted."

I said, quite firmly, "I know Steven will change his mind the minute he turns up on day one. I just know it."

So Connor [O'Sullivan] and I made the pieces anyway. We didn't have the budget for it, but we made them with the understanding that the minute we opened the first box of prosthetics we'd paid to produce, the production would pay us back. I don't recommend anyone does things this way.

So there we were, shooting the landing craft, and Steven turns around and says, "I want a forehead hit."

We opened the box, took out the first forehead piece, applied it there and then on the beach, and we were off to the races, creating new wounds on a daily basis.

Lois Burwell

Above: Kevin Haney rejuvenated Tim Robbins for the beginning of *The Shawshank Redemption* (1994).

Left: Few war movies are as authentic and immersive as Steven Spielberg's *Saving Private Ryan* (1998).

"Are you having fun?"

That was Stan Winston's mantra. He'd often say, when things got stressful, "Remember what we're doing here, guys. We're not curing brain cancer – we're making movies."

Obviously, everyone on Stan's team was expected to deliver. Everyone had to do their best work. But at the end of the day, they were making monsters! They were a bunch of fan boys and girls living their dreams.

My dad wasn't always so playful. In the Seventies, he was much more intense. What changed him was working on *Heartbeeps* (1981). Between the gelatine make-ups never wanting to stick, and then practically melting throughout the day, he almost had a nervous breakdown.

But then one day Bernadette Peters saw the worry on his face and asked him what was wrong. She listened while he reeled off the challenges, but then smiled and said, "Come on, Stan. It's only a movie. You gotta relax and enjoy yourself."

So from that day forward, thanks to Bernadette Peters, Stan made sure that fun was always the priority.

Matt Winston

Below: Stan Winston sculpts on a bust of Bernadette Peters for sci-fi comedy *Heartbeeps* (1981).

Opposite, top left: Bernadette Peters' Aqua hugs Andy Kaufman's Val in this charming continuity Polaroid for *Heartbeeps* (1981).

Opposite, top right: A continuity Polaroid for *Heartbeeps* (1981), featuring Aqua (Bernadette Peters, left), Catskil (voiced by Jack Carter, centre) and Val (Andy Kaufman, right). Stan Winston earned his first Academy Award nomination for the film.

Opposite, bottom: Stan Winston makes nice with Evillene of Oz, played by Mabel King in the musical *The Wiz* (1978).

"IT'S ONLY A MOVIE. YOU GOTTA RELAX AND ENJOY YOURSELF."

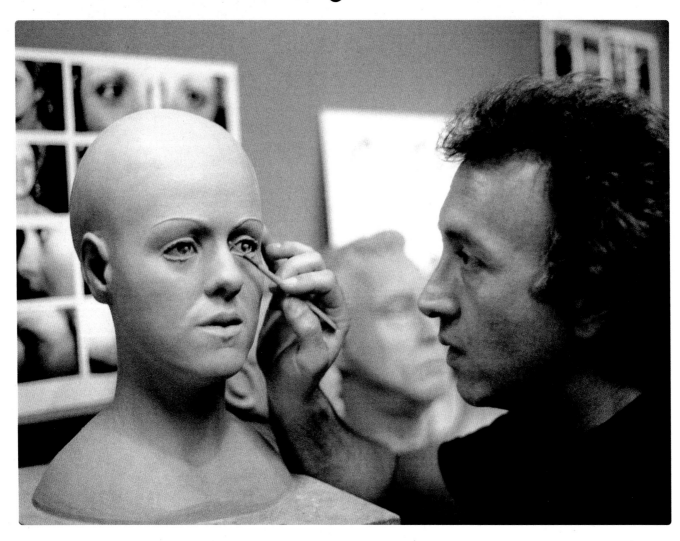

117 1ST position   67

While we were shooting *The Evil Dead* (1981), the time came to tell the actors about what we call "The Latex Point". That's the moment when you can no longer handle the make-up and you want to march off the set, crying hysterically, while trying to tear the appliances off your face.

On the original *Evil Dead* movies, almost every actor reached The Latex Point: "GET THIS OFF MY FUCKING FACE!"

And we'd have to calm them down. It was the same with Fede Alvarez's *Evil Dead* (2013). Jane Levy's walking away, like, "FUCK! FUCK THIS!"

There's only so much a person can handle. In *Evil Dead Rise* (2022), someone gets possessed for a third of the movie, and she's in full make-up that whole time. So it's tough. Of course it is. And we tell the actors, "Look. You're not going to like it. But you have no idea how bad it used to be."

Like on the first *Evil Dead*, Tom Sullivan, God bless him, was only working with what he had at the time. A hard-working and very creative make-up effects artist, but when he took a face cast of Betsy Baker using plaster of Paris, it ended up pulling all her eyelashes out. We looked inside the mould and there they were: two complete and beautiful sets.

Betsy also had a really tough time with the glass scleral contact lenses. You could only wear them fifteen minutes at a time, and no more than five times a day. We had strict instructions about that. Otherwise your eyes would be starved of oxygen and you'd go blind.

So we'd set up two or three shots to do in those fifteen minutes, which was absurd. One time she had to attack me with a knife, but she couldn't see shit because the lenses were completely opaque. Ash was really focused during those scenes as I really didn't want to get stabbed. It was all just so brutal.

In *Evil Dead Rise*, the lens work is all digital. There's no time limit and the actors can see, which is very helpful. And so we try to give our actors, now, that perspective. Because it could be SO MUCH WORSE.

Above: Bruce Campbell comes face-to-face with Mark Shostrom's Evil Pee Wee Head Demon, operated by Greg Nicotero for the horror-comedy classic *Evil Dead II* (1987).

"GET THIS OFF MY FUCKING FACE!"

Like on the first film, by the time we finished shooting, none of the actors were talking to us. And on the second, the true horror of that movie is what Ted Raimi had to endure.

The story is, Henrietta was played by Lou Hancock, an actress in her sixties. Because of her age, Sam [Raimi] didn't want to put her in the enormous, head-to-toe monster outfit. Meanwhile Ted, Sam's brother, wanted to be an actor and was trying to get into the Screen Actors Guild. So Sam hired Ted to play Possessed Henrietta, and he got in the union.

Oh, but God… On set…

Cut to North Carolina. It was summer and even the locals were apologising for how hot it was. They were like, "Oh Bruce, we're so sorry. Normally it's not over a 100 degrees [Fahrenheit/ 38°C] for THREE WEEKS IN A ROW."

So now here we are on an elevated set, where all the heat from the building went. There's no AC and there's Ted, baking in a full body monster suit, slumped over an apple box between takes. Oxygen on his face and he's just sucking down Gatorade after Gatorade.

There was one shot where Henrietta's floating and cackling and spinning round. For that, they got Ted in a harness and hoisted him up. His suit was so soaked with sweat, when they spun him, he splattered the crew. The sweat was just flying out of it.

And God bless the gallows humour of the KNB effects guys. At the end of every day, they'd take Ted's monster booties off his feet and, without him knowing it, they'd pour the sweat into a paper cup. Then they'd date it, put it on a shelf and be like, "Oh wow, he sweated a lot today. A little less yesterday…"

It was the most disgusting display of human sweat I've ever seen in my life.

On Sunday, the one day we weren't shooting, Sam would have a barbecue. Ted would come in, say hi and then collapse behind the couch for the rest of the day. He was just completely wiped out. But Sam was like, "It's not my problem. You want to be an actor? Be an actor."

So I tell these modern actors, "All the artists and technicians here have decades of experience. You'll never find a better crew. No one will ever take better care of you. And we're using the best, most modern appliances. So do please try to count your blessings."

Bruce Campbell

Opposite: Director Sam Raimi mugs behind Bruce Campbell's Evil Ash on the set of *Evil Dead II* (1987).

Right: "Finally monsieur, a wafer-thin mint?" Terry Jones as the vomitous Mr Creosote, virtually consumed by Christopher Tucker's grotesquely hilarious fat make-up for *Monty Python's The Meaning of Life* (1983).

Above: Terry Jones demonstrates Christopher Tucker's brilliant solution for manoeuvring Mr Creosote's enormous belly around the set of *Monty Python's The Meaning of Life* (1983).

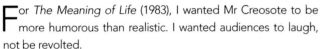

For *The Meaning of Life* (1983), I wanted Mr Creosote to be more humorous than realistic. I wanted audiences to laugh, not be revolted.

It was a dreadful thing to film, though, and certainly we were all revolted on the set. We shot the scene in a restaurant in West London over several hot, sunny days. The room became a furnace.

We used baby food for vomit, and it wasn't long before the whole restaurant was plastered in the stuff. In the heat, it quickly went off and smelled exactly like sick. The stench was overwhelming and it got worse every day. People were throwing up for real.

I'd go outside, take several deep breaths, run back into the restaurant, do whatever I had to do, then run out again, as quickly as I could. But Terry Jones was stuck there, trapped in that gory make-up and dripping with rancid baby food.

How he put up with it I don't know.

Christopher Tucker

"THE STENCH WAS OVERWHELMING AND IT GOT WORSE EVERY DAY."

I remember this one actress. She was always looking down at her phone. I'd say, "You have to lift your head up so I can see your face."

So she'd look up, but always eventually get back to her phone again. And this went on for several days. So finally, one day, I just made up her forehead. And said, "OK! You're done."

So she looks up and says, "Wait a minute. What about the rest of my face?"

I said, "Oh my gosh, you're right. I guess I could only see your forehead."

She didn't use her phone after that.

Leonard Engelman

I cold-called Rob Bottin's studio looking for work. Turned out they needed a sculptor, so they hired me right away. Like, I went in for my interview and ended up working there for thirteen hours.

Rob would come by every half hour to talk and hang out. He said, "You know, I worked on this film called *The Thing* (1982)."

I'm like, "Dude, I've seen *The Thing*!"

He said, "Once, on the movie, I stayed up for seven days straight. When I went to drive home, everyone's like, 'Don't drive yourself. You're too tired.'"

"But I said, 'I'm OK.'"

"Next thing I know, I'm waking up behind the wheel, because I hit the guard rail."

Mike Marino

The first time I ever worked with prosthetics was on Ridley Scott's *Legend* (1985). That was a really challenging shoot.

We'd get the call sheet, do the make-ups according to schedule, led by department head Peter Robb-King, but then we'd be told, "No, we're not shooting that. We're doing this instead…"

We often had lengthy make-ups on actors, three hours or more in the chair, then have to scrap those make-ups and start again on different characters for a scene. Poor Billy Barty won the prize for being the most needlessly made-up actor. He had thirty-one days, if I remember correctly, of being put in full make-up without being used.

You never knew who was coming in or what looks would be required. Once, we were asked to create a mummy, a character that Ridley Scott had come up with from absolutely nowhere. We went to the nurse and got bandages, I mixed up some colours, and Nick Dudman and I just made up the stuntman playing the mummy on the spot.

I was the make-up artist for David Bennent, who played Gump. One day on the set, he opened a bottle of water and threw it all over himself, ruining his make-up. Tom Cruise told him off. "Don't do that! It's disrespectful to me, to you, to Lois, to the film…"

I've always remembered that with gratitude, and it worked. David improved after that.

Obviously, one of the biggest make-ups in the film was Tim Curry as Darkness. It was immense, so Nick and I were going to do that together. We weren't allowed in the room the first time the make-up was applied. We only saw the finished result once Tim, as Darkness, walked on to the set to shoot the make-up test.

The next morning, Nick and I were to do the actual make-up on Tim, without really knowing in a hands-on way how we were going to apply the pieces. Nick and I arrived before 5 a.m. to set up. Tim was already there, a mass of red welts and blisters. It was horrifying for all of us.

Tim asked, "What are we going to do?"

And I said, "I'm not making you up, and nor is Nick. We're not doing anything until one of the grown-ups comes in."

So we just sat there, after placing some calls, and had a cup of tea. Tim couldn't shoot for three-and-a-half weeks while he recovered from whatever it was he'd gone through during the test make-up.

When he came back, not only were we applying this elaborate make-up, but we were doing it on someone with skin damage. Nick redesigned the skullcap that supported the horns to alleviate pressure, and that was just the first of many changes. The original make-up had taken twelve hours to apply, but we got it down to five-and-a-half.

The days we shot in the Hall of Darkness were the longest I've ever done on a film set. The earliest we ever finished was 12.30 a.m.,

and we'd been there since five in the morning. Some days we were there almost twenty-two hours. There wasn't time to go home. We'd just sleep a few hours in the studio, then start again.

Through it all, though, Tim was wonderful. He's one of the most marvellous actors I've ever worked with. Patience personified, good humoured, funny and a blindingly good actor, of course.

He deserved a medal for *Legend*.

Lois Burwell

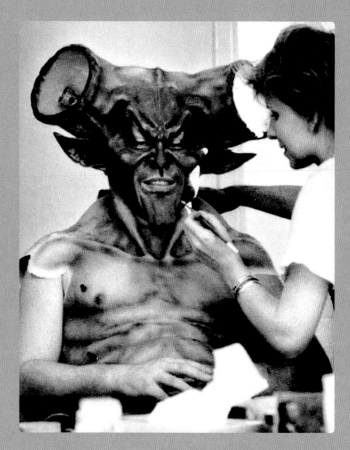

Above: Lois Burwell applies Rob Bottin's Darkness make-up to Tim Curry for Ridley Scott's *Legend* (1985).

I had the same driver on *Hellbound* (1988) and *Nightbreed* (1990). He'd pick me up every morning to take me to Pinewood Studios. Once he said, "I used to drive Tim Curry here, when he was making *Legend* (1985)."

I said, "Oh, really?"

He said, "Yeah. We made the same journey, sat right where you're sitting now. And I remember the first couple of days, he was very chipper, sitting upright, chatting away about this and that. Lovely guy.

"But he got quieter as the filming went on. And by the end of it, he looked grey. Just slumped in a corner of the car, and he never said a word."

Doug Bradley

Invaders from Mars (1986) was my first real experience of being in charge of a crew on set. It was a great education, but I remember being in the shower and seeing big clumps of hair falling out from the stress.

Stan [Winston] set everything up, then left for England to work on *Aliens* (1986). As soon as he left, the producers were like, "Listen, you son of a bitch, you're going to work eighteen hours a day."

This was back when producers felt free to demand you work ridiculously long shifts. Sometimes you'd even be expected to work for twenty-four hours straight. And they'd take no responsibility if you got into a car wreck on the way home.

My ace in the hole, though, was that I could call Stan and tell him exactly what was going on. So that's what I did. I called Stan and said, "They're threatening you'll be sued if I don't do the following things…"

Stan says, "Put him on the phone."

I hand the producer the phone and Stan starts yelling, quickly reducing him into a stammering mess. He's like, "Yes, Stan. No, no, no, Stan. Come on, Stan. Hey, it's me. What? No, Stan. Stan, calm down. Hey. What?"

He hands me the phone back and it was better after that. They were more respectful. I learned that day that when people are jerks, you have to fight for yourself and your crew.

You can't assume that everybody is going to be as cool to you as you are to them, especially when it comes to hard-driving producers. From that day on, I always held my corner.

Fortunately, my hair recovered and remains perfect to this day.

Alec Gillis

Below: Stan Winston left Alec Gillis to run the creature crew on Tobe Hooper's remake of *Invaders From Mars* (1986).

Opposite, top: Kevin Peter Hall cuts an imposing figure in the alien suit designed by the Stan Winston Studio for *Predator* (1987).

Opposite, bottom left: Kevin Peter Hall on set during reshoots for *Predator* (1997).

Opposite, bottom right Team *Predator* (1987), left to right: Shane Mahan, Steve Wang, Stan Winston, Brian Simpson, Kevin Peter Hall, Shannon Shea, Richard Landon and Matt Rose.

Jean-Claude Van Damme was originally hired to play the Predator back when they called it the Hunter. It was one of his first jobs and he had no experience as a creature performer.

Whenever he came in for a test, they'd put him in different variations of the suit, like the red one for the green screen and the proper painted one. Whatever suit he wore, though, they'd always cut the face out so he could breathe.

Later, when they put him in the full final suit, obviously, his face was covered, and that's when he started complaining. He was like, "Hey, wait a minute. Why are you covering my face? I'm an actor. You've got to be able to see my face."

And everyone was like, "Did no one explain to you what you're doing?"

Steve Wang

"I'M AN ACTOR. YOU'VE GOT TO BE ABLE TO SEE MY FACE."

Before it was outlawed, 355 adhesive was commonly used and very effective. Much better than spirit gum, which is like pine sap and gets itchy, crystally and breaks. Honestly, I've had moustaches get stiff and snap from being applied with it.

Actually, 355 was used in Vietnam. Field medics used to seal up wounds with it. Which was a handy thing to know when we were shooting *Mindwarp* (1991) and I cut my finger while digging around in this underground landfill. That place was the worst.

Anyway, I called for some 355, put it right in the wound and closed it up. God damn, it worked so well. Such a shame you can't get it any more.

Bruce Campbell

Dinosaurs (1991–94) was one of the highest stress shows I ever did. We had twenty-four mechanical heads, each with eighteen to thirty functions. During the first season, the downtime on set was horrible, because they just broke down constantly. And every time one broke and I was racing to fix it, the Disney guys would remind me that every minute of downtime cost 80,000 dollars. They put the fear of God in me!

For the second season, we tore those heads apart and completely rebuilt everything. By the third season, our downtime was literally zero. The show became a cakewalk and, still, after all these years, my absolute favourite thing to work on.

John Criswell

Above: Once a staple of prosthetic adhesives, 355 has long been discontinued and is today considered liquid gold.

Below: A sitcom sixty-five million years in the making: The Henson Creature Shop's *Dinosaurs* (1991–94).

Opposite, left: Jack Nicholson in Rick Baker's sparing werewolf make-up for Mike Nichols' *Wolf* (1994).

Opposite, right: A closer look at Rick Baker's innovative make-up for Jack Nicholson in *Wolf* (1994).

"THEY PUT THE FEAR OF GOD IN ME!"

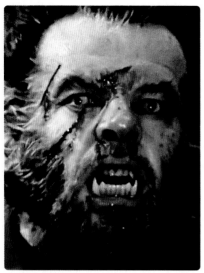

I didn't understand, at first, why the producers of *Wolf* (1994) approached me to do the movie. I told them, "The reality is there's not much make-up in it. Jack Nicholson's not an all-out crazy werewolf. He shouldn't change very much. It has to be subtle."

And they said, "That's why we're coming to you. Because you understand that."

So I told them that I'd have to meet with Jack to show him some designs and discuss the make-up. But they're like, "Whoa! No one sees the Great Oz."

So I said, "Well, I'm not going to do it then. Because there's no way the first time I meet him can be the first time I make him up."

Time passed.

They said, "OK, you can go to Jack's house. You've got forty-five minutes to talk things through and take any casts you need."

I told them, "That's not going to work either. I'm going to Jack's house to talk concept. I'm not taking a life mask in his kitchen."

So I go to Jack's house with my Photoshop design. And it's a modest house, only with Picassos and Renoirs on the walls. Eventually, Jack comes down the stairs in leopard skin shoes.

He tells me, "The way I see it, this'll be the first werewolf movie without any make-up."

And I said, "You know, I almost agree with that. I wouldn't say without any make-up, but definitely with very little, and carefully applied."

I showed him what I meant, and he was on board with it.

We ended up using a life mask from something else Jack had worked on, which worked out fine. And when I wanted to test the make-up, they found a little time for me, though I had to wait several hours for Jack to show up. And when I finally got him in the chair, he was chatting with a friend and smoking a cigar.

I say, "Jack, you know, this glue's kind of flammable."

But he just blows smoke in my face, and tells me, "So be careful."

I get him all made up. He looks at himself in the mirror and says, "My nose looks too cute. I want to change the shape. You got any of those nose plugs?"

I tell him, "No. I don't."

Then Jack's personal make-up artist, Steve Abrums, pipes up: "I'll cut up a sponge and shove bits up your nose."

The sponges widen his nose out, and Jack's like, "That's better."

And I go, "No. It isn't."

Jack shoots me a look.

I tell him, "You're supposed to be a wolf man, not a pig man. You look more like a pig man."

He got real pissed off. But by then, I didn't care. It's what I thought!

So I run up to Mike Nichols, the director, and tell him, "Jack's coming in. He's got shit shoved up his nose. Can you shoot the test with that, but then ask him, 'Is there something in your nose? Can you maybe pull it out?' Just to see what the make-up's supposed to look like?"

So Jack comes in, does a take and then Mike asks him to take the sponges out. Jack shoots me a pissed off look, because he knows I spoke to Mike.

Once we were done with the test, Jack's back in the chair and I'm taking his make-up off. I was pretty sure that was my last day on the movie. But when I'm done, he looks at me and grins. "Ricky boy, I think we're on the right track!"

I had no idea where the fuck that came from, but that's Jack. Jack is Jack, and you've got to take Jack on Jack's terms. And in the end, it was quite a fun shoot.

Rick Baker   281

We shot *District 9* (2009) in Johannesburg, South Africa, during a very tumultuous time. We were in the heart of the Soweto townships, while riots were happening in close-by Alexandra. Joe [Dunckley] and I were responsible for all kinds of make-up effects stuff like the Exo-suit, pulsing puppeteered alien eggs, the gruesome alien autopsy biolab scene, fabricated suits, Baby CJ costume, all the gore and, of course, the Wikus transformation. We also did the alien weapons – those really big guns – so there was a lot we were responsible for.

One time I'll never forget. We were in the middle of shooting a scene in the middle of a shanty town and it was late so we had to wrap. But because we hadn't finished the scene and would be coming back to it in the morning, the set was deemed "hot", so we had to leave all the props and set pieces exactly in place. There was a fella, a local guy who was our overnight security, so before we left we went to go see him to make sure he fully understood how irreplaceable everything was.

So Joe and I go to see him and there he is sitting on top of a pile of junk. And we said, "Hey man, this stuff is very important… Very expensive. So please be careful and, you know… Protect our stuff."

He looked at us, pulls a gun out of his pocket and says, "Anyone who comes near, I will shoot them!"

And we're like, "No! Whoa! Don't shoot anyone! We just want you to scare them away!"

Sarah Rubano

I've turned down every snow movie that's been offered to me since *The Grey* (2011). We shot it during the winter in Smithers, British Columbia, and it was brutal. I'm talking 40 degrees below freezing [-8°F/-22°C].

It was so cold, you'd take your gallon jug of blood, and even with vodka and antifreeze in it, the second you'd pour any out, it would freeze into icicles before hitting the ground.

Once I got stuck in a Portaloo because the door froze shut. I was stuck in there for half an hour, kicking the door and screaming for someone to come and get me the fuck out.

Obviously, you can't bitch too much when Liam Neeson's walking around in a jumper without complaining. Honestly, how he didn't get frostbite, or die of pneumonia, is beyond me. I had, like, fifty layers on, and I was still cold.

I did almost die, though. Probably that, even Liam would have bitched about.

We were about to shoot a scene and they're like, "We need a wolf out there by the tree line. Can you take it over?"

I said, "Sure. No problem."

I threw an animatronic wolf over my shoulders and started walking towards the trees. And immediately, I'm sinking in the snow, up to my shoulders. So I'm throwing the wolf in front of me, then grabbing it, and pulling myself towards it, slowly inching my way towards the tree line.

Eventually, I get there, I set up the wolf and then on the radio they're like, "OK, now hide behind that tree while we shoot."

So I stepped behind the tree, and immediately sank ten feet [3m] in the snow. I reached out and managed to grab a branch. And then I realised I'm right on the edge of a cliff. That this normal-sized tree is actually a 100-foot [30.5m] tree on the edge of a fucking cliff that no one even knew was there.

And I was like, "OH, MY FUCKING GOD. I'M GOING TO DIE!"

Somehow I didn't. Though it did almost scare me to death. And, yeah… I never did a snow movie again.

Mike Fields

Above: Sarah Rubano applies contact lenses to Sharlto Copley for his demanding role as the hapless Wikus Van De Merwe in *District 9* (2009).

Make-ups are often very delicate, yet directors routinely start with wide shots and only get round to close-ups by the end of the day, by which time the make-ups don't look nearly as good.

Working with Mila Kunis on *Oz the Great and Powerful* (2013) was a great partnership. She's magnificent. But I constantly had to be at her side to make sure she didn't damage her witch make-up by eating a big sandwich or lying down on a pillow. And she was great about that, as I know I annoyed the shit out of her by constantly checking on the make-up and touching it up. Because I had to! Honestly, I never got a break on that show.

So after fourteen hours of shooting, by which time Mila's make-up was ratty and way beyond fixing, Sam Raimi would call for her close-up. And when I'd protest, Sam would say, "We'll fix it later."

But I didn't want it to get fixed in post. I wanted it to look pristine on camera. So there were a couple of times when I managed to talk Sam into shooting Mila's close-up first thing in the morning, and it was beautiful.

That's how you shoot a make-up.

Howard Berger

"I NEVER GOT A BREAK ON THAT SHOW."

Left: Peter Montagna adds a final layer of beauty make-up to Mila Kunis as Theodora in *Oz the Great and Powerful* (2013).

Below: Mila Kunis brought the magic to Sam Raimi's *Oz the Great and Powerful* (2013) as Theodora, the Wicked Witch of the West.

Following pages: For *Oz the Great and Powerful* (2013), Gino Crognale ensured every Winkie soldier was ready to stand guard in Emerald City.

"GETTING IT ON, AND KEEPING IT ON, WAS HARD AS HELL."

Every day, Werner Pretorius and I applied Idris Elba's make-up for *Star Trek Beyond* (2016). It was an extremely heavy, multi-piece, silicone make-up, and Idris was sweating before we even put anything on him. So getting it on, and keeping it on, was hard as hell.

The whole film, I was never further than arm's length from him. Before and after each take, I'd use these great, big bath towels to soak up all the sweat that, like, fountained from his ears, or burst from a pinhole someplace else.

At the beginning of the movie, I was like, "Can we make him look shiny? That would be so much easier."

But they're like, "No. We want him flat."

Oh my God.

For the end of the movie, when his character goes from alien to human, Idris wanted to look as gaunt as possible, so he'd sneak off to work out, which obviously made the sweat situation even worse.

The costume people would come out of a tent and tell me, "You know he's in there doing press-ups, right?"

I'd run in. We had these big, industrial fans, so I'd say, "Here, let me cool you down."

But he's like, "I don't want any of that. I can handle the heat."

It was the make-up I was worried about, though! I've never worked so hard in my life.

Mike Fields

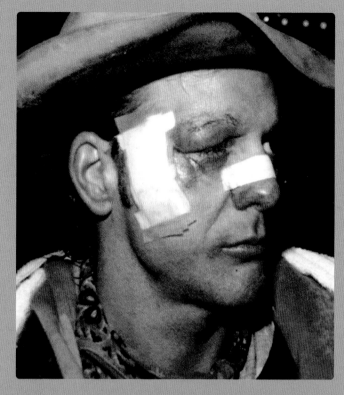

I first worked with Mickey Rourke on *Heaven's Gate* (1980). He was this hotshot actor from New York and they were giving him special treatment. I had to do a make-up test on him on a Sunday, my day off. So we're in his hotel and Ben Nye Jr tells me to set up my stuff. "This could take a while," he says.

"This guy's a real piece of work."

Apparently, Mickey was giving wardrobe and props a hard time with all this quirky stuff he wanted, like a cowboy hat with a little string and bead, and a broken sword like the one Chuck Connors had in the TV show *Branded* (1965–66).

So he comes in and I gave him the same look we gave everybody else: a stained tan make-up, light dirt and a little bit of redness, like he'd been out in the sun. And he goes, "I think my cheeks should be redder."

And I go, "I'll give you a little more, but push it too far and you'll look like a clown."

I added as much red as I could without ruining his make-up, and he goes, "I still think it needs more red."

So I bent over and whispered in his ear, "You know how you've got people breaking swords and tying strings on hats for you? I think that's pretty cool. But don't fuck with me."

I straightened up and clapped my hands. "All right," I said, "you're done!"

"PUSH IT TOO FAR AND YOU'LL LOOK LIKE A CLOWN."

And he just looked up at me and gave me the Mickey smirk. That's how we got introduced to each other.

Later on, he was doing a big scene with Christopher Walken and Geoffrey Lewis inside a cabin. We were shooting it over two days. So he's working with Walken, who'd just won a Best Supporting Actor Academy Award for *The Deer Hunter* (1978), and Michael Cimino, who'd won Best Director and Best Film. And I think Mickey was a little nervous.

After they'd wrapped for the day, I found him sobbing. Evidently, he'd started flubbing his lines and Michael Cimino had taken off his baseball cap and beaten him across the face with it, screaming, "You stupid idiot. How come you don't know your lines?"

Opposite, above: On *Star Trek Beyond* (2016), Idris Elba sorely tested his Krall make-up, designed by Joel Harlow and applied by Werner Pretorius and Mike Fields, who'd spend the remainder of his day shadowing the star on damage control.

Top: Mickey Rourke took his licks on *Homeboy* (1988), courtesy of make-up artist Ken Diaz.

Above: A beaten and battered Mickey Rourke in *Homeboy* (1988).

Now, Mickey and I were boxing fans. We had that in common. So before he came to work the next day, I went to the costume truck and found a blue terrycloth robe. I got some aluminium foil from catering, cut out some letters and glued them to the back of the robe. When Mickey showed up, he sat quietly in the chair as I did his make-up. Later, when it was time to go to set, I pulled out the robe and held it up and said, "Hey Mickey, check this out!"

On the back it said 'Mickey Montana' with a star in the middle. And I threw it over his shoulders and said, "Come on, champ. Let's go get 'em."

We marched to set like a fighter and his trainer on their way to the ring. I'm rubbing his shoulders. I spritz him down, gave him a slap on the cheek and said to him, "Take him out, Champ!"

He went in there and smoked that scene! And that was the beginning of our relationship.

Our next movie together was Barfly (1987).

Now, Mickey always wants a lot of make-up. He loves it. He uses it to create his character. But after a week or two, he doesn't need it to find the character any longer, and he doesn't want to be bothered with it. So once we'd established his make-up, it was a constant battle for me to maintain it. And I do mean, literally, a battle. Like, we'd end up having fist fights on set.

If I bent over to grab something out of my make-up kit, he'd punch me on the arm. And it escalated. One time, he backed me into a closet. I confused him by acting more hurt than I really was, then I grabbed his wrist and punched him as hard as I could on his forearm. He screamed. Then I kneed him in the stomach and punched him in the chest. We were tripping over equipment and knocking over furniture. It was crazy.

But you know what? In that film it worked for him, because he was doing all these fights with Frank Stallone and it helped get his energy up. A big part of the relationship I had with Mickey was getting him ready to smoke a scene, and that continued in our next film together, a boxing drama called Homeboy (1988).

I found a lot of times that directors were jealous of our relationship. They hated it. As a result, my work on Homeboy was sabotaged. I did three levels of prosthetic injury make-ups on Mickey for the big boxing scene at the end. But the director edited the rounds of the fight out of sequence, totally messing up the injury progression. He also flipped the negative at times, causing Mickey's swollen eye to switch back and forth from one side of his face to the other.

By the time we worked on Johnny Handsome (1989), Mickey was kind of bored of acting. He didn't think it was a manly enough occupation. So on that movie, I think he was just collecting a pay cheque. Our fights were less about his performance and more about frustration.

One morning my sciatic nerve went out and I couldn't get my

"MICKEY LET OUT THIS BLOOD-CURDLING SCREAM."

socks and shoes on, which, in turn, made me late for work. For some reason, Mickey felt I was late because I'd been out all night partying. When I bent down carefully to put some brushes away in my make-up box, Mickey put his foot on my shoulder and shoved me over hard to the side. This wrenched my back even more and caused excruciating pain.

I was so pissed off at him, but because my back was out I needed to get an equaliser. I went and found an 8-foot [2.4m] stick and taped a powder puff to the end. When Mickey came out of rehearsal, I loaded powder on the puff and said, "Hey Mickey, it's time for your touch-up!"

I swung the stick at his head. Mickey went to block the hit with his arms, so I adjusted my swing and cracked him across the shins. I then backed him up, stabbing at him with the broken pieces.

It got ridiculous. Mickey was beginning to feel claustrophobic and didn't want to wear the facial deformity prosthetic any more. One day, we were about to shoot the scene where bandages are removed, revealing his freshly surgically reconstructed face. I believe that Mickey's anticipated claustrophobia, from having his face wrapped in bandages, was causing him to have high anxiety. He would not allow me to paint on his fresh surgical scar before going to set.

Once on set, we did multiple rehearsals. After each rehearsal, I attempted to apply the scars. Each time Mickey would turn and walk away. Now camera was ready and I needed to quickly paint on the scars, wrap his face and shoot the scene. This time I snuck up behind him, which surprised Mickey. He quickly turned, walked away and found himself trapped in a corner of the set where he could find no exit.

He was like a caged animal. He went nuts! To create an immediate escape route, he started knocking over lights and C-stands. Mickey then went to his fancy motorhome, took a broom handle and smashed all the cabinets and mirrors. We had to stop production for a few hours that day.

Towards the end of filming, Mickey started talking about the next movie he wanted me to do with him. I said, "Mickey, we can't do another movie together right now. One of us is gonna end up in the hospital, man."

We took a break and came back together for a film called *F.T.W.* (1994). Mickey was in a much better place, and this time it was all about the performance. He did some sense memory exercises prior to this big emotional scene. Talked about how his mother had left their father when he was like, eleven. And then she married an abusive cop and he'd always have to protect his younger brother Joey.

So he did this big scene and he was great, but I asked the director to give him another take. And I went up to him, acting like I was

Above: Mickey Rourke quickly learned to turn to Ken Diaz when required to look the part. Here, his Charles Bukowski-inspired character from Barfly (1987) was right up Ken's alley.

doing a touch-up, and I whispered in his ear, "Hey Mickey… Joey's dead."

Mickey let out this blood-curdling scream, which startled the crew.

I tell the director, "Roll, roll!"

The camera started rolling and Mickey went into dialogue. He was incredible. Tears were running down faces of crew members. It was the most emotional scene I've ever seen filmed. And those are our bookends: from the boxing thing for *Heaven's Gate* to breaking everyone's heart in *F.T.W.* I played a major part in that performance and Mickey dedicated that scene to me.

That's our relationship in a nutshell.

LESSONS LEARNED

You don't interview fifty-plus make-up masters, and a bunch of brilliant actors and filmmakers, without gathering a little wisdom.

We're not just talking about tricks of the trade, or industry survival tips, but also good, general life advice. Insights that apply to really anyone making their way in the world.

So even if you're not pursuing a career in make-up effects, don't skip this final chapter. Because everyone we spoke to worked hard to get where they are. And they all have something interesting to impart.

Growing up in South Side, Pittsburgh, felt like growing up on an island. We were so cut off from the rest of the world. So make-up effects was not a job I even realised existed.

Later, when I learned it was a real thing, it didn't occur to me that black people could do it, because I never saw anybody of colour doing it. Still today, kids directly link what they can do based upon who they see doing it, and I'm not just talking colour, but gender, size and shape.

After I graduated from high school, I made it a point to help out at other schools, running the make-up departments for school plays.

Once this little kid came up to me, and he goes, "You can be a make-up artist?"

I told him, "Yes."

After that, every day I was there, he'd come back to watch me. He wasn't even a part of the play. And I've no idea what happened to him after. But maybe that was the spark that set him on his path.

Sometimes that's all it takes, I think – seeing someone like yourself doing something you'd never imagined you could do. Suddenly it becomes an option. Suddenly it's a possibility.

Carey Jones

I always loved masks.

The Eighties were the heyday of mask sculpture, for me, because that heavy rubber monster style echoed what was going on in the movies then.

There's so much involved in producing multipiece make-ups. It's so technical. But masks you can make by yourself. So just sculpt something. Make a mould. Pour a mask. Paint the mask. From concept to completion, you can do it all at home, alone, at your kitchen table.

That's how I built my portfolio. So when anyone asks me how to get started, I always tell them, "Make some masks."

Just sit there and do it. Blast out some sculptures. All you need is clay and your hands. You don't even need any tools.

Dive headfirst in, and the more you produce, the better you'll get. It's inevitable.

Masks have been so great for me. Masks put me on the map.

Mikey Rotella

Previous pages: Kazu Hiro applies a finishing touch to his larger-than-life Andy Warhol sculpture.

Top: Greg Nicotero spritzes Carey Jones' River Ghost Alien for *Predators* (2010).

Above: Mikey Rots strikes a pose with a couple of his creations.

Opposite, top: Richard Taylor menaced by orcs, behind the scenes of *The Lord of the Rings* trilogy (2001–03).

Opposite: Eryn Krueger Mekash on mould duty.

I'd like to think that anyone can be successful at what they aspire to do if they have a combination of passion, enthusiasm, tenacity and a dose of talent. I see passion as what's in your heart. Enthusiasm is the ability to turn passion into action. Then you need tenacity, which is possibly the core of my ability.

I'm not greatly talented, but boy, I've got grit and I will never let go of the bone until the job is done. Of course, you need some talent, but that's possibly irrelevant if you don't possess the first three things in large amounts.

Richard Taylor

"ALL YOU NEED IS CLAY AND YOUR HANDS."

When I was younger, I didn't ask enough questions. Early in my career, I worked with Rick Baker on a miniseries called *Something Is Out There* (1988), and I just always wanted to ask him stuff. But I didn't, because I thought maybe he'd get mad at me or something.

Really though, what's the worst that could have happened? Maybe he'd have said, "I can't answer that right away, but I'll get back to you later."

We've been friends a long time now and these days I ask him questions all the time. Which, of course, he's always happy to answer. I could have known all these things years ago, if only I'd not been so worried about speaking up.

So I always tell people, "Ask questions."

Eryn Krueger Mekash

Don't be afraid of trying things. No matter what, you'll get something out of it. If you try something that doesn't work, it's not a failure – that's the process. You can't get to where you need to be without first trying all sorts of different things.

Don't let the pressures get to you. Respect the brief, trust your instincts. Create mood boards, storyboards… Really dig in and experiment with textures, colours… You'll get there!

David White

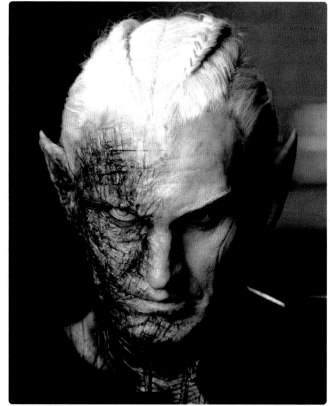

If I'd known at ten years old that someday Rick Baker would be posting photos of his stuff on the internet, every day, for everyone to see, my head would have just been blown.

I hope kids today appreciate how lucky they are, because back in our day we had to hunt for photos in magazines, then study them with magnifying glasses for clues about what materials he used, and how he did things.

Norman Cabrera

Top, Left: Sofia Boutella as Ahmanet in David White's make-up creation for *The Mummy* (2017).

Top, right: David White's make-up on Christopher Eccleston as Malekith in *Thor: Dark World* (2013).

Left: A young Norman Cabrera – and friends – in his Florida bedroom.

Above: Norman Cabrera and his mentor Rick Baker during prep on *Gremlins 2: The New Batch* (1990).

Back when I started, I wanted to be Dick Smith. I copied everything he did, but nothing ever came out as well. I realised that as my brain, my hands and my eyes weren't Dick's, I could never be as good at what he did. That I had to find my own voice.

As soon as I figured that out, I improved.

So while it's fine, of course, to admire and be inspired by great make-up artists, what's most important is that you figure out what it is that YOU really want to do.

Find your own voice.

Kazu Hiro

Most people who watch me apply a make-up, they don't know where I'm headed. A lot of times I don't either! But I know I'm going somewhere.

Don't believe step-by-step instructions that tell you this is the way. There's no such thing as THE way. It's just A way.

To me, a make-up's only wrong if it doesn't look great. And I don't care how you get there. I don't care what you use. I don't care if you stand on your head when you do it.

All that matters is the end result. And that's not how it looks to the eye, but to the camera.

So do it YOUR way. Because that's how you'll grow as an artist.

Greg Nelson

Top, left and right: Kazu Hiro's beautiful larger-than-life sculptures of Abraham Lincoln and Jimi Hendrix, respectively.

Above: Kazu Hiro sculpts another one of his amazing larger-than-life art works.

Right: Designed by Rick Baker, Sharon Baird's *Ratboy* (1986) make-up is applied by Greg Nelson.

Dick Smith showed me a photograph once of a make-up that had been sent to him by someone wanting to take his course. And it was truly terrible.

He then pulled out another photograph, of the most exquisite sculpture of Alfred Hitchcock I'd ever seen. There were close-ups of the neck and jaw area where you could see pores stretched with fat. It was perfect.

Dick said, "These are both from the same artist. I told him after the first photo to go take some art courses and then come back to me. And this is what happened."

I learned in that moment that you can never judge from a person's early work what they might become.

Todd McIntosh

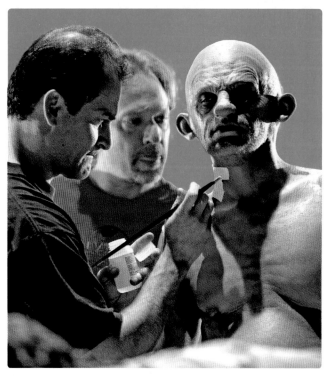

Keep practising.

So many times, I'm interviewing people. Young artists. I'm looking through their book, and the only thing I see is what they did in school.

Thing is, when you're at school, you've got an instructor who'll push you and give you tweaks. But I want to see what you've done since. What you've done on your own. What you've managed without being spoon-fed everything.

The more you do, the more you learn. Sure, you'll screw up, but that's OK. Next time, you'll know what to do. So don't be afraid to screw up.

Just do it!

Louie Zakarian

The most interesting potential employees are always the most well-rounded, so make sure your portfolio represents a variety of techniques.

Greg Nicotero

Opposite, top: Dick Smith applies the old-age Barnabas Collins make-up to actor Jonathan Frid for *House of Dark Shadows* (1970).

Opposite: Gino Crognale and Greg Nicotero ready Nick Stahl as Yellow Bastard for *Sin City* (2005). Made up blue for the shoot, the character's colour was digitally altered to yellow during the VFX process of this highly stylised film.

This Page: The many faces of zombified Greg Nicotero on *The Walking Dead* (2010–22).

Don't be too good at what you don't want to do.

I've seen people get trapped, like if they're a pretty good artist but great at making moulds, often they're stuck making moulds and they're unhappy.

So if you don't want to do something, don't be good at it. Or at least, don't let people know you're good at it.

Steve Wang

Perc Westmore once told me to observe everyone, as that way, you either learn what to do, or what not to do.

Leonard Engelman

How you get on with the actor in your chair is no less important than how you do your make-up.

Greg Nelson

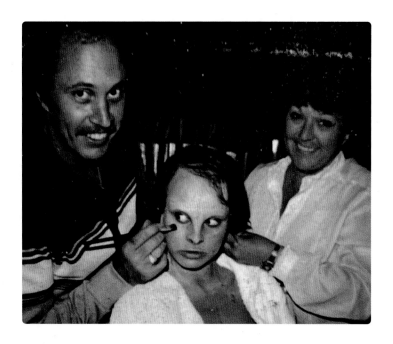

"DON'T BE TOO GOOD AT WHAT YOU DON'T WANT TO DO."

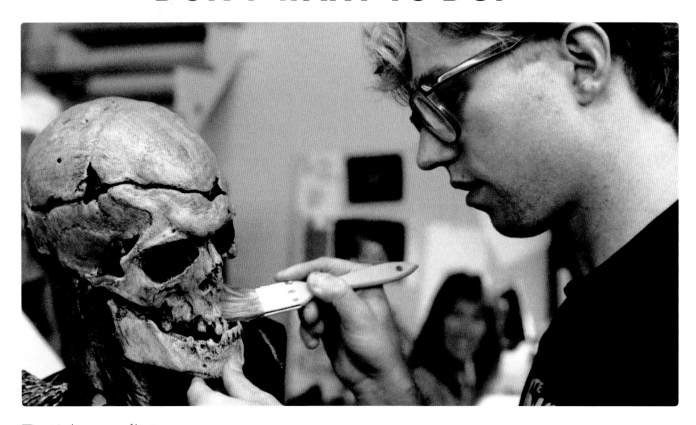

Best is the enemy of better.

Take pride in your work, but don't be precious, because it's not all about your make-up.

Garrett Immel

Top: Leonard Engelman and Janice Brandow apply an early-stage transformation make-up, designed by Thomas and Bari Burman, to actress Nastassja Kinski for *Cat People* (1982).

Above: Garrett Immel prepares a Deadite for battle on Sam Raimi's *Army of Darkness* (1992).

on't bullshit. When you're young, if you make a mistake and try to hide it, you might think you can pull the wool over everybody's eyes, but it'll come out.

Everything always comes out.

Rob Freitas

"EVERYBODY CALM THE FUCK DOWN."

When you're young you make mistakes. There were times I was nearly driven to tears. You just feel incompetent. Like you let the production down. The first time it happened, I was young, I almost ran away.

I was having an anxiety attack, then I looked across the sound stage, saw the big stage door open and I said to myself, "Hey, guess what? I can walk out that fucking door, and none of you can stop me. What are you going to do about it? Nothing!"

Then you mature and you realise, "Hey, let's just stipple a little colour over it."

You get to the point where you're like, "All right, everything's gonna be OK. Everybody calm the fuck down."

Mike McCracken Jr

Everybody suffers, sometimes, from not being able to finish their make-up. You could do it for hours. Do it forever!

That's when you have to walk away. Take a break. Let the actors go put on their costumes or something. Because when they come back, usually you realise you've done enough. That it doesn't need any more red or whatever else you were stuck on.

Eryn Krueger Mekash

Top, left: Rob Freitas marks out his mould division line on a sculpture by Moto Hata. Rob has made it a mission to help complete the artwork Moto created before his untimely passing in 2009.

Above: Two McCrackens for the price of one: Mike Jr and his prolific father, Mike Sr.

Opposite: Eryn Krueger Mekash completes a make-up on Mirjam Clement for a MAC demonstration on combining prosthetics and beauty.

299

Take what you're doing very seriously. Believe absolutely that what you're doing is important. But at the same time, understand it is only part of the process.

Don't make the mistake of thinking you're at the centre of it all. We are just a cog. So keep your head down and just do the best you can.

Jeremy Woodhead

Below: Michael McCracken Sr transforms his daughter with a cybernetic design of his own.

Bottom: Todd McIntosh completing one of the many demons he helped bring to life for *Buffy The Vampire Slayer* (1997–2011), created with John Vulich of Optic Nerve, who made the prosthetics.

"DON'T MAKE THE MISTAKE OF THINKING YOU'RE AT THE CENTRE OF IT ALL."

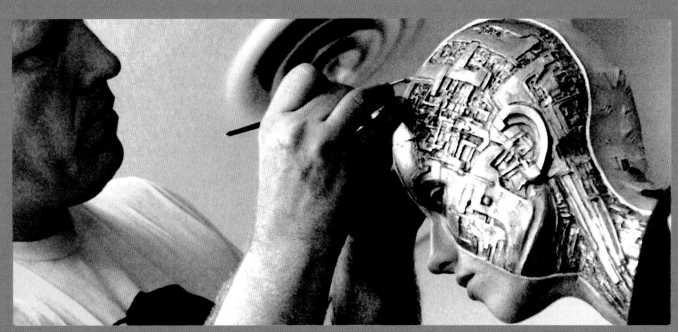

In application, you have to know your parameters. Say you've got an hour-and-a-half before they want your make-up on set. You have to evaluate what you can do in an hour-and-a-half to get the desired effect.

If painting the prosthetic is going to take a lot of time, you have to figure out the quickest way to do the gluing process. Or maybe it's the other way around and you take time with the gluing and simplify the painting. Either way, you have to parse the process in your head before you start.

A lot of people don't do that, though. They prefer to wing it and end up wasting a great deal of time on one thing, or going over their time limits on another.

The thing is, make-up artists are not alone in the room, so to speak, although some definitely think they are. You have to learn that the entire medium is one big mess of connecting wires and times and schedules and limits and money and that other people have to do their job, too. We just have to plug ourselves into whatever our time slot is and make it work.

Todd McIntosh

Above: Stephen Immel is transformed into Abraham Lincoln by his aspiring make-up artist son, Garrett Immel.

Right, top to bottom: Tom Savini is made up as The Creep by Everett Burrell, who designed the make-up in his hotel room while shooting *Creepshow 2* (1987) on location in Prescott, Arizona.

"MAKING A MOVIE ISN'T JUST ABOUT APPLYING A PERFECT MAKE-UP."

Don't get bogged down and lose focus trying to make something perfect when you can make it excellent and fulfil your other obligations. Because making a movie isn't just about applying a perfect make-up.

It's also about getting to set on time, keeping the make-up fresh all day and making sure your actor isn't ready to kill you by the time you're done.

Garrett Immel

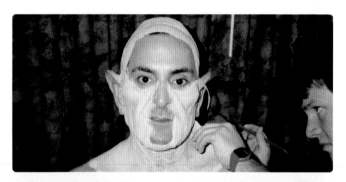

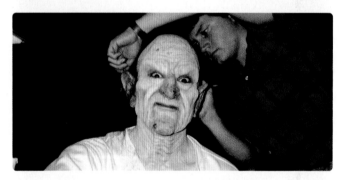

I was a little Italian kid reading *Famous Monsters*. Suddenly I'm in the fucking Vietnam war. Seeing all these horrible things, thinking about make-up effects actually saved me. I'd focus, not on the death, but how to recreate it.

I'm probably the only make-up artist who has seen the real thing. That's why everything I do has to be anatomically correct. I have to get the same feeling from the fake stuff that I did from the real stuff, or else it doesn't work for me.

Like in a movie where they go to the crime scene the next day and the blood's red. After 24 hours, though, it should be dark brown. I also hate it when an actor playing a cadaver closes his mouth, trying to look pretty for the camera. But when you're dead, none of your muscles work. Your jaw is slack.

Danny Trejo is excellent at portraying a dead body. He just lets everything go. I think maybe he had to play dead in his life, like when he was in prison? So yeah. I hate fake things. I brought that back from Vietnam.

Tom Savini

It drives me nuts to see a great wound make-up ruined because it's covered in too much blood. It's not realistic and it's not artistic. You have to be strategic about where you place the blood. It has to look organic.

Tami Lane

"YOU'RE THERE TO MAKE IT WORK."

If you're going to set and, let's say you're doing a slit throat, know two other ways to do that gag. Because, what if you go to Albuquerque, you open your box, and your slit throat's not in there?

You gotta go to Home Depot. You've gotta find a craft store. You've gotta figure out a way to make a slit throat out of what you can find. Because the movie shoots tonight and production doesn't want to hear, "Oh, the pieces got lost."

What they want to hear is, "I'll make it work."

That's what keeps you working. That's what gets you respect in this business. Just being able to pull shit out of your ass without complaining about it.

So don't bitch. Just make it work. You're there to make it work.

Stephen Prouty

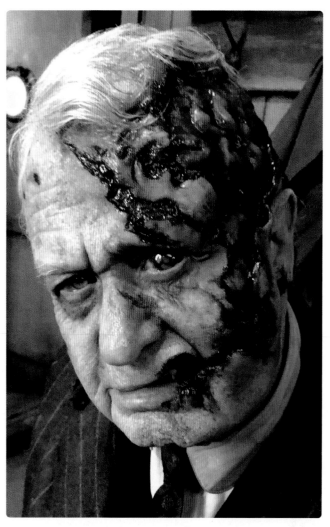

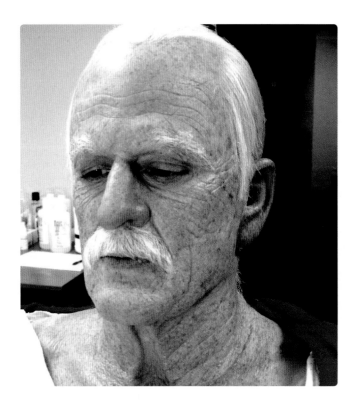

Opposite: The Maestro of Gore, Tom Savini, mingling with a menagerie in his mask room at home.

Top: Richard Blackburn made up as Dead Chester Sampson for the Netflix series *Jupiter's Legacy* (2021). Tami Lane was the prosthetic make-up supervisor on the show under the KNB EFX banner.

Left: Johnny Knoxville made up as Irving Zisman for *Bad Grandpa* (2013), by Stephen Prouty, Bart Mixon, Jamie Kelman and Will Huff.

Above: Stephen Prouty refreshing his alien on the set of *The Orville* (2017–2022).

Beyond even your talent, what matters most is your attitude, personality and focus. Even if you're not the best artist, if you try hard, you're dedicated and you go with the flow, you'll get hired all the time, because people will like you and they'll see that you care.

We all know amazing artists who are pains and you just can't be around them for long. They could be Rembrandt for all I care, but no one will want to hire them.

So be positive, friendly and enjoy yourself. Be the sort of person who people want to hang out with. If you can do that and love what you do, that's the key to success.

Bill Corso

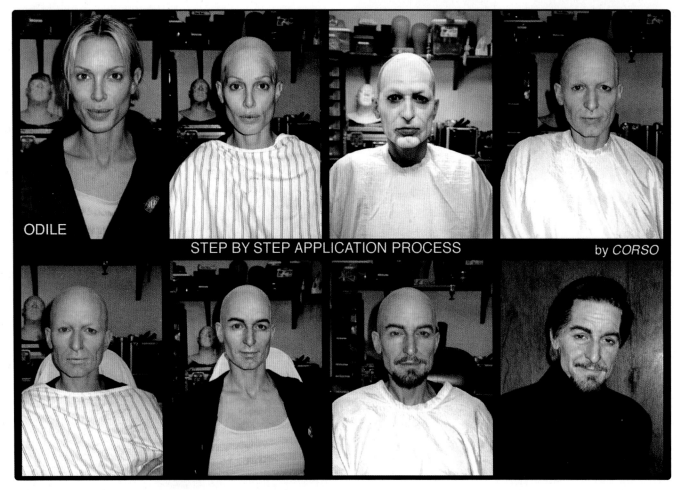

ODILE

STEP BY STEP APPLICATION PROCESS

by *CORSO*

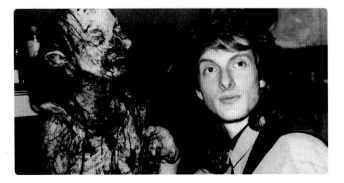

"BE THE SORT OF PERSON WHO PEOPLE WANT TO HANG OUT WITH."

Half of this job is designing, sculpting and having fun creating make-ups, but the other half is business, and you have to learn to take care. You have to be wary of the people around you, because it's amazing what some of them will do, given the opportunity.

That said, I love what I do and I have lots of fun. Just be careful who you work with.

Greg Cannom

"WHAT MATTERS MOST IS THE CRAFT ITSELF."

What film you're on is less important than the work you produce. What matters most is the craft itself.

You're going to be involved in a variety of projects. Some will be good. Others will be shit. But all of them are going to present obstacles and challenges, and they're what you have to embrace. It's when you overcome those things, that you produce work you can be proud of.

Blair Clark

Opposite, top left: Alex Winter in his amazing Ricky make-up, created by Bill Corso under Steve Johnson's supervision, for the film *Freaked* (1993).

Opposite, top right: Ruby Dee as Mother Abagail, another outstanding make-up created and applied by Bill Corso for Mick Garris's adaptation of Stephen King's *The Stand* (1994).

Opposite, centre: How to transform a beautiful woman into a distinguished, older man – Bill Corso uses prosthetics, hairpieces and skill to successfully gender swap his wife Odile.

Opposite, bottom: Bill Corso on *The Boneyard* (1991), his first time as department head. Some say Bill's strength flows from his mighty locks.

Above: Greg Cannom's iconic Ozzy Osbourne werewolf make-up for the music video, *Bark at the Moon* (1983).

Left: In the final shot of *Thriller* (1983), Greg Cannom enters the frame as this iconic zombie. Many of the make-up team played zombies in Michael Jackson's music video, including Rick Baker and Kevin Yagher.

Mick: For years there was a fight between practical and digital effects, but when the two sides come together, when the best of both combine, it's pure magic.

Computer effects alone, to me, look like video-game graphics. They have no heft. But when sophisticated animatronics or make-ups are enhanced by, say, CGI to make a creature's pupils dilate, it's that extra 5 per cent that breathes life into the effect.

Howard: You're absolutely right. It was like on the first *Narnia* movie where James McAvoy was in the Mr Tumnus make-up from the waist up and all-digital below. The CG effects guys kept inviting me into the editing room to see what they were doing, but I wanted to wait until everything was finished. Then the first time I saw James walk out from behind the lamp post, it took my breath away.

Mick: It used to be a competition, but now, if people are smart about it, it's a marriage. Together, practical and digital can achieve more than either can manage alone.

Mick Garris and Howard Berger

"THEY'RE BOWLING TROPHIES."

Tom [Woodruff] and I worked together on *Death Becomes Her* (1992). There was only room for one of us, though, to be included in the submission for the Best Visual Effects Academy Award.

It was our first nomination and we tossed a coin to see whose name would be on it. Before we tossed it, we agreed that the winner had to feel really bad for the other guy.

Tom took heads and won the toss. After he left the room, I kept flipping the coin, but it just kept coming up heads. I double checked, but it was not a two-headed coin.

Tom had won, fair and square.

I love the Oscars. It's always a great show, and the drinks are free. But it's like Stan [Winston] used to say: "They're bowling trophies."

If you obsess over them, they'll mess you up. They're a thrill. They're validation. But they're not the goal.

Alec Gillis

Opposite, top: On the set of *Splice* (2009) with KNB team members (left to right) Kyle Glencross, Shane Zander, Chris Bridges, Howard Berger and Tami Lane.

Opposite, bottom: Standing proud with the Aslan riding puppet on *The Chronicles of Narnia: The Lion, the Witch and the Wardrobe* (2005) are (left to right) David Wogh, Jeff Himmel, Sonny Tilders, Rob Derry and Howard Berger.

Left: The Jack Nicholson werewolf puppet created by ADI for *Wolf* (1994). The puppet's design was based on Rick Baker's make-up.

Above: Rather than split the Oscar in half, Tom Woodruff (l) took the entire award home after he and Alec Gillis won it for their work on *Death Becomes Her* (1992).

We were just about done with *Predator* (1987), and I remember Stan [Winston] came up to me one night and said, "I just want to say, you did a really great job on this thing."

Being a kind of self-hating perfectionist at the time, I was like, "No, you know, I could have done better. I wish we'd had more time…"

And Stan's like, "You know, you should just take a compliment. It's OK to be proud of something you've done. You don't have to hate everything, because if you're not enjoying this, what are you doing it for?"

That made a lot of sense to me and helped me get into a healthier frame of mind. Today, I subscribe to James Cameron's philosophy: Don't be a perfectionist. Be a greatist! It doesn't have to be perfect. It just has to be great.

I can live with that!

Steve Wang

"IT'S OK TO BE PROUD OF SOMETHING YOU'VE DONE."

Richard Taylor gave me some of the best advice ever: "A good career is not just made up of the projects you do – it's also made up of the projects you don't do."

Tami Lane

Above: On the set of *The Lord of the Rings: The Return of the King* (2003), Richard Taylor reveals Lawrence Makoare's Gothmog to director Peter Jackson for the first time.

Below: Richard Taylor was instrumental in helping Peter Jackson populate the world of J. R. R. Tolkien's *The Lord of the Rings* with all creatures great and small.

To survive in this business, you have to be resilient, and in a thousand different ways. You have to be able to do the hours. To think on your feet. To have a vision, and know how to execute that vision.

You need staying power.

Lois Burwell

"ENJOY THE SURPRISE OF EACH NEW DISCOVERY."

If I'd known how hard this job was, how long the hours are and how much stress you have to deal with, I might never have become a make-up artist. And that would have been a great shame.

I say then, simply, follow your heart. Do what you want to do. Do things your own way. And enjoy the surprise of each new discovery.

Close your eyes, and jump!

Montse Ribé

Stay focused, be humble, keep learning. Trust your creative intuitions and be grateful that you get to work in such an amazing industry.

Sarah Rubano

Top: Sarah Rubano makes up Dane DeHaan for his role as the Green Goblin in *The Amazing Spider-Man 2* (2014). The make-up was designed and created by the magicians at the Weta Workshop, who entrusted Sarah with the final on-set visualization.

Left: Montse Ribé sculpts the maquette of Young Hellboy for *Hellboy II: The Golden Army*, a character she later played in the film.

AFTERWORD

BY SETH MACFARLANE

I believed in Sloth.

If you've bought this book, I probably don't need to tell you who Sloth is, but just in case there are upsetting gaps in your film education, he was the deformed younger brother of the Fratelli crime family in *The Goonies*, and was also the prosthetic make-up creation of artists Craig Reardon and Tom Burman. And when I say, "I believed in Sloth," I mean it. I didn't know this was a football star in make-up. I thought this was a real actor whose facial characteristics made him a perfect fit for the role. He scared me at first, then delighted me when he freed Chunk and joined the heroes.

This was decades before CGI became something filmmakers could rely on as needed for storytelling, an era when such visions could still only be realized with prosthetics, make-up and animatronics. The totality of the entertainment industry's effects makeup work during those decades is a great and often unheralded achievement – yet the creativity and sweat that brought Sloth to life was never the point; the point was for me to believe he was real.

It certainly wasn't the only time in my life a prosthetic make-up effects artist made me believe. In 1985, I saw the movie *Mask*, which was the story of real-life Rocky Dennis, and his struggle to cope with craniodiaphyseal dysplasia, a serious form of bone disorder. I was unfamiliar with Eric Stoltz, so, at twelve years old, I just assumed that Rocky Dennis was portrayed by an actor with a similar disability. Little did I know that I was seeing the work of make-up artist Michael Westmore, whose prosthetic creation captured both the medical reality of Rocky's condition, as well as the humanity of the individual beneath.

And of course, we all remember Rick Baker and Stuart Freeborn's achievement in which they brought a Tatooine cantina to life, where aliens drank while other aliens performed what sounded like Glenn Miller tunes, a tour de force which is still a benchmark regularly acknowledged by people in the industry. (This is a *Star Wars* reference, and if you didn't know that, I really don't know why you're buying this book, but whatever.)

That was my life as an audience member, and I don't think I truly understood the significance of the make-up artist until I created my science fiction series, *The Orville*, and began working with make-up wizard Howard Berger and his team of practical magicians at KNB EFX Group. Here I was engaged with a true artist, who would take an at-best vague stage direction that identified a character as an alien, and somehow bring it to life.

Howard wasn't just designing Halloween masks (although all his work would make GREAT Halloween masks); his creations lived on their own and worked with the actor inside the prosthetic to create a new species. And he did it every week – not just for our alien lead characters, like the authoritarian-minded Krill, or the single-sex Moclans, or Dann the engineer, or Rob Lowe's Darulio, but for literally dozens of others lurking in the background of our spaceship.

Right from the beginning, when I saw what he could do, I took it for granted that Howard would be able to fill up the world that was in my head with an unending variety of believable aliens (I'm not exaggerating that I took him for granted – episode two took place in an intergalactic zoo). And he never let me, or the audience, down. Howard's designs were always filtered through his own extensive experience, striking a sophisticated and intelligent balance between what was exciting but achievable, fantastic but believable, adding humor, pathos and/or menace where necessary, and always – always – retaining some identifiable spark of relatability in even the most exotic designs.

His work cemented my appreciation not just for his talent, but the talent of all his colleagues and their predecessors, many of whom are celebrated in this book. They are true artists who make believers of us all.

FILMOGRAPHIES

I grew up with *Fangoria*. I'm a Fango Kid! Make-up effects guys were my rock stars.

The artistry involved in what they do is really no different than that of any fine artist.
Their pieces belong in museums.

Fred Raskin

As a director I work with actors, cinematographers, composers… All sorts of
talented, creative people. But if the make-up effects don't work, nothing works.

That's why I think of make-up effects guys as the ultimate magicians. The
suspension of disbelief is what their magic's all about, and I'm in awe of them.

Mick Garris

Gino Acevedo *Wes Craven's New Nightmare (1994), Wishmaster (1997), Spawn (1997), The Lord of the Rings: The Two Towers (2002), The Lord of the Rings: The Return of the King (2003), King Kong (2005), 30 Days of Night (2007), The Lovely Bones (2009), The Hobbit: The Battle of the Five Armies (2014).*

Rick Baker *The Autobiography of Miss Jane Pittman (1974; E), An American Werewolf in London (1981; AA), Greystoke: The Legend of Tarzan, Lord of the Apes (1984), Harry and the Hendersons (1988; AA), Coming to America (1989), Ed Wood (1994; AA), The Nutty Professor (1996; AA), Men in Black (1998; AA), How the Grinch Stole Christmas (2000; AA), The Wolfman (2011; AA).*

Vivian Baker *Great Expectations (1998), 21 Grams (2003), A Series of Unfortunate Events (2004), Grey Gardens (2009; E), Pirates of the Caribbean: On Stranger Tides (2011), Oz the Great and Powerful (2013), Jurassic World (2015), Bombshell (2019; AA), The Rhythm Section (2020).*

Howard Berger *(Co-founder of KNB EFX Group) Day of the Dead (1985), Aliens (1986), Predator (1986), Harry and the Hendersons (1987), Casino (1995), Boogie Nights (1997), Kill Bill Vol. 1& 2 (2003/04), The Chronicles of Narnia: The Lion, the Witch and the Wardrobe (2005; AA), Hitchcock (2012), Oz the Great and Powerful (2013), Lone Survivor (2013), The Orville (2017-Present).*

Doug Bradley *Star of Hellraiser (1987), Hellbound: Hellraiser II (1988), Nightbreed (1990), Hellraiser III: Hell on Earth (1992).*

Lois Burwell *Gregory's Girl (1980), Legend (1985), Highlander (1986), The Muppet Christmas Carol (1992), Braveheart (1995; AA), Mission: Impossible (1996), Saving Private Ryan (1998), The Last Samurai (2003), War of the Worlds (2005), Lincoln (2012).*

Norman Cabrera *Harry and the Hendersons (1987), Beauty and the Beast (1987-1990), Gremlins 2: The New Batch (1990), From Dusk Till Dawn (1996), Spawn (1997), Kill Bill: Vol. 1 (2003), Hellboy (2004), The Cabin in the Woods (2011), The Walking Dead (2010-2022), Scary Stories to Tell in the Dark (2019).*

John Caglione Jr *C.H.U.D. (1984), Dick Tracy (1991; AA), Chaplin (1992), Zelig (1983), Angels in America (2003; E), The Insider (1999), 3:10 to Yuma (2007), The Dark Knight (2009), The Amazing Spider-Man 2 (2014), The Irishman (2019).*

Bruce Campbell *Star of The Evil Dead (1981), Evil Dead II (1987), Army of Darkness (1992), Hercules: The Legendary Journeys (1995-1999), Escape from L.A. (1996), Bubba Ho-Tep (2002), Sky High (2005), My Name is Bruce (2007), Burn Notice (2007-2013), Ash vs Evil Dead (2015-2018).*

Greg Cannom *The Howling (1981), The Lost Boys (1987), Hook (1991), Hoffa (1992), Bram Stoker's Dracula (1992; AA), Mrs Doubtfire (1994; AA), Titanic (1997), A Beautiful Mind (2001), The Curious Case of Benjamin Button (2008, AA), Vice (2018; AA).*

Blair Clark *Enemy Mine (1985), The Fly (1986), RoboCop (1987), Dragonheart (1996), Starship Troopers (1997), Armageddon (1998), Hellboy (2004), The Spiderwick Chronicles (2008), Ted (2012), Clifford the Big Red Dog (2021).*

Bill Corso *The Stand (1994; E), The Shining (1997; E), Galaxy Quest (1999), A Series of Unfortunate Events (2004; AA), Click (2006), Grey Gardens (2009; E), 42 (2013), Foxcatcher (2014), Deadpool (2016), Bill & Ted Face the Music (2020).*

Mark Coulier *Merlin (1998; E), Arabian Nights (2000; E), Harry Potter and the Goblet of Fire (2005), X-Men: First Class (2011),*

The Iron Lady (2012; AA), The Grand Budapest Hotel (2014; AA), Dracula Untold (2014), Suspiria (2018), Stan & Ollie (2018), Pinocchio (2019).

John Criswell *Critters (1986), Cellar Dweller (1987), Dinosaurs (1991-1994), The Chronicles of Narnia: The Lion, the Witch and the Wardrobe (2005), Where the Wild Things Are (2009), Predators (2010), Fright Night (2011).*

Ken Diaz *Heaven's Gate (1980), Roar (1981), Fright Night (1985), Dad (1989), Star Trek: The Next Generation (1987-1994; E), Alien Nation (1989 1990; E), The Mask of Zorro (1998), Pirates of the Caribbean: The Curse of the Black Pearl (2003), Black Panther (2018), Westworld (2016-2021; E).*

Nick Dudman *Return of the Jedi (1983), Legend (1985), Labyrinth (1986), Willow (1988), Batman (1989), Interview with the Vampire: The Vampire Chronicles (1994), Penny Dreadful (2014-2016), The Harry Potter Octology (2001-2011).*

Leonard Engelman *Night Gallery (1969-1973), Cat People (1982), Ghostbusters (1984), Rambo: First Blood Part II (1985), The Witches of Eastwick (1987), Batman Forever (1985), How the Grinch Stole Christmas (2000), Oz the Great and Powerful (2013).*

Robert Englund *Star of V (1983-1985), A Nightmare on Elm Street (1984), A Nightmare on Elm Street Part 2: Freddy's Revenge (1985), A Nightmare on Elm Street 3: Dream Warriors 1987), The Phantom of the Opera (1989), Wes Craven's New Nightmare (1994), The Mangler (1995), 2001 Maniacs (2005).*

Mike Fields *Final Destination (2000), Thir13en Ghosts (2001), Masters of Horror (2005-2007), The Grey (2011), The Cabin in the Woods (2011), Fear the Walking Dead (2015-Present), R.L. Stine's Monsterville: Cabinet of Souls (2015; E), Star Trek Beyond (2016), The Predator (2018), Chilling Adventures of Sabrina (2018-2020).*

Ben Foster *Star of Alpha Dog (2006), 3:10 to Yuma (2007), 30 Days of Night (2007), The Messenger (2009), Lone Survivor (2013), The Program (2015), Hell or High Water (2016), Leave No Trace (2018), The Survivor (2021).*

Rob Freitas *The Nutty Professor (1996), Hellboy (2004), Land of the Dead (2005), Hostel (2005), The Chronicles of Narnia: The Lion, the Witch and the Wardrobe (2005), Star Trek (2009), Men in Black 3 (2012), Bombshell (2019).*

Carl Fullerton *Friday the 13th Part 2 (1981), Ghost Story (1981), The Hunger (1983), Remo Williams: The Adventure Begins (1985), Warlock (1989), The Silence of the Lambs (1991), Philadelphia (1993), Munich (2005), The Book of Eli (2010), Ma Rainey's Black Bottom (2020).*

Toni G *How the Grinch Stole Christmas (2000), Planet of the Apes (2001), Pirates of the Caribbean: The Curse of the Black Pearl (2003), Monster (2003), Blades of Glory (2007), The Road (2009), Oz the Great and Powerful (2013), Maleficent (2014), Unbroken (2014).*

Mick Garris *Director of Critters 2 (1988), Sleepwalkers (1992), The Stand (1994), The Shining (1997); Creator of Masters of Horror (2005-2007), Fear Itself (2008-2009), Post Mortem with Mick Garris (2009-Present).*

Alec Gillis *(Co-founder of Amalgamated Dynamics, Inc.) Invaders from Mars (1986), Aliens (1986), Pumpkinhead (1988), Tremors (1990), Death Becomes Her (1992), Alien³ (1992), Jumanji (1995), Starship Troopers (1997), Spider-Man (2002), It (2017).*

Pamela Goldammer *Hellboy II: The Golden Army (2008), The Wolfman (2010), Harry Potter and the Deathly Hallows: Part 2 (2011), Game of Thrones (2011-2019), Border (2018), X-Men: Dark Phoenix (2019), Future Man (2020).*

Neill Gorton *The Unholy (1988), Nightbreed (1990), Judge Dredd (1995), Little Britain (2003-2006), Doctor Who (2005-Present), Torchwood (2006-2011), Thor (2011), All is True (2018), This Sceptred Isle (2022).*

Barrie Gower *28 Days Later... (2002), Shaun of the Dead (2004), Stardust (2007), The Iron Lady (2011), Game of Thrones (2011-2019; E'14, '16 & '18), Life of Pi (2012), Rocketman (2019), Chernobyl (2019), Doctor Strange in the Multiverse of Madness (2022), The Last of Us (2022).*

David Grasso *Spy Kids (2001), Serenity (2005), The Chronicles of Narnia: The Lion, the Witch and the Wardrobe (2005), The Walking Dead (2010-2022), This is the End (2013), Preacher (2016-2019), Legion (2017-2019).*

Kevin Haney *Driving Miss Daisy (1989; AA), Dick Tracy (1990), Mark Twain and Me (1991; E), Hocus Pocus (1993), The X Files (1993-2018; E), The Shawshank Redemption (1994), Friends (1994-2004), The Show Formerly Known as the Martin Short Show (1995; E), Kissinger and Nixon (1995; E), Life with Judy Garland: Me and My Shadows (2001; E), Primetime Glick (2001-2003; E), Oz the Great and Powerful (2013).*

Joel Harlow *The Stand (1994; E), The Shining (1997; E), Buffy the Vampire Slayer (1997-2003), Pirates of the Caribbean: Dead Man's Chest (2006), Star Trek (2009; AA), Inception (2010), Dark Shadows (2012), The Lone Ranger (2013), Logan (2017), Black Panther (2018).*

Mike Hill *Apocalypto (2006), The Wolfman (2010), Men in Black 3 (2012), The Shape of Water (2017), Scary Stories to Tell in the Dark (2019), Nightmare Alley (2021).*

Kazu Hiro *How the Grinch Stole Christmas (2000), Planet of the Apes (2001), Click (2007), Norbit (2008), The Curious Case of Benjamin Button (2008), Looper (2012), Darkest Hour (2017; AA), Mindhunter (2017-2019), Bombshell (2019; AA).*

Garrett Immel *Army of Darkness (1992), Scream (1996), Boogie Nights (1997), The Green Mile (1999), Sin City (2005), The Chronicles of Narnia: The Lion, the Witch and the Wardrobe (2005), Drag Me to Hell (2009), Predators (2010), The Walking Dead (2010-2022; E '11 & '12), Fright Night (2011).*

Carey Jones *The Walking Dead (2010-2022; E), Lone Survivor (2013), Preacher (2016-2019), Legion (2017-2019), Watchmen (2019); Suit performer in Predators (2010), This is the End (2013), The Orville (2017-Present), Creepshow (2019-Present), The Book of Boba Fett (2021).*

Doug Jones *Star of Hocus Pocus (1993), Hellboy (2004), Pan's Labyrinth (2006), Fantastic 4: Rise of the Silver Surfer (2007), Hellboy II: The Golden Army (2008), Falling Skies (2011-2015), Crimson Peak (2015), The Strain (2014-2017), The Shape of Water (2017), Star Trek: Discovery (2017-Present).*

Paul Katte *The Island of Dr. Moreau (1996), The Matrix Reloaded (2003), The Chronicles of Narnia: The Lion, the Witch and the Wardrobe (2005), The Hobbit: An Unexpected Journey (2012), Childhood's End (2015).*

Jamie Kelman *The Ring (2002), House M.D. (2004-2012; E), Iron Man (2008), Star Trek (2009), Zombieland (2009), Behind the Candelabra (2013; E), Lone Survivor (2013), Vice (2018), The Mandalorian (2019-Present), The Book of Boba Fett (2021-Present).*

Eryn Krueger Mekash *Sabrina, the Teenage Witch (1996-2003), Nip/Tuck (2003-2010), Alpha Dog (2006), Glee (2009-2015), Eat Pray Love (2010), American Horror Story (2011-Present; E '15 (x2), '16 & '17), The Normal Heart (2014; E), American Crime Story (2016; E x2), Feud: Bette and Joan (2017; E), Hillbilly Elegy (2020).*

John Landis *Director of Schlock (1973), The Kentucky Fried Movie (1977), National Lampoon's Animal House (1978), The Blues Brothers (1980), An American Werewolf in London (1981), Trading Places (1983), Michael Jackson: Thriller (1983), Spies Like Us (1985), Three Amigos! (1986), Coming to America (1988), Innocent Blood (1992).*

Tami Lane *The Lord of the Rings: The Fellowship of the Ring (2001), The Chronicles of Narnia: The Lion, the Witch and the Wardrobe (2005; AA), The Chronicles of Narnia: Prince Caspian (2008), The Hobbit: An Unexpected Journey (2012), Ted 2 (2015), The Shallows (2016), The Orville (2017-Present), Jupiter's Legacy (2021), Interview with the Vampire (2022-Present).*

Love Larson *The Girl with the Dragon Tattoo (2011), Skyfall (2012), The Hundred Year-Old Man Who Climbed Out of the Window and Disappeared (2013), A Man Called Ove (2015), Bohemian Rhapsody (2018), Amundsen (2019), Dune (2021), Moon Knight (2022-Present).*

Mike Marino *I Am Legend (2007), Black Swan (2010), Men in Black 3 (2012), The Irishman (2019), True Detective (2014-2019), I Know This Much is True (2020), Coming 2 America (2021), The Batman (2022).*

David Martí *Pan's Labyrinth (2006; AA), The Orphanage (2007), Hellboy II: The Golden Army (2008), The Impossible (2012), Mama (2013), Crimson Peak (2015), A Monster Calls (2016).*

James McAvoy *Star of The Chronicles of Narnia: The Lion, the Witch and the Wardrobe (2005), The Last King of Scotland (2006), Starter for 10 (2006), Atonement (2007), X-Men: First Class (2011), Filth (2013), Trance (2013), Split (2016), It Chapter Two (2019), His Dark Materials (2019-2022).*

Mike McCracken Jr *Twilight Zone: The Movie (1983), The Kindred (1987), Star Trek VI: The Undiscovered Country (1991), Deep Blue Sea (1999), Sky High (2005), Inception (2010), The Butler (2013).*

Todd McIntosh *Masters of the Universe (1987), Dracula: Dead and Loving It (1995), Buffy the Vampire Slayer (1997-2003; E), Dark Shadows (2005), Torchwood (2006-2011), Pushing Daisies (2007-2009; E), Legion (2017-2019), The Orville (2017-Present), Space Jam: A New Legacy (2021).*

Greg Nelson *Ratboy (1986), Harry and the Hendersons (1987), The Tracey Ullman Show (1987-1990; E), Coming to America (1988), Dad (1989), The Rocketeer (1991), Star Trek: Voyager (1995-2001; E), How the Grinch Stole Christmas (2000), Tropic Thunder (2008).*

Greg Nicotero *(Co-founder of KNB EFX Group) Day of the Dead (1985), Evil Dead II (1987), Army of Darkness (1992), From Dusk Till Dawn (1996), Dune (2000; E), Death Proof (2007), Inglourious Basterds (2009), The Pacific (2010), The Walking Dead (2010-2022; E '11 & '12), Fear the Walking Dead (2015-Present), Creepshow (2019-Present).*

Margaret Prentice *The Howling (1981), The Thing (1982), RoboCop (1987), Beauty and the Beast (1987-1990), Coming to America (1988), How the Grinch Stole Christmas (2000), Planet of the Apes (2001), Tropic Thunder (2008), Star Trek (2009), Oz the Great and Powerful (2013).*

Stephen Prouty *The Mask (1994), How the Grinch Stole Christmas (2000), The Cat in the Hat (2003), Zombieland (2009),*

Thor (2011), Bad Grandpa (2013), Baby Driver (2017), Captain Marvel (2019), The Survivor (2021).

Fred Raskin Editor of The Fast and the Furious: Tokyo Drift (2006), Django Unchained (2012), Guardians of the Galaxy (2014), Bone Tomahawk (2015), The Hateful Eight (2015), Guardians of the Galaxy Vol. 2 (2017), The House With a Clock in its Walls (2018), Once Upon a Time... In Hollywood (2019), The Suicide Squad (2021), Peacemaker (2022-Present).

Montse Ribé Pan's Labyrinth (2006; AA), The Orphanage (2007), Hellboy II: The Golden Army (2008), The Impossible (2012), Mama (2013), Crimson Peak (2015), A Monster Calls (2016).

Mikey Rotella The Walking Dead (2010-2022), The Cabin in the Woods (2011), Star Trek Beyond (2016), The Orville (2017-Present), Hellboy (2019), Lovecraft Country (2020), Them (2021), Jupiter's Legacy (2021).

Sarah Rubano 30 Days of Night (2007), The Chronicles of Narnia: Prince Caspian (2008), District 9 (2009), The Hobbit: An Unexpected Journey (2012), Elysium (2013), Chappie (2015), Childhood's End (2015), Ghost in the Shell (2017), Mortal Engines (2018), Avatar 2 (2022).

Tom Savini Dawn of the Dead (1978), Friday the 13th (1980), The Burning (1981), Creepshow (1982), Day of the Dead (1985), Invasion U.S.A. (1985), Monkey Shines (1988). Actor in Knightriders (1981), Creepshow 2 (1987), From Dusk Till Dawn (1996).

Mike Smithson The Fly (1986), The Blob (1988), Austin Powers: The Spy Who Shagged Me (1999), Gilmore Girls (2000–2007; E), Little Nicky (2000), Planet of the Apes (2001), Avatar (2009), Men In Black 3 (2012), The Lone Ranger (2013), Star Trek: Discovery (2017), Deadpool 2 (2018).

Richard Taylor Meet the Feebles (1989), Braindead (1992), The Lord of the Rings: The Fellowship of the Ring (2001; AA x2), The Lord of the Rings: The Two Towers (2002), The Lord of the Rings: The Return of the King (2003; AA x2), King Kong (2005; AA), The Chronicles of Narnia: The Lion, the Witch and the Wardrobe (2005), The Hobbit: An Unexpected Journey (2012).

Christopher Tucker I, Claudius (1976), Star Wars (1977), The Boys From Brazil (1978), The Elephant Man (1980), Quest for Fire (1981), The Meaning of Life (1983), The Company of Wolves (1984), High Spirits (1988).

Vincent Van Dyke Grey's Anatomy (2005-Present), Dexter (2006-2013), Feud: Bette and Joan (2017), I, Tonya (2017), Halloween (2018), Bombshell (2019), Star Trek: Picard (2020-Present; E).

Eva Von Bahr The Girl with the Dragon Tattoo (2011), The Hundred Year-Old Man Who Climbed Out of the Window and Disappeared (2013), A Man Called Ove (2015), Bohemian Rhapsody (2018), Amundsen (2019), Dune (2021).

Steve Wang Harry and the Hendersons (1987), Predator (1987), The Monster Squad (1987), Gremlins 2: The New Batch (1990), Godzilla (1998), Planet of the Apes (2001), Reign of Fire (2002), Underworld (2003), Hellboy (2004), Bill & Ted Face the Music (2020).

David White Krull (1983), Lifeforce (1985), Mary Shelley's Frankenstein (1994), Lost in Space (1998), Blade II (2002), In Bruges (2008), Captain America: The First Avenger (2011), Snow White and the Huntsman (2012), Guardians of the Galaxy (2014), Maleficent: Mistress of Evil (2019).

Matt Winston (Co-Founder at Stan Winston School of Character Arts) Actor in Arli$$ (1996-2002), Fame L.A. (1997-1998), Fight Club (1999), Enterprise (2001-2005), Scrubs (2001-2010), Six Feet Under (2001-2005), Little Miss Sunshine (2006), John from Cincinnati (2007).

Jeremy Woodhead Mary Shelley's Frankenstein (1994), The Lord of the Rings: The Fellowship of the Ring (2001), Alexander (2004), V For Vendetta (2005), Cloud Atlas (2012), Snowpiercer (2013), Doctor Strange (2016), Stan & Ollie (2018), Judy (2019), Morbius (2022).

Kevin Yagher (Founder of Kevin Yagher Productions, Inc.) A Nightmare on Elm Street 2: Freddy's Revenge (1985), The Hidden (1987), 976-EVIL (1988), Child's Play (1988), Tales from the Crypt (1989–1996), Face/Off (1997), Sleepy Hollow (1999), Mission: Impossible II (2000), A Series of Unfortunate Events (2004), Bones (2005-2017).

Louie Zakarian Saturday Night Live (1975-Present; E x9), Requiem for a Dream (2000), The Producers (2005), The Magnificent Seven (2016), The Gong Show (2017-2018), Bohemian Rhapsody (2018), Vampires vs. the Bronx (2020).

Key: Academy Award (AA), Emmy (E).

INDEX

CREDITS

/ Working Title 2 Productions / Big Talk Productions 168T, 168C

Sin City (2005), Troublemaker Studios / Dimension Films 268-269, 296B

Splice (2009), Dark Castle Entertainment / Copperheart Entertainment / Gaumont / Telefilm Canada / Ontario Media Development Corporation 306T

Stan & Ollie (2018), BBC Films / Fable Pictures / Sonesta Films / Entertainment One 265

Star Trek (1966-69), Desilu Productions / Paramount Television / Norway Corporation 48T

Star Trek (2009), Spyglass Entertainment / Bad Robot Productions 186B

Star Trek Beyond (2016), Skydance Media / Bad Robot Productions / Sneaky Shark Productions / Perfect Storm Entertainment 155, 286

Star Trek: Picard (2020-Present), Secret Hideout / Weed Road Pictures / Escapist Fare / Roddenberry Entertainment / CBS Studios 154

Star Wars (1977), Lucasfilm / 20TH Century Fox 136-137

Summer School (1987), Paramount Pictures 164TR

Superman: The Movie (1978), Dovemead Ltd. / International Film Production 27C

Teen Wolf (2011–17), Adelstein Productions / DiGa Vision / First Cause, Inc. / Lost Marbles Television / Siesta Productions / MTV Production Development / MGM Television 190TL

The Amazing Spider-Man 2 (2014), Marvel Enterprises / Avi Arad Productions / Columbia Pictures / Matt Tolmach Productions 309T

The Autobiography of Miss Jane Pittman (1974), Tomorrow Entertainment 244TR

The Boneyard (1991), Backbone Productions / Backwood Film / Prism Entertainment 304B

The Chronicles of Narnia: Prince Caspian (2008), Walt Disney Pictures / Walden Media 139, 142, 230T, 231

The Chronicles of Narnia: The Lion, The Witch and the Wardrobe (2005), Walt Disney Pictures / Walden Media 103, 218, 306B

The Curse of the Werewolf (1961), Hammer Film Productions 19

The Dark Knight (2008), Warner Bros. Pictures / Legendary Pictures / DC Comics / Syncopy 106

The Elephant Man (1980), Brooksfilms 192-193, 195, 196-197

The Empire Strikes Back (1980), Lucasfilm Ltd. 27T, 70

The Exorcist (1973), Hoya Productions 28B, 30, 88-89, 180BR

The Green Mile (1999), Castle Rock Entertainment / Darkwoods Productions 237T

The Hunchback of Notre Dame (1939), RKO Radio Pictures 17

The Hunger (1983), Metro-Goldwyn-Mayer 28T, 29

The Irishman (2019), TriBeCa Productions / Sikelia Productions / Winkler Films 247, 248-249

The Iron Lady (2011), DJ Films / Pathé / Film4 / Canal+ / Goldcrest Pictures / UK Film Council / CinéCinéma 255

The Island of Dr. Moreau (1977), Cinema 77 / Major Productions 90

The Lone Ranger (2013), Walt Disney Pictures / Jerry Bruckheimer Films / Infinitum Nihil / Blind Wink Productions 187

The Lord of the Rings (2001–03), New Line Cinema / WingNut Films 37, 216, 293T, 308

The Lost Boys (1987), Richard Donner Production 124L

The Mummy (1932), Universal Pictures 56

The Mummy (1959), Hammer Film Productions 53

The Mummy (2017), Perfect World Pictures / Conspiracy Factory Productions / Sean Daniel Company / Secret Hideout / Chris Morgan Productions 294TL

The Nutty Professor (1996), Imagine Entertainment 21

The Orville (2017–22), Fuzzy Door Productions / 20TH Television 190TR, 214-215, 303BR

The Outer Limits (1963-65), Daystar Productions / Villa DiStefano Productions / United Artists Television 14TL

The Monster Squad (1987), Taft Entertainment Pictures / Keith Barish Productions 18R, 18B

The Phantom of the Opera (1925), Jewel Productions 14TR, 71B

The Rocketeer (1991), Walt Disney Pictures / Touchstone Pictures / Silver Screen Partners IV / Gordon Company 213BL, 213BC

The Shallows (2019), Columbia Pictures / Weimaraner Republic Pictures / Ombra Films 174

The Shape of Water (2017), Fox Searchlight Pictures / TSG Entertainment / Double Dare You Productions 112-113, 205

The Shawshank Redemption (1994), Castle Rock Entertainment 271T

The Silence of the Lambs (1991), Strong Heart Productions 162T, 163

The Stand (1994), Laurel Entertainment / DawnField Entertainment / Greengrass Productions 304TR

The Survivor (2021), Bron Studios / New Mandate Films / Creative Wealth Media / Endeavor Content / USC Shoah Foundation 95T, 226, 238-239

The Terminator (1984), Hemdale / Cinema '84 / Pacific Western Productions / Euro Film Funding 114

The Thing (1982), The Turman-Foster Company 24, 160-161

The Walking Dead (2010-2022), Idiot Box Productions / Circle of Confusion / Skybound Entertainment / Valhalla Entertainment / AMC Studios 32T, 169, 170-171, 190BR, 297

The Wiz (1978), Motown Productions 273B

The Wolf Man (1941), Universal Pictures 12-13

Thir13en Ghosts (2001), Warner Bros. Pictures / Columbia Pictures / Dark Castle Entertainment 165L, 165BL

This Is the End (2013), Columbia Pictures / Mandate Pictures / Point Grey Pictures 150-151

This Sceptred Isle (2022), Fremantle / Passenger / Revolution Films 264T

Thor: Dark World (2013), Marvel Studios 294TR

Tropic Thunder (2008), Red Hour Productions / DreamWorks Pictures 186T

True Detective (2014–19), Anonymous Content / HBO Entertainment / Passenger 245TC, 246

White Chicks (2004), Columbia Pictures / Revolution Studios / Gone North Productions 202

Wolf (1994), Columbia Pictures 281, 307L

Wonderguy (1993), Take Twelve Productions 82TR

Young Frankenstein (1974), Gruskoff/Venture Films / Crossbow Productions, Inc. / Jouer Limited 16B

Zombieland (2009), Columbia Pictures / Relativity Media / Pariah 168B

PHOTOGRAPHY CREDITS

The publishers would like to thank the following sources for their kind permission to reproduce the pictures in this book:

Gino Acevedo Collection: 57 (BOTH), 79
Alamy Stock Photo: AA Film Archive 281L; Album 11T, 225R; Album/HBO 254T; Album/American Filmworks 270R; Allstar Picture Library Ltd. 266B; Moviestore Collection Ltd 271T; Photo12 271R; PictureLux/The Hollywood Archive 11B
Amblin: Universal Studios 94
AMPAS: 105T
Jason Baker Photography: 302
Howard Berger Collection: 7 (BOTH), 14TR, 14BL, 14BR, 15 (BOTH), 16T, 33T, 47 (ALL), 48T, 51 (BOTH), 52 (ALL), 55L, 73T, 74, 86-87, 103 (BOTH), 142, 150-151 (ALL), 158L, 159T, 162B, 164BL, 164BR, 165 (ALL), 175 (BOTH), 176-177, 183B, 186T, 188L, 210T, 211, 214-215, 220 (BOTH), 230T, 231, 237TR, 243 (ALL), 244TL, 252-253, 256-257 (ALL), 274, 279TR, 279BL, 280T, 283 (BOTH), 284-285, 292B, 299BL, 301TR, 301R, 301BR, 303TR, 303BR, 306 (BOTH), 309T; 20TH Century Fox 16B, 34; 20TH Century Fox/Lucas Films 26TL, 27T, 70 (BOTH), 136-137 (BOTH); Hammer Films 19, 53; Graham Humphrey 4; KNB EFX 128-129 (ALL), 134-135, 139, 166TL; MGM 26BL, 26BR; MGM UA 29 (BOTH); Sony Pictures 22T; Universal Studios 12-13, 17, 18TR, 20 (BOTH), 21, 40-41 (BOTH), 45, 56, 71B; Warner Brothers Studio 27C, 30
Phil Bray Photography: 218
John Buechler Archives: 125B
Lois Burwell Collection: 277
Norman Cabrera Collection: 126-127, 149 (BOTH), 294BL, 294BR
John Caglione Jr Collection: 106, 199 (BOTH), 227 (BOTH)
Greg Cannom Collection: 124L, 202 (BOTH), 229 (ALL), 251 (ALL), 305 (BOTH)
Cinefex Magazine: 22B
Blair Clark Collection: 138 (ALL)
Andrew Cooper Photography: 172 (BOTH)
Bill Corso Collection: 50 (BOTH), 258-259 (ALL), 304 (ALL)
Mark Coulier Collection: 99, 167 (ALL), 255 (ALL)
John Criswell Collection: 280B
Ken Diaz Collection: 24, 160 (BOTH), 250 (ALL), 270L, 287 (BOTH), 289
Nick Dudman Collection: 96-97 (BOTH), 98 (BOTH), 143 (BOTH); 20TH Century Fox/Lucas Films 179 (BOTH)
Empire Pictures: 125T
Leonard Engelman Collection: 42-43 (BOTH), 298T
Mike Fields Collection: 133 (BOTH), 286
Rob Freitas Collection: 299TL
Carl Fullerton Collection: 68-69, 162T, 163 (BOTH), 237L, 237C
Toni G Collection: 183T
Alec Gillis Collection: 140 (BOTH), 200-201 (BOTH), 278, 307 (BOTH)
Neill Gorton Collection: 100-101 (ALL), 144-145 (ALL), 146-147, 148 (ALL), 264T
Barrie Gower Collection: 168T, 168C, 244C, 245TL, 267B; HBO 107 (BOTH), 232-233, 234-235 (BOTH)
David Grasso Collection: 48B, 102, 112T, 131
Kevin Haney Collection: 28T, 212 (ALL)
Joel Harlow Collection: 115, 132, 155, 186B, 187 (BOTH), 203, 208-209, 244TC

Margaret Herrick Library: 88-89, 164TL, 180BL, 180BR, 181 (ALL), 319; 20TH Century Fox 25 (ALL); Lois Burwell 198 (ALL); Universal Studios/John Landis Collection 23 (BOTH), 116-117, 120-121 (BOTH), 122; Warner Brothers 28B
Mike Hill Collection: 19TR, 112B, 113, 205 (BOTH)
Kazu Hiro Collection: 35, 58-59 (BOTH), 95B, 260-261, 262-263, 290-291, 295TL, 295TC, 295C
Garrett Immel Collection: 166TR, 298B, 301TL
Doug Jones Collection: 81T
Marshall Julius Collection: 8-9 (BOTH)
KNB EFX Archives: 190 (ALL), 222-223
Paul Katte Collection: 54, 55R
Jamie Kelman Collection: 60-61 (ALL), 226 (ALL); HBO: 95T, 238-239
Eryn Krueger Mekash Collection: 38-39, 264B, 293B
Tami Lane Collection: 76 (BOTH), 174 (BOTH), 219B
Love Larson Collection: 207; Warner Brothers 111
Goran Lundstrum Collection: 221
Mike Marino Collection: 91 (BOTH), 206, 236 (ALL), 240-241, 244B, 245TC, 246-247 (ALL); Niko Tavernise Photography 248-249
David Martí Collection: 104, 105B, 219T
Mike McCracken Jr Collection: 14TL, 90, 299R, 300T
Todd McIntosh Collection: 49 (ALL), 78B, 81L, 81BL, 81BR, 124BR, 130 (BOTH), 296T, 300B
Greg Nelson Collection: 164TR, 213BL, 213BC, 245BR, 295BR
Greg Nicotero Collection: 73BC, 169 (BOTH), 170-171, 230B, 268-269, 275, 292T, 296B, 297 (ALL); AMC 32T; KNB EFX 173 (ALL)
Margaret Prentice Collection: 161
Stephen Prouty Collection: 168B, 180TL, 245TL, 303BL
Fred Raskin Collection: 84-85 (BOTH)
Montse Ribé Collection: David Marti 184-185 (ALL), 309B
Mikey Rotella Collection: 75 (BOTH)
Sarah Rubano Collection: 282
Tom Savini Collection: 32B, 33B, 71T, 73BL, 73BR, 123 (BOTH), 156-157, 158T, 159B
Starlog Publishing: Fangoria Magazine 66-67 (ALL)
Art Streiber Photography: 311
Richard Taylor Collection: 31 (BOTH), 37, 63, 64-65, 166BR, 216 (BOTH), 293T, 308 (BOTH)
Christopher Tucker Collection: 192-193, 195, 196-197 (BOTH), 276 (BOTH)
Vincent Van Dyke Collection: 86TL, 154, 242 (BOTH), 267T
Steve Wang Collection: 18R, 18B, 77, 110L, 141 (ALL), 217 (BOTH)
Warren Publishing: Famous Monsters of Filmland 44 (ALL)
David White Collection: 80 (ALL), 92, 108-109 (ALL), 110R, 152-153 (ALL), 294TL, 294TR
Stan Winston Archives: 114 (BOTH), 118-119 (ALL), 180TR, 182, 204 (BOTH), 244TR, 272-273 (ALL), 279BR
Jeremy Woodhead Collection: 265 (BOTH), 266TR, 266R
Kevin Yagher Collection: 46, 78T, 93 (BOTH), 178, 210B, 228 (BOTH), 244L, 245BL
Louie Zakarian Collection: 82-83 (ALL), 213TC, 213TR

Every effort has been made to acknowledge correctly and contact the source and/copyright holder of each picture. Any unintentional errors or omissions will be corrected in future editions of this book.

ACKNOWLEDGEMENTS

Thanks, first, to our incredible cast of contributors, for their wonderful stories and fantastic photographs: Gino Acevedo, Eva Von Bahr, Rick Baker, Vivian Baker, Doug Bradley, Lois Burwell, Norman Cabrera, John Caglione Jr, Bruce Campbell, Greg Cannom, Blair Clark, Bill Corso, Mark Coulier, John Criswell, Ken Diaz, Nick Dudman, Vincent Van Dyke, Leonard Engelman, Robert Englund, Mike Fields, Ben Foster, Rob Freitas, Carl Fullerton, Toni G, Mick Garris, Alec Gillis, Pamela Goldammer, Neill Gorton, Barrie Gower, David Grasso, Kevin Haney, Joel Harlow, Mike Hill, Kazu Hiro, Garrett Immel, Carey Jones, Doug Jones, Paul Katte, Jamie Kelman, John Landis, Tami Lane, Love Larson, Mike Marino, David Martí, James McAvoy, Mike McCracken Jr, Todd McIntosh, Eryn Krueger Mekash, Greg Nelson, Greg Nicotero, Margaret Prentice, Stephen Prouty, Fred Raskin, Montse Ribé, Mikey Rotella, Sarah Rubano, Tom Savini, Mike Smithson, Richard Taylor, Christopher Tucker, Steve Wang, David White, Matt Winston, Jeremy Woodhead, Kevin Yagher and Louie Zakarian.

Thanks to our editor Ross Hamilton, our designer Russell Knowles, and to everyone else who helped us along the way: Heidi Berger, Holly and Maisy Berger, Paula Comesaña, Russell Binder, Stacie, Josh, Rowan and Rhys Finesilver, Ronald Fogelman, Roland Hall, Russell Julius, Heather, Allan, Jordan and Keala Kruse, Jeannie and Sonny Raffle, William Strauss, Ri Streeter and our parents, Susan and Kenneth Berger, and Myrna and Morris Julius.

Thanks to John Chambers, Lon Chaney, Stuart Freeborn, Jack Pierce, Dick Smith, Daniel Striepeke, William Tuttle and Stan Winston for a lifetime of inspiration.

The authors would also like to thank the following people, without whose help and artistry this book would not have been possible: J.J. Abrams, Forrest J. Ackerman, Andrew Adamson, David Anderson, Allan Apone, Roy Ashton, Drew Barrymore, Peter Berg, Javier Botet, Rob Bottin, Richard Brake, Mel Brooks, John Buechler, Tom Burman, Everett Burrell, Bill Butler, Sasha Camacho, John Carpenter, Robert Carrelli, Regina Castruita, Lon Chaney Jr, Chad Coleman, Steve Coogan, Odile Corso, Gino Crognale, Tom Cruise, Tim Curry, Charles Dance, Warwick Davis, Johnny Depp, Peter Dinklage, Doug Drexler, Stephan Dupuis, Mike Elizalde, David Emge, Kevin Feige, Gunnar Ferdinandsen, Mike Fontaine, Harrison Ford, Karen Gillan, Evan Goldberg, James Gunn, Kevin Peter Hall, Tom Hanks, Ray Harryhausen, Kane Hodder, Sir Anthony Hopkins, Dawn Hudson, John Hurt, Michael Jackson, Peter Jackson, Mark Johnson, Angelina Jolie, Boris Karloff, Bob Keen, Stephen King, Kathleen Kinmont, Heidi Klum, Johnny Knoxville, Bill Kramer, Mila Kunis, Robert Kurtzman, Blake Lively, Domenick Lombardozzi, George Lucas, Goran Lunstrom, David Lynch, Peter Macon, Nick Maley, Tyler Mane, Neal Martz, Michael McCracken Sr, Lorne Michaels, Peter Montagna, Donald Mowat, Naimie, Jack Nicholson, Connie Nicotero, Jim Nicotero, Gary Oldman, Veronica Owens, Daniel Parker, Simon Pegg, Sam Raimi, Craig Reardon, Robert Rodriguez, Seth Rogen, George Romero, Matt Rose, Mickey Rourke, Richard Rubenstein, Matt Severson, Mark Shostrom, Stellan Skarsgård, Steven Spielberg, Meryl Streep, Quentin Tarantino, Charlize Theron, Tony Timpone, Wayne Toth, Johnny Villanueva, John Vulich, KISS, Mark Wahlberg, Chris Walas, Hugo Weaving, The Westmore Family, Debbie Winston, Karen Winston, Edgar Wright, Bernie Wrightson, Renée Zellweger and Robert Zemeckis.

Thanks also to ABC Television, The Academy Museum of Motion Pictures, The Academy of Motion Picture Arts and Sciences, Altered States FX, Alterian Inc, Amazon Studios, Amblin Entertainment, AMC, Aurora Monster Models, Autonomous FX, Bad Robot, BBC, CBS, Cinefex, Cinovation, Columbia Studios, DDT, Disney Studios, Don Post Studios, Dreamworks Pictures, Empire Pictures, Famous Monsters of Filmland, Fangoria, Fractured FX, Frends Beauty Supplies, Hammer Studios, HBO, Henson Productions, ILM, KNB EFX Group, Inc, Legacy Effects, Lucasfilm, Makeup Effects Lab, Margaret Herrick Library, Marvel Studios, MEG, MGM Studios, NBC, Netflix, New Line Cinema, Optic Nerve, Paramount Pictures, Point Grey, Pronrenfx, Saturday Night Live, Searchlight Films, Sony Studios, Stan Winston Studios, Starlog Publications, StudioADI, 20th Century Fox, United Artists, Universal Studios Warner Bros. Studios, Vincent Van Dyke Studios, WETA Workshop and Wingnut Films.

Finally, extra special thanks to our wives, Mirjam and Ruta, for all their help, encouragement, patience and love. We couldn't have done it without them.

AUTHOR BIOGRAPHIES

Special Make-up Effects Artist **Howard Berger** has over 800 feature film credits that span four decades. Over the course of Howard's career, he has worked on such films as *Dances With Wolves* (1990), *Casino* (1995), *From Dusk Till Dawn* (1996), *The Green Mile* (1999), *Kill Bill 1 & 2* (2003), *Oz the Great and Powerful* (2012) *Lone Survivor* (2013) and *The Amazing Spider-Man 2* (2014).

In recognition for his work on *The Chronicles of Narnia: The Lion, The Witch and the Wardrobe* (2004) Howard won the Academy Award for Best Make-up as well as a British Academy Award for Best Achievement in Make-up. In 2012 Howard was again nominated for an Academy Award for designing and creating Sir Anthony Hopkins' portrait make-up for the FOX Searchlight feature *Hitchcock* (2012).

In 1988 Howard co-founded KNB EFX Group, Inc. For the past 34 years KNB has garnered its reputation as the most prolific Special Effects Make-up studio in Hollywood. He resides in Sherman Oaks, CA with his artist wife, Mirjam.

A veteran nerd with unbound enthusiasm for everything you love, **Marshall Julius** is a film critic, blogger, broadcaster, quizmaster and collector of colourful plastic things. Also the author of *Vintage Geek* (September Publishing, 2019) and *Action! The Action Movie A-Z* (Batsford Film Books, 1996). Marshall lives in London, England with his wife Ruta, and though his lifestyle appears sedentary, actually he's wildly active on Twitter: *@MarshallJulius*